THE REVIVAL OF METAPHYSICAL POETRY

The Revival of
METAPHYSICAL
POETRY

THE HISTORY OF A STYLE, 1800 TO THE PRESENT

Joseph E. Duncan

1969

OCTAGON BOOKS

New York

Reprinted 1969
by special arrangement with the University of Minnesota Press

OCTAGON BOOKS
A DIVISION OF FARRAR, STRAUS & GIROUX, INC.
19 Union Square West
New York, N. Y. 10003

LIBRARY OF CONGRESS CATALOG CARD NUMBER: 79-75991

Printed in U.S.A. by
TAYLOR PUBLISHING COMPANY
DALLAS, TEXAS

TO MY MOTHER

Acknowledgments

I AM deeply grateful to all who have helped me in the preparation and publication of *The Revival of Metaphysical Poetry*. For their care in examining the entire manuscript or large portions of it, I am indebted to the following persons: Professor Marjorie Hope Nicolson, Professor William York Tindall, and Professor Lionel Trilling, all of Columbia University, and Professor Robert Hart and Professor William Rosenthal, both of the University of Minnesota, Duluth Branch. For giving me the benefit of some of their own research in American literature, I wish to thank Professor George Arms, of the University of New Mexico, and Mr. Jay Leyda, who has been working with unpublished Emily Dickinson material. For her careful work on the index, I am very grateful to LeAne Haase Rutherford.

I am especially indebted to Dame Edith Sitwell, Sir Francis Meynell, and Robert Penn Warren for their gracious permission to use material on which they hold copyrights. To the many publishers listed on the copyright page who released material for my use, I also wish to express my gratitude.

To *Studies in Philology* for permission to reprint material from my article "The Intellectual Kinship of John Donne and Robert Browning" and to *PMLA* for permission to use material from my "The Revival of Metaphysical Poetry, 1872–1912," I owe further thanks and appreciation.

J. E. D.

Table of Contents

THE REVIVAL OF METAPHYSICAL POETRY

Introduction

EVERY revival is a new interpretation. Each period seeks out those elements in its cultural past with which it has an affinity and reshapes them in its own image to meet its own needs. Sometimes this tendency is a search for self-understanding and for a kind of cultural companionship. In reviving classical culture the Renaissance interpreted it anew, and the nineteenth century similarly reinterpreted Renaissance culture. Our own century has displayed a distinct taste for the seventeenth century's mature thoughtfulness and its self-conscious awareness of tensions and problems. Evidence of this affinity is seen in efforts to reestablish a poetic drama and to revitalize the musical tradition of the English Renaissance as well as in the response to new scientific concepts and the renewed interest in the political movements that preceded and accompanied the Puritan revolution.

However, the affinity has been most clearly revealed in the metaphysical revival, the pronounced interest in the seventeenth-century "metaphysical" poets who in varying degrees employed a style found in its most distinguished and distinguishable form in the poetry of John Donne. The metaphysical revival began almost imperceptibly in the earlier nineteenth century, increased in vigor and importance, and has flourished in the twentieth century. Merritt Y. Hughes has asserted that the only forces comparable to Donne's power over modern poetry are Shakespeare and Milton's influence in the eighteenth century, and Douglas Bush has called the metaphysical revival "the main single factor in effecting the modern revolution in taste." Similarly, Mario Praz has said that the "revaluation of the metaphysicals has been an

3

earthquake in the English Parnassus, reshaping the outline of its summit as if it were a volcano," and has noted the revival's significance in helping to popularize common speech rhythms and superficially unpoetic language.[1] Any anthology of modern poetry or any bibliography of recent English studies testifies to the revival's vitality. Because of the recent importance, then, of this metaphysical tradition, a consistent study of the movement as a whole should fill a need and cast some additional light on the history of British and American poetry and criticism during the last century and a half.

Throughout the whole span of the revival there are two important characteristics that stand out: its continuity and its variety. The course of the revival shows no sharp breaks, but an abundance of fresh interpretation. The closest analogy is a musical theme and variations. While critics and poets made an about-face and were affected by events such as the Catholic revival and the Second World War, throughout the revival the later stages nevertheless developed organically and logically from the earlier ones. The examination of the nineteenth-century phases of the revival, which particularly needed investigation, gives added stature and perspective to the whole movement. In addition to its essential continuity, the movement always had life and interest because it was always changing. New generations of critics explored new paths of interpretation, and new generations of poets transmuted metaphysical techniques into a genuine modern poetic idiom. For both critics and poets, new interpretation — rather than imitation — has been most rewarding.

This study attempts to show in what ways the metaphysical style, as it was interpreted and varied through successive periods, was both like and unlike the metaphysical style of the seventeenth century. The first section examines metaphysical poetry entirely from a seventeenth-century point of view. The second and principal section traces the revival from its beginnings in the early nineteenth century to the present. This section includes an examination of changing critical attitudes toward metaphysical poetry and a study of shifting interpretations of the metaphysical style in the poetry of Robert Browning, Gerard Manley Hopkins, Emily Dickinson, W. B. Yeats, T. S. Eliot, and others.

Analysis of the metaphysical qualities in these poets illuminates both the main lines of the revival and the poets themselves. Hopkins and Eliot, for instance, have helped shape the revival in crystallizing conceptions basic to one phase of the movement and in influencing other poets. Also, poets like Eliot, William Empson, and the Fugitives can probably be best understood as a part of the mainstream of the metaphysical revival. Similarly, thinking of Browning, Yeats, Wallace Stevens and Edith Sitwell as metaphysical poets reveals some important characteristics of their work, and even when a poet's knowledge of the seventeenth-century metaphysicals is doubtful, as with Emily Dickinson, an investigation of the poet's use of metaphysical techniques yields new insights into the poetry.

This study is related to two forms of literary research: studies in reputations and in influences. However, while it shares in both of these, it is essentially neither. Unlike the usual study in reputations, it emphasizes the line of successive interpretations, rather than individual evaluations, and treats poetic style as a vital force guiding creative efforts in a later period. Unlike the usual investigation of influences, this study relates the poetry to changing critical trends, treats similarities that may be independent of an influence, and is concerned about equally with similarities and dissimilarities in the analysis of new poetic interpretations of the metaphysical style.

While including some investigation of both reputations and influences, this work may be best thought of as the history of a style — or as the history of a particular kind of idea and attitude. It is an attempt to treat the history of the imitations, adaptations, and interpretations of the metaphysical style in relation to the metaphysical revival. A part of what is said is always expressed only through a style or the ways of saying something, perhaps something seemingly quite different. As this sort of "idea" and attitude is completely and faithfully expressible only through style, the history of the metaphysical style is also the history of this special kind of idea.

Early Conceptions
of Metaphysical Poetry

CRITICS have been in much more general agreement about who the principal seventeenth-century metaphysical poets were than about what metaphysical poetry is. But fortunately this general agreement provides valuable clues to an understanding of both the seventeenth-century and modern conceptions of metaphysical poetry. Metaphysical elements have been recognized in the work of Sidney, Shakespeare, Marlowe, Chapman, and other English and Continental poets. However, the most representative metaphysical poets were John Donne, Edward Herbert, George Herbert, Aurelian Townshend, Henry King, John Cleveland, Andrew Marvell, and Abraham Cowley. Richard Crashaw was a metaphysical poet, but he was a special case. In the work of Henry Vaughan and Thomas Traherne there are some important metaphysical elements, but other qualities are so pronounced that it is deceptive to consider these poets with Donne.

Many later sixteenth-century poets wrote some more or less metaphysical poetry. Sidney's twenty-ninth sonnet ("Like some weak lords") depends on an extended metaphysical conceit, and his "In a grove most rich of shade" suggests Donne's "The Extasie." Shakespeare's sonnets 44, 45, 87, 134, and 137 have pronounced metaphysical characteristics, and Fulke Greville, Lord Brooke, sometimes approached Donne in his bare, irregular verse and abstract, involved, unconventional conceits. Both Marlowe and Chapman employed metaphysical conceits in their "Hero and

Leander." Also, in "Ovids Banquet of Sense" Chapman sometimes expressed the emotional in terms of abstract relationships and scientific processes. Robert Southwell combined the Jesuit poetic of Pontanus with the pointed manner of Martial and Ovid in a poetry that sometimes anticipated Donne, Herbert, and Crashaw. His long translation "The Tears of St. Peter" is sown thick with conceits and displays a striking mixture of wit and deep seriousness.

While the seventeenth-century metaphysical poets were never so self-consciously allied as was the "tribe of Ben," neither were they only individuals working independently. King and both the Herberts were friends of Donne. Townshend was the traveling companion of Edward Herbert. Donne, George Herbert, and Crashaw had a common friend in Nicholas Ferrar. Cowley and Crashaw were intimate friends, and Marvell was at Cambridge at the same time that they were. However, each of these poets left his distinctive mark upon the metaphysical style. Donne was the leavening force in the rise of the style and its most consistent and extreme adherent. His poetry abounds in probing analogies and ingenious wit, and recent critics have found in Donne their most prized examples of ambiguity and the unified sensibility. Following Donne's lead, Edward and George Herbert helped establish, respectively, the secular and devotional lines in metaphysical poetry. In his structures and figures Edward Herbert, who praised the expression of "common things ingeniously and wittily" and "somewhat out of the ordinary road," [1] resembled Donne more closely than any of his other followers. Apparently influenced by Marino, he incorporated Italian techniques into Donne-like structures. Cowley and Cleveland mark two successive steps toward the forfeiture of meaning for the sake of wit — and, incidentally, toward a broader and less aristocratic popularity. Marvell, whose tone is often closer to that of Lovelace and the Cavalier Platonists than to Donne's, absorbed the metaphysical style with an easy grace into his own. George Herbert channelled the metaphysical style into a true devotional poetry. Like Donne, he married a careful logic to a metaphorical vision. Both Donne and Herbert depended in their figures on abstract knowledge and everyday experience. However, Herbert's work smells less of the lamp than Donne's and has more of the freshness of the garden and the sanctity of the chapel. Crashaw stood apart. His metaphysical style is intertwined with a Continental Catholic baroque style. His poetic structures are frequently loose, almost epigrammatic, while his conceits tend to depend on an all-suffusing sensuous and emotive appeal rather than on aptness and precision. All of these poets contributed to the development of the style known as metaphysical, but defined in many different ways.

SEVENTEENTH-CENTURY APPROACHES

Modern critics and scholars have vied with each other in explaining and defining metaphysical poetry. But how was the metaphysical style regarded during the period of its flourishing? There are many references to wit and metaphor, but only a few specific allusions to metaphysical poetry. William Drummond saw that there was a new style and noted its characteristics. "Some men of late, transformers of everything," he wrote, "consulted upon her [poetry's] reformation, and endeavored to abstract her to metaphysical ideas and scholastic quiddities, denuding her of her own habits and those ornaments with which she hath amused the world some thousand years." [2] Then in his conversation with Drummond, Ben Jonson revealed that he considered Donne's poetry witty and excellent in some ways, metrically rough, difficult to follow, and occasionally sacrilegious. There is also just the hint of the enticing idea that he had recorded his own and Donne's ideas in his lost dialogue introduction to his translation of Horace's "Ars Poetica," in which Donne was to take the apparently important role of Criticus, [3] the kind of part that Jonson usually reserved for himself in his plays.

Several of the elegies on Donne's death shed some light upon the way in which Donne's contemporaries regarded his style. Thomas Carew mentioned Donne's revolt against imitation and conventional imagery of "gods and goddesses," his pregnant fancy, his masculine line that bends "our troublesome language," and

8

Donne's "strict laws" which will be "too hard for libertines in poetry." [4] In this allusion is another tantalizing hint that perhaps Donne had taken some steps toward the formulation of a new poetic. Edward Herbert, noting that Donne did "so refine Matter with words, that both did seem divine," praised both his "Idiom and sence," [5] and apparently felt that Donne had been able to express something new through the handling of the language. A distinct, slightly puzzling point of view is seen in Arthur Wilson's praise of Donne for his concern with beauty and his attention to out-of-doors nature.

The marginal references in an early Donne edition are also illuminating. The seventeenth-century owner, identified as Giles Oldisworth, an Anglican clergyman and nephew of Sir Thomas Overbury, found hidden references and allegories throughout Donne's poetry. The amorous "The Good Morrow" was understood to be an address to God, the three-in-one union of "The Flea" was "doing despight to ye blessed Trinitye," and the lesbianism of "Sappho to Philaenis" was interpreted allegorically to represent the relationship between Christ and Christianity. Like Jonson, Oldisworth found profanity in Donne's extravagant praise of mortal women. He also saw concealed allusions to Presbyterians and Independents. [6] Other contemporaries probably allegorized Donne's poetry, and Donne himself may easily have seen a suggestion of the Trinity in any union of three in one.

Scanty evidence of this kind still leaves many questions unanswered. How was the poetry of Donne and his followers related to the philosophical, rhetorical, and poetic theories of the Renaissance (the term will usually refer to the sixteenth and early seventeenth century)? What basis — if any — was there in early seventeenth-century criticism for conceptions that have been popular in twentieth-century criticism? Although the poetry changed more rapidly than the criticism, by correlating various writings known to the seventeenth century one can discover the prevailing attitudes of the period toward the characteristics of metaphysical poetry generally recognized by critics from Drummond to Dr. Johnson and from Coleridge to T. S. Eliot. Seventeenth-century writers did not have much to say about metaphysical poetry as such, but they did discuss the kind of logical structure, metaphor, and wit usually regarded as typical of Donne and his followers. One can also test the insights of the "new critics" by examining from a seventeenth-century point of view the knotty problems of the precise expression of personal experience, ambiguity, and the relation of thought and feeling. One can indeed gradually approach a seventeenth-century conception of metaphysical poetry. If the approach today seems tangential and indirect, it is because the seventeenth century conceived of metaphysical poetry tentatively, obliquely, and in its own terms.

LOGIC AND METAPHOR

During the Renaissance many writers forged new links between rhetoric and logic. "I wish that every man should desire, and seeke to haue his *Logique* perfit, and before he looke to profite in *Rhetorique*, considering the ground and confirmation of causes, is for the most part gathered out of Logique," wrote Thomas Wilson.[7] Part of the new interest in logic was due to Peter Ramus, who in his drastic revision of Aristotle stressed the subordination of other sciences to logic and greatly simplified the logical processes of investigation and disposition. There was a new emphasis upon the so-called figures of thought, such as definition, distinction, cause and effect, comparison, example, dilemma, and the imaginary dialogue, which could be dealt with under the heads of logic. These figures of thought were distinguished from the figures of words treating chiefly tropes and schemes including spelling, diction, syntax, and devices for arousing emotion. Logical disposition, figures of thought, and the metaphysical conceit flourished in the logic-conscious Renaissance climate.

Writings familiar to the metaphysical poets could have given them considerable support for their conceits. In fact, Aristotle could be regarded as the father of the conceit. He stressed the need for appropriateness in figures, but he also emphasized the pleasure given by strangeness, originality, and surprise. He approved metaphors derived from well-constructed enigmas and explained that "it is proper to derive metaphors from objects which are closely related to the *thing itself*, but which are not *immediately* obvious," as in philosophy "it is a mark of sagacity to discern resemblances in things which are widely different." [8] Similarly in sixteenth-century France, Ronsard and Du Bellay objected strenuously to trite images and called upon poets to use analogies ("the nerves and tendons of the Muses") based on the work of painters, engravers, mariners, and other groups.[9]

English writers approved of both the logical extension of conceits and a new subject matter in metaphors. Abraham Fraunce praised the consistent extension of one figure. Later Cowley, showing himself aware of his own technique, explained that "the old fashion way of writing was like *disputing* in *Enthymemes*, where half is left out to be supply'd by the Hearer; ours is like *Syllogisms*, where all that is meant is exprest." [10] Perhaps the most convincing evidence of the interest taken in the logically elaborate metaphor during the seventeenth century is provided by the many manuals giving explicit directions for working out comparisons by substance, quality, relation, action, and the other logical aids to invention. The extension of subject matter was noted by Hoskins. "It is true," he wrote, "that we study according to the predominancy of courtly inclinations: whilst mathematics were in request, all our similitudes came from lines, circles, and angles." He added that he had "outworn six several styles since he was first fellow of New College." Hoskins, however, writing at a time when he could have been familiar with some of Donne's poetry, praised analogies in which "things seeming unequal are compared, and that in similitudes as well as examples." [11]

An extension of this broadening process to include progressively more erudite comparisons continued well into the seventeenth century. Ralph Johnson recommended figures drawn from "Laws and Customs" of the Jews, Greeks, Romans, and Egyptians and from "the whole series of Natural and Artificial things, especially Pyramids, Labyrinths, Temples, Fish, Fowls, Stars, etc." While Hobbes emphasized judgment as a necessary restraint on wit, he also observed that "the more unlike and unproportionable the things be otherwise, the more *grace* hath the Metaphor." Similarly, Thomas Fuller praised John Cleveland for avoiding obvious comparisons in his metaphors, which carried with them "a difficult plainness, difficult at the hearing, plain at the understanding thereof." [12]

Henry Peacham's discussion of the metaphorical relation of qualitatively different realms of being shows a clear understanding of several functions of the metaphysical conceit. Metaphors are taken from many places, he wrote, but chiefly from the following: from the sense as applied to the mind, from the mind to the body or senses, from the unreasonable (the animal) to the reasonable (man), from the reasonable to the unreasonable, from the living to the lifeless, from the lifeless to the living, and from men's doings and from substances. [13]

Renaissance criticism, then, recognized and partly defined its penchant for the kind of metaphor that has come to be regarded as the metaphysical conceit — the metaphor that connected logically subjects not obviously analogous and that often linked different levels in the great chain of being. The Renaissance concern with this kind of metaphor was apparently largely the product of the intense interest in the theory of correspondences. The theory assumed that there were intimate, interlocking relationships between the heavens, the earth, the body politic, and man, all of which were an expression of God. Because God, man, and nature were joined through the Incarnation and Eucharist, one could find sacramental and incarnational symbols in the world. Analogies between the infinite and the finite were justified by dogma. In the Incarnation, God had become man, who himself contained in small the earth and its mineral, vegetable, and animal realms. Through the Eucharist, too, partakers were felt to be united with each other, with Christ, and thus with God. The union, living and continuous, was embodied in history. These mysteries justified not only the discovery of divine symbols, but also the use of surprising unions achieved through metaphors, paradox, and puns. Crashaw, for instance, found "new similes to Nature" proclaimed in "the wealth of one Rich Word." [14] However, as the universal church became a national church assailed by sectarianism, symbols often lost their roots in dogma and sometimes became rather trivial metaphors. Writers tended to find the spiritual element "just behind" rather than within the concrete or to abandon nature for a private inner world of spirituality. Probably the use of analogical symbols and other kinds of correspondences was often a desperate attempt to reunite the natural and divine orders.[15]

But for one of any faith, man was in truth a microcosm or "little world," whose four "humors" corresponded to the four elements. Astronomy and geology were organically related to physiology and medicine. Man was connected not only with the stars, but with the mineral, vegetable, and animal realms. Nor was it an accident that there were seven spheres, seven ages of man, seven days, seven sins, and seven notes in the scale. Although the belief in correspondences and an organic universe had existed for centuries, Renaissance thinkers were particularly eager to bring order into complexity by finding connections not only between the macrocosm and the microcosm, but between all created things. The great chain of being, which extended from the lowest to the highest orders of creation, involved a series of corresponding realms, each with its head and own internal order. The basic system of course had numerous variations due to the influence of Platonism and other modes of thought.

It is highly important for metaphysical poetry that the system of correspondences both inspired further analogical reasoning and provided the methods and tools for it. Since correspondences were regarded as both literal and meaningful, logical analogy could be thought of as an instrument for discovering truth. The metaphysical conceit was apparently a product of the Renaissance tendency to discover significant analogies almost everywhere. As the heart was sometimes regarded as the body's sun, only a slight departure from an accepted idea would lead to the construction of a conceit around the idea that true love, or a mistress, is the poet's sun. Sometimes, as in the best of Donne and Andrew Marvell, this analogizing produced true insights of a high order; sometimes, as in the worst of Cowley and Cleveland, it produced only forced and superficial comparisons. While a dependence on a system of correspondences was common to most Renaissance thinkers, it is at the core of much metaphysical poetry and is one of the most important characteristics of the metaphysical style, contributing to various witty devices besides the conceit.

WIT

Carew and others recognized Donne's sovereignty of "the universal monarchy of Wit," and during the earlier seventeenth century the metaphysicals were known and praised for no one thing so much as for their wit. The new aesthetic criterion of wittiness, freshened and refurbished almost beyond recognition, was one of the most significant of the many new intellectual influences upon later Elizabethan and Jacobean literature.

This interest in wit was derived mainly from classical, medieval, and earlier Renaissance rhetorical theory. Aristotle had recommended a decorous use of most of the elements conventionally attributed to wit: surprise, deception, antithesis, and the pun. He was interested in wit as a stylistic device that could enliven and make more effective the matter in hand, and was aware of its close relationship to an underlying logic. He pointed out that the antithetical style was pleasant because contraries could be more easily understood when juxtaposed, and he approved of unexpected puns that expressed a truth.[16]

Cicero made an important distinction between jests that excited laughter and those, such as plays on ambiguous words, that were "rather commended as jests of elegance and scholarship." It was this intellectual wit, sometimes referred to in both classical and Renaissance works as a kind of "urbanity," with which the metaphysicals had the greatest affinity. Quintilian likewise praised urbanity, with its tincture of learning, and recognized wit's close relation to logic, especially its frequent dependence on false reasoning. With the elder Seneca, wit became associated with superficial ingenuity and epigrammatic development with little attention to a unifying aim. This conception, which flourished in the

Gallic schools of the fourth and fifth centuries, continued as a potent influence even into the Renaissance.[17]

To the Renaissance, however, wit seemed something new and fresh. The challenge of adapting it to bring refinement to modern languages lent it an air of novelty and opened new potentialities. Castiglione's courtiers were familiar with Cicero's approval of the urbane jests that incited wonder rather than laughter. They admired "doubtful expressions," those "contrary to expectation," and indeed virtually all forms of ambiguity, including the pun, the "privie signification," and other kinds of word-play.[18] The ideal was the continual flash of novelty from surprising intellectual relationships. As the Hoby translation of *The Courtier* was widely read and respected in Renaissance England, it probably provided both poets and readers with an important criterion for wit, particularly since it treated wit more thoroughly than most English manuals.

At about the turn of the century wit assumed its commanding position in England. It became associated with ingenuity, the novelty of the problem, paradox, and metaphysical lyric, and with the logical juggling with which these were developed. Wit was no longer seen as the ornament of a work, but as its soul and quintessence. Gabriel Harvey defended wit as an "affluent Spirit,"[19] and Cowley in his ode to wit intimated that wit was in the spirit, not the elements, of a work.

Two early seventeenth-century attempts to treat the psychology of wit reveal more than most of the vague, repetitious allusions to wit in the rhetorics. Sir William Cornwallis explained that wit "leaues postes between the senses and the fancie, which speedily conuey intelligence and as speedily answered." It is, he continued, a fancy "well-disposed to the abilities of both neighbors, the common sense and the memory," that differs from judgment not in success but in its quickness and copiousness, its "ready payment." It is a "colour of the Soule," but partakes of the body so much that always it "must be doing, though to no end doing." "It is a fruitful land sowed and reaped at an instant." Cornwallis evidently thought of wit both as an active impulse that interrelated in an instant all the faculties of the mind as they were then understood and as the product of this impulse. Cornwallis's words are particularly interesting because he knew Donne and would probably have had him in mind in any consideration of wit.[20]

A more erudite effort to define wit psychologically was made by a T. W., usually identified as Thomas Walkington, who defined nine different kinds of wit in terms of the theory of humors. Wit, he explained, has its seat "in the Active Understanding, which doth offer the Species and ideas of Objects to the Passive, there to be discerned and judged of according to their real essence." The great wits are of a fiery temperament and are consequently always in motion. Wit gives its possessor an "active nature," a "quick insight into a thing" and "a sence of feeling most exact." Like Cornwallis, T. W. stressed the chameleon-like character of wit, and he recommended judgment as its proper consort.[21]

While the conception of wit at the turn of the century was organic, dynamic, and synthetic, men of letters still studied the witty figures of rhetoric that could be learned and produced more or less mechanically. Hoskins approved of the "pleasant touch" given by various types of puns, but warned against a too liberal use of word-play.[22] Various kinds of puns and antitheses were mentioned by most of the rhetoricians. Paradox, becoming increasingly popular as a literary form, reflected the effort to chain the finite and the infinite and to find the oneness in all things. It became the idiom of the no-man's-land between spirituality and skepticism, faith and reason, and was an integral part of the skeptic pattern and the core of the great Christian mysteries. In the later seventeenth century Isaac Barrow included in his description of wit references to a "crafty wresting" of matter and a "plausible reconciling of contradictions, as in acute Nonsense." [23]

During the early decades of the seventeenth century wit was primarily intellectual and logical and, despite the ideal of spontaneity, extremely self-conscious. Many Renaissance rhetoricians followed Aristotle in stressing the logical nature of antithesis. Paradox and the farfetched conceit, both of which present novel and surprising relationships, were considered in terms of logic or pseudo-logic. Despite conservative critics' warnings against wit, the literary-minded of the earlier seventeenth century admired wit — and chiefly for its superficial brilliance and urbane elegance.

THE PROBLEM OF PERSONAL EXPRESSION

Some recent critics have gloried in the metaphysicals as expressing precisely the flux and flow of particular experience. But while these poets' aesthetic theories would not have justified this kind of expression, there is nevertheless a fascinating new personal element in their work. Renaissance writers were chiefly interested in universals and were more concerned with communicating these abstract ideas to a reader than in expressing personal feelings because of a private need. In the seventeenth century, however, and particularly in metaphysical poetry, the experiences through which these ideas were presented became increasingly complex and individual. Both in prose and in poetry there was a trend toward styles that reflected thought processes and the personality of the author. The metaphysical style occupies in poetry a position similar to that of the anti-Ciceronian styles of Rabelais, Lipsius, Montaigne, and their English imitators in prose.

The idea of the poet as physician to himself was familiar. George Puttenham observed that "it is a peece of ioy to be able to lament with ease, and freely to poure forth a mans inward sorrowes and the greefe wherewith his minde is surcharged." He explained that sorrows were appeased "not with any medicament of a contrary temper, as the Galenistes use, to cure (*contraria contrariis*) but as the *Paracelsians*, who cure (*similia similibus*), making one dolour to expel another." Half-serious developments of the theory are also found in Sidney's thirty-fourth sonnet and in Donne's "The Triple Foole," which maintains that grief is tamed when fettered in verse. Owen Felltham wrote that the poet shall "vent his *passions* by his Pen, and ease his *heart* of their weight," and Samuel Daniel praised the sonnet for expressing a "present passion," which might often be "without measure." [24]

But the stress was upon poetry as a release from emotional strain, not upon the realistic description of personal experience.

Statements by the metaphysicals about the personal element in poetry are both rare and ambiguous. There are none by Donne sufficiently clear to prove anything. George Herbert in his dying message to Nicholas Ferrar described his poems as "a picture of the many spiritual conflicts that have passed betwixt God and my soul," but he also made it clear that the poems were intended as a public as well as a private statement when he asked Ferrar to judge them solely according to their potential benefit to other Christians. Similarly, Cowley emphasized that poetry was not "the *Picture* of the *Poet*, but of *things* and *persons* imagined by him," but he also stressed the effect upon the poet of cares and misfortunes.[25] While there is no evidence that the metaphysicals attempted to give an exact poetic expression of a particular personal experience, it is clear that there was a growing interest in the kind of intimate personal statement that was written to communicate a deep universal meaning in a form that would move the reader to adopt the writer's point of view. Donne's "Holy Sonnets" and Herbert's devotional poems are the best examples.

Renaissance writers, however, were fascinated with styles that exhibited not only character, but also the actual act of thinking and the natural idiom of conversation. The theory that style was the image of the man was developed by Puttenham, who explained that style, by which one could best judge a man, reflected the warp and woof and temper of a man's mind. "Speake that I may see thee," declared Jonson, who wrote that language "springs out of the most retired, and inmost parts of us, and is the Image of the Parent of it, the Mind." A call for a more personal type of writing was also issued by both English and French prose writers. Nashe wrote, "Let our speech accorde with our life," and one of the French advocates of the Senecan style recommended that the writer not only present clear ideas, "but also the movements with which one conceives them." [26] Closely related to the demand for a more personal style was a growing interest in cultivating colloquial diction and rhythms. Poets probably felt that these contributed to a kind of expression that was both personal and sincere. Although their contemporaries at times regarded the metaphysical poets, particularly Donne, as obscure, these poets shared the interest in the plain language and conversational rhythms for which Jonson and others were striving. Donne, whose poetry often seems like impassioned conversation, referred to his poetry as masculine and straightforward, and George Herbert rejected rheotrical devices which he considered to be artificial and merely decorative.

This accent on a conversational, personality-revealing style accounts for most of the "personal" quality of Donne and his followers. Some critics have assumed that the rebellious Donne flouted all critical dicta, but it is more probable that he took seriously the increasingly popular conception of the function of style. Several characteristics of his poetry — the remote analogies, the ellipses, the qualifying parenthetical remarks, and the natural diction and rhythms — suggest the thinking process. As Donne's style is so fundamentally consistent in poems, letters, devotions, tracts, and sermons, it evidently reflected his personality and thought processes while still adhering to the basic demands of Renaissance rhetoric. Donne and the other metaphysicals often combined a flexible use of rhetoric with intimate personal detail while still dealing in a large measure with universals.

THE RELATION OF THOUGHT AND FEELING

It has become fashionable to echo Eliot's remark about "the direct sensuous apprehension of thought" and the "recreation of thought into feeling" [27] found in the metaphysicals — and more recently it has become even more fashionable to dismiss the "unified sensibility" as an incomprehensible private myth of Eliot. In any case, Eliot has understood the metaphysical poets at least somewhat better than the metaphysical poets could have understood his theories about their work.

Though Donne and his contemporaries did not find in metaphysical poetry a distinctive relation of thought and feeling, they did sometimes think in terms somewhat similar to those employed by modern critics. Donne himself seems to have felt an opposition between the "rational" and "feeling" aspects of man. Speaking of the rational soul that "hath swallowed up a Negative, and feeling soul," Donne concluded that "God himself, who onely is one, seems to have been eternally delighted with a disunion of persons." More significantly, Donne and others emphasized the close relationship between body, mind, and soul. Burton's *Anatomy of Melancholy* and other Renaissance treatments of psychology stress the body's influence on the mind. Donne, as is revealed in "The Extasie" and throughout his work, felt particularly strongly about the close relationship between body, mind, and soul in the psychological process. He found thoughts "ever leavened with passions and affectations." In a letter to Henry Goodyere, he wrote:

We consist of three parts, a Soul, and Body and Mind: which I call those thoughts and affections and passions, which neither soul nor body hath alone, but have been begotten by their communication, as Musique results out of our breath and a Cornet.[28]

It is important that the metaphysical style received its determining impetus at a time when men were keenly aware of the close relationship between thoughts, passions, and the senses — after the reaction against the medieval concentration upon the spiritual and before the Cartesian dichotomy of mind and body.

Neither Renaissance nor modern academic psychology resorts to the imprecise oversimplification of treating thought and feeling as disparate entities. However, Donne and other Renaissance intellectuals frequently spoke of thoughts, passions, and affectations and had a fine sense of their complex relationship, but not of their fusion in a creative process. The relationship was viewed in moral, not aesthetic, terms.

AMBIGUITY

Cleanth Brooks and a good many other modern critics have regarded ambiguity as a distinguishing characteristic of metaphysical poetry. The metaphysical poets, they have explained, showed a lively awareness of different attitudes toward a given situation. Did the metaphysicals, then, understand ambiguity in something like the modern sense? If so, when was ambiguity approved or censured?

There are of course several kinds of ambiguity. It is unlikely that the metaphysicals, as some critics have suggested, used words and images connotatively to give an "ironic" or "dissonant" dimension to their work for its own sake. Poets used images to adorn or to disparage, but not to do both simultaneously. However, they were aware of the ambiguity resulting from directly conflicting attitudes and of the problem of using wit in a serious context.

Burton spoke of the "mixed affections and passions" experienced when perturbations arose simultaneously from both the concupiscible and irascible faculties, and Vives believed that one hated most strongly where there was a basis for love. But traditional Renaissance rhetoric continued to demand the expression of one attitude at a time. William Webbe classified all poetry under the heads of comical, tragical, and historical, and Puttenham wrote that the joys of love were to be uttered in one sort of poetry and the sorrows in another.[29] Although many metaphysical poems express single basic attitudes, some others such as Donne's "A Valediction: Of My Name, in the Window" express conflicting attitudes.

Numerous Renaissance writers, including Shakespeare, apparently found no inconsistency in the use of wit in serious matters. In his letters Donne used a conceited manner in treating serious topics — even in writing of the death of one of his children. After Donne's death Sidney Godolphin praised him as a "prodigie of wit and pietie" and Lord Falkland alluded to his most obvious witty tour de force, "The Crosse," as an "Antheme" and "Psalme." Thomas Pestell lauded Donne, with whom he associated George Herbert, for "intertissu'd *Wit* and *Holiness*." Later in the century Dean Duport hailed Herbert as a "poet at once most witty and most devout."[30]

The seventeenth-century metaphysicals and their readers could have found among the ancients and their own contemporaries abundant authority for a way of thinking and writing with which they apparently had an affinity. Both Cicero and Quintilian had recommended the use of wit and humor in a serious context because it provided a relaxation from gravity and showed the author to be a man of taste and polish. Praising a "seriously jocose" manner and "an elegant kind of humor, satirical with a mixture of gravity," Cicero asserted that "there is no time of life in which wit and polite humor may not very properly be exercised." Sir Thomas More defended his use of wit in religious discussions by pointing out that "as Horace sayeth, a man maye sometyme saye full soth in game," and Thomas Blount remarked that Persius "never *sports*, but after the most *serious* manner in the World." [31]

Along with its serious didacticism the humanistic spirit also brought with it several types of wit that made for a kind of ambiguity. More, with whose work Donne was certainly familiar, consistently used puns, other witty devices, and merry tales in his religious discussions, although not without misgivings, and continued his show of wit even upon the scaffold. Another humanist with his own brand of ambiguity was Erasmus, who termed More an "English Democritus" and insisted that More had "made" him write *The Praise of Folly*, which after much serious fooling reaches a climax in the conclusion that "all Christian Religion seems to have a kind of allyance with folly" and that "there are no sort of fools seem more out of the way than are these whom the zeal of Christian Religion has once swallow'd up." [32] More's ambiguous attitude is illustrated in a rather startling way as one realizes that the man who delighted in such a work was also a Christian martyr.

The Italian concept of *sprezzatura*, one of the ideals of the Renaissance gentleman, also inspired a style of writing in which a playful wit danced through the most serious matter. Castiglione's courtiers, for instance, sharply condemned any great show of care and seriousness, advising gentlemen to conceal these by grace and urbanity. [33] Probably most fashionable Renaissance verse was influenced by this idea, and the metaphysicals apparently agreed with Castiglione that it was well to avoid an exaggerated earnestness and to invite praise by nonchalantly hinting at great knowledge.

The most obvious proof that at least a large group at the turn of the century saw no impropriety or indecorum in combining extreme wit with extreme seriousness is the popularity enjoyed by the Anglo-Catholic "witty" preachers. The most famous of these, Lancelot Andrewes, began during the 1590's to interlard his sermons with startling comparisons, antitheses, paradoxes, puns, and word-play. Binding all together was a fine mesh of logic. Donne approved such devices "*used ad ancillationem*, to convey, and *ad vehiculum*, as a chariot," but condemned going to extremes.[34]

Similar tendencies were manifested in a more extreme and sometimes bizarre fashion on the Continent. There was a general belief in the Catholic countries that conceits, puns, and various pleasantries in religious works caught the reader's attention, aided comprehension, chased away the devil, opened the way for divine inspiration, and were completely compatible with saintly aims. Tesauro conceived of God as speaking through nature in witty subtleties and wrote explicit instructions for unveiling these and for the use of witticisms in the pulpit.[35]

Another kind of ambiguity significant for metaphysical poetry was the grotesque, particularly the witty grotesque. A marked concern with sickness, death, and the grave in their most naturalistic aspects appeared in many types of late Renaissance work. *Hamlet* is one of the best examples. However, when the grotesque is merged with witty devices and with humor, the result is distinguishable as a new product. This distinct kind of ambiguity occurs in Donne's prose paradoxes and problems treating suicide, in Dekker's *Plague Pamphlets*, in most of the work of Sir Thomas Browne, and pre-eminently in metaphysical poetry. It sets the tone in the treatment of graves in Donne's "The Relique" and Marvell's "To His Coy Mistress," while Donne's "The Autumnall," beginning as a compliment to a lady, tops off a description of shapeless "Winter-faces" with an account of souls seeking their lost teeth at the resurrection.

The metaphysicals' habit, then, of intersprinkling various kinds of wit with serious treatments of one's soul and one's mistress was the product of an old and widespread tradition that experienced a significant florescence during the late Renaissance. But this is only one side of the total picture. There was a distinctly different point of view that sometimes directly influenced the metaphysicals. Virtually always during the history of this tradition there were careful qualifications from within or questionings from without.

Despite their general approval of a witty seriousness, Cicero had warned against jokes violating dignity and Quintilian had particularly disapproved of the metaphysical habit of punning on names. The witty More apparently suffered recurring misgivings. In the *Apologye* he quoted Horace to justify bringing in "among the most serious matters fansyes and sports and mery tales," and he submitted the *Dialogue* to learned men for approval because he feared that the jests "should unto sad men seem over light and wanton for the weight and gravity of such an earnest matter." [36] Nor had the "witty" preachers escaped criticism for their strange figures, wit, and extensive use of tenuous logical analysis. And during the first decade of the seventeenth century T. W. seemed to feel some necessity for defending a touch of lightness where one might expect an untempered gravity. Citing Erasmus's praise of Folly and Beza's praise of Nihil, he concluded: "Tragical Melpomene hir self will now and then put on the Comicall . . . and wise men will sometimes play with Childrens Rattles." [37]

The metaphysical poets themselves were sometimes troubled in glimpsing a cleavage between the scintillating exhibition of wit and the expression of the deeply serious. Donne, for instance, in two passages from his letters suggested that wit and elegance were not consistent with sacred matters:

I find little errour in that Grecians counsell, who saies, If thou ask anything of God, offer no sacrifice, nor ask elegantly, nor vehemently, but remember that thou wouldest not give to such an asker.

I would also rather make short prayers than extend them, though

God can neither be surprised, nor besieged: for, long prayers have
more of the man, as ambition of eloquence, and a complacencie
in the work, and more of the devil by often distractions; for, after
in the beginning we have well intreated God to hearken, we speak
no more of him.

In one poem he grouped wit with fame and hopes as "profane
mistresses" and again wrote:

> When we are mov'd to seeme religious
> Only to vent wit, Lord deliver us.[38]

Donne felt at times that wit was incompatible with truly serious
matter, but he was more suspicious of the spirit inspiring the wit —
the desire to enhance the writer rather than the matter. Furthermore, Donne went far beyond the courtly convention in depre-
cating "giddie fantastique Poets," and seemed to feel that it was
inappropriate even to versify the serious.[39] Perhaps partly because
of his Catholic background he participated enthusiastically in a
tradition that regarded conceits and witty devices as legitimate
enhancements of the most serious subjects, but even while continuing to employ them he came to question wit and the motives
behind it.

George Herbert during his earlier years regarded wit and seriousness as congenial complements. He wrote conceited Latin
verse on his mother's death, addressed two witty sonnets to God,
and treated religious subjects with the "false wit" later ridiculed
by Addison. In "Jordan" (II), which apparently refers to his
use of metaphysical wit, he wrote:

> Nothing could seem too rich to clothe the sunne,
> Much lesse those joyes which trample on his head.

However, he now found unnecessary the "curling" metaphors,
the "trim invention," the "thousands of notions" offered by the
brain and the general striving after liveliness and popular appeal.
He felt God was obscured in "dust blown by wit." He attacked
the "witty" preachers' style and declared that the character of
the parson's sermons was holiness: "he is not witty, or learned,
or eloquent, but holy."[40] Similarly, Marvell in "The Coronet" in-

timated that wit presumably used to glorify Christ was in reality intended to glorify the poet.

Probably classical rhetoric, the humanists, the courtiers, the Jesuits and others helped to give the metaphysicals the authority and example for pursuing their own particular penchant in intermingling the witty and the highly serious. Although its lighter side was usually recognized, wit was regarded as a decorous means of expressing deep truths effectively. This merging of wit and seriousness, while not intended as today to reflect the complexity and ambiguity of personal experience, reveals a broad view and an integration of diverse elements that later periods have sometimes found strange. The seventeenth-century metaphysicals, while they seldom regarded wit as actually frivolous, approached some moderns' views in finding the spirit behind the wit out of place in serious discussions. In using wit with a full awareness that some considered it inappropriate, they approached the practice of some modern metaphysicals.

A POETRY OF INTEGRATION

In the light of all of these current Renaissance ideas about poetry and related fields, how would Donne's contemporaries have conceived of metaphysical poetry? An attempted reconstruction of the seventeenth-century interpretation or conception of metaphysical poetry is all that is possible. But, in accordance with such a reconstructed definition, metaphysical poetry is poetry in which the emotional or intuitive element is subjected to a highly intellectual consideration that usually emphasizes rational relationships through the use of logical modes of organization, wit, and tenuously logical metaphors that are frequently extended. This poetry assumes that the poet and his readers share an interest in certain abstract systems of thought, particularly the conception of the interlocking relationship between the physical and supersensible through a system of correspondences. Wit results from an emphasis on the logical relationships between words and ideas such as are found in antithesis, paradox, the pun, and the conceit. These devices, when exploited apparently for their own sake in a serious context, give the effect of ambiguity and sometimes produce the witty grotesque. The logical metaphor characteristic of metaphysical poetry is – in I. A. Richard's terminology – one in which the "tenor" (the term being compared), usually an emotional or intuitive experience, is examined in terms of a precise and complex "vehicle" (the term to which the tenor is compared). The vehicle typically is exact, consistent, and essentially abstract. Although the logical relationship between the two is often very tenuous, the metaphor frequently links two qualitatively different realms (e.g., the physical and spiritual) in a way that has meaning for the poet and his contemporaries.

Although Donne remains the best representative of the metaphysical style, poetry need not be "just like" Donne's to be genuinely metaphysical. The essential qualities of metaphysical poetry should not be confused with the adjuncts of Donne's style, such as his own rhythms, meters, grammatical structures, and technical vocabulary. Donne's style and the metaphysical style are not synonymous. The metaphysical style is an abstraction derived from analysis of basic and distinguishing features in the work of a group of poets who are considered as a group only because each poet's work exhibits in a considerable degree at least some of these fundamental characteristics.

But metaphysical poetry at its best goes far beyond these distinguishing features and becomes a poetry of sweeping imagination and perceptive integration. Through correspondences and incarnational and sacramental symbolism metaphysical poetry attempts to grasp and hold together a bursting universe. An imaginative expansiveness results from the tensing of the metaphorical relationship, the broadened subject matter, and the virtuosity in wit. The conceit, paradox, and pun, with their linking of different domains, and ambiguity, with its union of the witty and serious, appear as two related aspects of the imaginative range and integrative drive of metaphysical poetry. While the grotesque often indicates a half-realized awareness of incongruity or discontinuity, the use of a witty grotesquerie in a serious amorous or religious poem is a kind of symbolic integration of the incongruous, an effort to remove the discontinuity by bridging the gap. Whether metaphysical poetry displays a "unified sensibility" or not, it is characterized by a particularly close relationship between feeling and thinking, life and learning. In individual poems the integration may vary between perfect unity and a kind of colloidal state in which different elements are held suspended in solution together. In any case, metaphysical poetry may be conceived of as the produce of the tensions between an imaginative centrifugal force and an integrative centripetal force.

The metaphysical style, which attained its full development in the earlier seventeenth century, decayed and disappeared in the later seventeenth century. Not until the romantic revival of the early nineteenth century, when the metaphysical style was interpreted anew by poets and critics, did it again become a shaping and vitalizing influence on English poetry.

❧ I I ❧

Seeds of the Revival

CAREW had praised Donne for planting blossoms of "fresh invention" in the muses' garden, but during the late seventeenth century and earlier eighteenth century the blossoms drooped sadly and went to seed. Under the influence of romanticism these seeds of the recent metaphysical revival slowly came to life, struggled to become adapted to an unfavorable intellectual climate during most of the nineteenth century, and finally flowered again during the later nineteenth and earlier twentieth centuries.

Early nineteenth-century critics frequently praised the "beauties" of seventeenth-century metaphysical poetry with the enthusiasm of the discoverer while condemning its "faults" with the vigor of the intellectual vigilante. Their attitudes marked a very discernible break with those of the eighteenth century when the metaphysicals were known chiefly through highly unsympathetic criticism, such as Addison's essays on "mixed wit" and "false wit" and Johnson's essay on Cowley, or through adaptations, such as Pope's neoclassic revisions of some of Donne's satires and Wesley's Methodist hymns based on George Herbert's lyrics.

ROMANTICS AND ELIZABETHANS

The germ of the modern metaphysical revival was in the Elizabethan revival of the earlier nineteenth century, which in turn was a part of the general European interest in older literatures which accompanied the growth of romanticism. Many older poets were made available by editors, re-evaluated by critics, and drawn upon by poets. During the first three quarters of the nineteenth century many new editions of the metaphysical poets appeared. There were at least ten new editions of George Herbert alone, mostly during the 1850's and 1860's. Donne, Crashaw, and Cowley were included in Alexander Chalmer's editions in 1810. Then Donne, Cowley, and Marvell appeared between 1822 and 1855 in F. J. Child's "The British Poets" series, while Donne, Herbert, Cowley, and Marvell were represented in Alexander Grosart's "The Fuller Worthies" editions of the early 1870's. In the United States, Ezekiel Sanford edited the works of Donne, Crashaw, and Cowley between 1819 and 1823. As knowledge of the seventeenth-century metaphysical poets spread, some nineteenth-century poets such as Beddoes, Hood, and Browning became strongly metaphysical, while others such as Wordsworth and Tennyson showed some slight metaphysical influence. Wordsworth, for instance, referred to the "heaven taught skill of Herbert" and perhaps depended both on Herbert and on Crashaw in his "Intimations of Immortality" ode. Tennyson admired some poems by Donne and Marvell, echoed Herbert's "The Flower" in the prologue to "In Memoriam," and perhaps depended on his "The World" in "The Palace of Art." [1]

The revival of the Renaissance lyric, though less ostentatious than the revival and imitation of the plays of Shakespeare and Marlowe, was ultimately more significant. The rediscovered older lyric forms, free from the domination of Milton or Pope, were richly suggestive for earlier nineteenth-century poets who, despite their often grandiose literary plans, found the short personal lyric most congenial. For instance, the interspersed lyrics are by far the most valuable part of Thomas Lovell Beddoes's dramatic work. Most romantic writers, while regarding the age of Elizabeth as the high point of the English Renaissance, failed to distinguish between the Elizabethan and Jacobean eras. The kinds of lyrics popularized by the Elizabethan song writers and the "tribe of Ben" were widely imitated. Among those able to capture the savor and technique of seventeenth-century lyrics while retaining much of the subject matter and diction of the romantic poets were Beddoes, George Darley, Thomas Hood, Thomas Wade, and Charles Lamb.

The time was ripe for a reinterpretation of the seventeenth-century metaphysical style since there were both significant similarities and dissimilarities in the philosophical and aesthetic attitudes of the metaphysicals and the romantics. It would seem at first that an almost impassable chasm separated the Renaissance and romantic points of view. The Renaissance poet was interested in illuminating the unchanging truths of a complex, but divinely-ordained, well-ordered, and knowable universe; the romantic poet, with a century of British empiricist aesthetics behind him, felt that the imagination continuously created its own world according to its own laws. The Renaissance placed its faith in general ideas derived from the constancy of human nature and apprehended through reason and logic, while the romantic era centered its faith in the particular feelings of the individual ("minute and remote distinctions of feeling," as Shelley wrote to Godwin December 11, 1817, in describing his own imaginative process) which were the product of association guided by intuition. The Renaissance poet was primarily concerned with revealing truths to a reader, but the romantic poet tended to believe in poetry for the sake of the poet. For the Renaissance, metaphors pointed out actual logical analogies; but for the romantic era, metaphors more characteristically reflected a subjective emotional sympathy, compared feelings rather than ideas.

One of the first qualities of the metaphysicals' work that attracted the sympathetic attention of the nineteenth century was the apparently personal tone of many of the lyrics. The metaphysicals' adherence to the Renaissance theory that style should reveal the man and his thought processes often deceived the nineteenth-century critics and prompted them to attribute an exaggerated personal significance to metaphysical poetry. Leigh Hunt reflected a characteristic attitude when he asserted that Donne's "On His Mistris" ("By our first strange and fatall interview"), which earlier critics felt sure Donne had written for his wife, was "full of as much nature and real feeling, as sincerity ever put into a true passion." Later in the century George Macdonald wrote that "George Herbert goes beyond all that have preceded him, in the expression of feeling as it flows from individual conditions, in the analysis of his own moods." [2]

The romantics also approached the metaphysicals sympathetically because of some fundamental similarities in their world-views, although these similarities were shot through with differences. The romantics thought of man as a little world less literally than had the Renaissance writers, but they did return to a belief that nature, like man, was an organic whole and not just a concourse of atoms. Reacting against a mechanistic point of view, they restored to the universe much of the Renaissance sense of the supersensible, the supernatural, and the invisible — although they saw through an alluring veil of mystery many things taken for granted in the Renaissance. They believed that there were correspondences between man and his world and that the proper study of mankind was not so much man as man's relation to everything else, particularly the mysterious powers that were abroad in the universe. However, the Renaissance cosmology had crumbled under the impact of science, and with it had collapsed the belief in a complex, all-embracing, unitive system of correspondences and the faith in logical analogy as an instrument for discovering objective truth about the universe. In the earlier nineteenth century correspondences were less systematically analogical, less concrete and particularized, and less literal. God was further removed from the world, but was somehow expressed in nature. The universe was sometimes conceived of as a process involving an ascent from the material to the ideal. Analogies confined to the material realm were frequently regarded as superficial and the more mystic relations between the world-soul and man's soul were stressed by a number of poets and critics.

Writers of the romantic era often apprehended correspondences as separate intuitive insights hinting at the inexpressible, rather than as a complex system. They saw an organic interrelationship between nature (particularly out-of-door "beauties"), imagination (particularly the poetic imagination), and symbols, which were thought of as depending on the creativity of the human mind. Study of the association of ideas stimulated interest in sympathetic analogies resulting from the mind's supposed tendency to fuse itself with kindred forces and forms. Marvell's comparison of an amorous relationship to two parallel lines and Hogarth's comparison of the serpentine "line of beauty" to a state of volition and ease were arrived at by very different processes, but the similarity between the two might nevertheless be richly suggestive. Despite the differences between Renaissance and romantic conceptions of analogy, the very belief in the existence of some kind of correspondences between man and nature, the finite and the infinite, helped provide an intellectual climate favorable to an appreciation of metaphysical poetry.

Although the flavor of seventeenth-century wit was on the whole foreign to the seriousness of nineteenth-century aesthetics, the conception of romantic irony, as developed in the aesthetic theories of Schlegel and the literary works of Tieck, included a kind of wit and played a role similar to that of wit. Asserting the sovereign superiority of the artist over the world which his imagination continuously creates, the theory of romantic irony enabled the artist to sport playfully with his materials, to decline to adhere to only one point of view, and to mix the seemingly frivolous with the serious.

COLERIDGE AND THE REVIVAL

If Eliot has been the messiah of the recent metaphysical cultism, Coleridge was its John the Baptist, crying out the merits of the metaphysicals in a wilderness of aesthetic prejudice and misunderstanding and preparing the way for the present revival. His contribution was twofold and incalculable. He communicated his enthusiasm for the metaphysicals to an important circle of literary friends and acquaintances through his letters and brilliant conversation and brought an understanding and appreciation of their poetry to a much wider group through his lectures and published writings. Probably of more ultimate importance, however, were some of his aesthetic theories, particularly that of the reconciliation of opposites, that have become the cornerstone of much of the recent critical praise of metaphysical poetry.

Coleridge's discussions of the metaphysicals are often fragmentary, but in general his position is clear. He felt that Donne had untold reserves of intellectual, imaginative, and personal power. Coleridge declared that the "popolousness" and "activity" were as great in Cowley as in Donne, but that the "will-worship in squandering golden hecatombs on a fetish" was Donne's own. Coleridge sought to define the distinctive qualities of Donne's wit:

Wonder-working vigour, intenseness and peculiarity of thought, using at will the almost boundless stores of a capacious memory, and exercised on subjects where we have no right to expect it — that is the wit of Donne!

Coleridge was one of the first of a new era to appreciate Donne in somewhat the same way as did the seventeenth century. His description of Donne's wit resembles those of T. W. and Cornwallis, who also had emphasized copiousness, memory, quickness, surprise, and "ready payment." Coleridge's notes on "The Canonization" show a growing insight into the logical, metaphorical, and dramatic structures of Donne's style. He observed that he formerly sought out "grand lines and fine stanzas," but that his delight had greatly increased since it consisted more "in tracing the leading thought throughout the whole." He asserted that "nothing was ever more admirably made out than the figure of the compass" in "A Valediction: Forbidding Mourning," and in his comment on "The Extasie" he noted that he "could never find fault with metaphysical poems, were they all like this, or but half as excellent." [3]

Although Coleridge believed that Donne's wit occasionally approached blasphemy, he was often sympathetic to wit and to ambiguity. In one of Donne's verse letters to the Countess of Bedford he discovered a happy specimen of "that white flattery in which the wit unrealises the falsehood, and the sportive exaggeration of the thoughts, blending with a delicate tenderness, faithfully conveys the truth as to the feelings." He observed that sometimes regret was expressed most naturally through "intellectual effort and activity." [4]

Although he apparently never carried out the proposal, jotted down in one of his notebooks, to write "2 Satires in the manner of Donne," he imitated the Donnean measures in a verse commentary scribbled in his copy of the Chalmers edition of Donne:

> With Donne, whose muse on dromedary trots,
> Wreathe iron pokers into true-love knots;
> Rhyme's sturdy cripple, fancy's maze and clue,
> Wit's forge and fire-blast, meaning's press and screw. [5]

Coleridge's comments on the other metaphysicals are less extensive. He was fond of George Herbert, but was sometimes disturbed by the "too frequent quaintness of the thoughts" in *The Temple*. Nevertheless, he preferred Herbert's "enigma of thoughts" to the nineteenth-century "riddle of words." In December 1818, he wrote to Collins that he had ceased to laugh at Herbert's quaintness and found more comfort in *The Temple* "than in all the poetry since the poems of Milton," and particularly recommended "The Flower." Coleridge thought Crashaw unsurpassed when he combined richness of thought and diction, as in the latter part of his hymn to Saint Teresa. He recalled that the passages treating her martyrdom were ever present to his mind during the composition of the second part of "Christabel" — "if, indeed, by some subtle process of the mind they did not suggest the first thought of the whole poem." [6]

While Coleridge's literary theories were no doubt intended to be of universal application and were apparently formulated with metaphysical poetry only incidentally in mind, there are striking parallels in the fortunes of Coleridge's aesthetics and Donne's poetry. Coleridge's theories serve to interpret Donne's poetry and Donne's poetry serves to illustrate Coleridge's theories. The two have shed a radiant aura of critical approval upon each other and together have acted as a guiding beacon for modern metaphysical poets. The example of Donne and the precepts of Coleridge, as both have been interpreted by Richards, Brooks, Eliot, and other "new critics," have become almost indistinguishably blended.

Richards has maintained that Coleridge's aesthetics opened up new fields in the study of language comparable to the new universe discovered by Galileo insofar as both made the significant shift from a preoccupation with the "what" and "why" to the "how." [7] Most of Coleridge's present significance as a critic pivots around his definition of the synthetic power of the imagination. "This power," he explained, "first put in action by the will and understanding, and retained under their irremissive, though gentle and unnoticed, controul . . . reveals itself in the balance or reconciliation of opposite or discordant qualities." He regarded it as harmonizing the general with the concrete, the idea with the image, emotion with order, and the natural with the artificial.[8]

From Coleridge's theory of the imagination Richards derived his own theory of two principal types of poetry: exclusive, in which the psychological impulses run parallel, and inclusive, characterized by "the extraordinary heterogeneity of the distinguishable impulses," as in Donne's "Nocturnall upon Saint Lucies Day" and Marvell's "The Definition of Love." [9] With polite bows of acknowledgment to Richards and Coleridge, Brooks re-examined metaphysical poetry, put Donne and Coleridge together, and got a definition for moderns:

It is a poetry in which the oppositions of the impulses which are united is extreme, or, to base oneself directly on Coleridge: it is a poetry in which the poet attempts the reconciliation of qualities which are opposite or discordant in the extreme.[10]

Donne, could he have seen such a definition, would probably have felt quite undone, since he apparently felt he was expressing a single significant truth rather than a mass of divergent impulses, and even Coleridge, who was frequently able to approach the seventeenth-century point of view, would no doubt have been gravely perplexed. The idea of ambiguity, of which Renaissance critics were only vaguely aware in their growing suspicion that wit was inappropriate to a highly serious theme, is central to Brooks's discussion of metaphysical poetry. Nevertheless, the definition provides a suggestive working concept and is symptomatic of the twentieth century's demands upon the seventeenth century.

OTHER CRITICS OF THE REVIVAL

There were a number of other earlier nineteenth-century men of letters who shared Coleridge's interest in the metaphysicals. Lamb's enthusiasm perhaps surpassed even that of Coleridge. Lamb apparently had a mind delicately attuned to appreciate the wit, metaphors, and grotesquerie of the metaphysical poets. Hazlitt wrote of Lamb that "his jests scald like tears: and he probes a question with a play upon words." He recalled how Lamb read Donne's "On His Mistris" to Southey and himself "with suffused features and a faltering tongue." "But with what a gusto would he describe his favourite authors, Donne, or Sir Philip Sidney, and call their most crabbed passages *delicious*." Defending the depth of personal feeling in the poems of Donne and Cowley, Lamb insisted that "in the very thickest of their conceits, — in the bewildering mazes of tropes, — a warmth of soul and generous feeling shines through." Once Lamb inquired of Coleridge his opinion of "a poet very dear to me, the now out of fashion Cowley," and asked if "no inconsiderable part of his verse be not delicious." [11]

Indeed, no inconsiderable part of Lamb's own verse has been found "delicious" in the seventeenth-century manner. Although Lamb's seventeenth-century vein owes more to the Jonsonian tradition than to the metaphysicals, several poems and frequent flashes of wit indicate some influence by the metaphysicals. A mixture of wit and undoubted seriousness graces his punning "Epicedium: Going or Gone" and his "On an Infant Dying as Soon as Born":

> She did but ope an eye, and put
> A cleare beam forth, and strait up shut
> For the long dark: ne'er more to see
> Through glasses of mortality.

Another poem reminiscent of the metaphysicals treats the insanity of Lamb's sister, "Her sense lock'd up, and herself kept out." [12]

Lamb's criticism of the metaphysicals was personal and impressionistic, but Thomas De Quincey and William Hazlitt analyzed the logical and rhetorical basis of the metaphysical style and more than any other critics of the age came to understand the dress, if not the spirit, of metaphysical poetry from a seventeenth-century point of view. De Quincey, treating the metaphysicals in his essay on rhetoric, ransacked his own store of rhetoric in extravagant praise of Donne, while Hazlitt from virtually the same premises lashed out bitterly against the metaphysicals.

De Quincey insisted that the seventeenth-century metaphysical poets were essentially rhetorical in that they placed "the principal stress upon the management of the thoughts, and only a secondary one upon the ornaments of style." Attacking Johnson's essay on Cowley, he maintained that "the artifice and machinery of rhetoric furnishes in its degree as legitimate a basis for intellectual pleasure as any other." He asserted that Donne "combined — what no other writer has ever done — the last sublimation of dialectical subtlety and address with the most impassioned majesty." "Massy diamonds compose the very substance of his poem on the Metempsychosis . . . whilst a diamond dust of rhetorical brilliancies is strewed over the whole of his occasional verses and his prose." [13]

Hazlitt saw only the glitter of cheap tinsel where De Quincey had discovered diamond dust. He explained that metaphysical poetry was a poetry of definitions that "proceeded in mode and figure, by *genus* and specific difference" and was in general the "logic of the school." He branded metaphysical poetry as "an oblique and forced construction of dry, matter-of-fact, decked out in a robe of glittering conceits, and clogged with the halting shackles of verse." He defined it as an "ill-assorted unprofitable union" of what he called severe poetry and lively poetry. [14]

A different kind of an attempt to restore to the metaphysicals some of their lost prestige was made by Walter Savage Landor, who introduced Marvell as a character, although chiefly as a political figure, into three of his *Imaginary Conversations* and discussed Donne and his poetry in a dramatic conversation between Izaak Walton, Charles Cotton, and Oldways, who is presented as in possession of some of the poet's earliest verses. In a pastoral setting redolent of the atmosphere of *The Compleat Angler* the three praise the passion, wit, and even majesty of Donne's poetry and discuss an imagined early love affair with Mistress Margaret Hayes, a red-haired, white-eyebrowed beauty to whom the "lost verses" were addressed before the twenty-year-old Donne, forced to renounce his older mistress, joined Essex's Azores expedition in order to forget her. Both the criticisms and the quoted poems, presumably written by Landor himself in imitation of Donne, show that he felt the exuberant vitality of Donne's work. In the conversation Walton explains that Donne's "spring torrent of passion" cast up ingenious thoughts over the "green meadows of still homely life" just as a raging brook tosses up sharp and sparkling rocks. The cosmic extravagance of Donne's flattery, as in his "The Feaver," is caught in Landor's imitation:

> She was so beautiful, had God but died
> For her, and none beside,
> Reeling with holy joy from east to west
> Earth would have sunk down blest,
> And, burning with bright zeal, the buoyant Sun
> Cried thro' his worlds *well done!*

Landor represented all the characters as in agreement about Donne's genius. They are impressed by his imaginative power and are not disturbed by his mixture of wit and sacred subject matter.[15]

REACTIONS TO SEVENTEENTH-CENTURY TASTE

Despite the eminence of many of its participants, the metaphysical revival of the early nineteenth century was essentially a minority movement. Although the first brilliant burst of enthusiasm faded, an afterglow of understanding and approval remained during the middle of the century and helped prepare for the new upsurge of interest in the 1870's.

During the earlier nineteenth century many critics still maintained that the metaphysicals' "cold conceits" ruined their poetry. Alexander Chalmers attacked conceits as "ludicrous," Thomas Campbell regarded them as disgraceful, and Henry Hallam asserted that the metaphysicals' conceits "unite coldness of subtlety with the hyperbolic extravagance of counterfeited passion."[16] These critics believed that the main thing in a poem was deep personal feeling, that metaphysical conceits were essentially logical, that logical reasoning about scientific and philosophical abstractions was virtually impossible in a state of sincere and deep feeling, and that consequently the conceits were like a killing frost that destroyed the feeling in a poem.

During the course of the nineteenth century the metaphysical metaphor was gradually reconciled with the natural expression of personal feeling. Although almost all shades of opinion were current at the same time and some critics even were — in Madame de Sévigné's phrase — not altogether of their own opinion, it is still possible to view this acclimation as taking place in four distinct steps. The first step in the revolt against the extreme view that metaphysical poetry contained nothing of value was the development of the idea that conceits were, indeed, quite bad, but chiefly because they obscured the real beauties and true feelings hidden away in metaphysical poetry. This idea was probably the one most widely held. "Almost every beauty we meet with, goes hand in hand with some striking deformity," wrote one critic in *The Retrospective Review*. "No sooner has Donne kindled the fancy with a splendid thought," declared Mrs. Anna Jameson, "than it is as instantly quenched in a cloud of cold and obscure conceits." Taking issue with De Quincey's sympathetic interpretation of the conceit, George Gilfillan pictured Donne as a "great genius ruined by a false system," for "in no writing in the language is there more spilt treasure — a more lavish loss of beautiful, original, and striking things than in the poems of Donne." [17]

The second step was taken when the critical scales were tipped slightly and the beauties were thought of as outweighing and compensating for the faults. George Cunningham explained that the inappropriate figures in George Herbert's poems were so offensive that they nearly — but not quite — destroyed the pleasures derived from the beauties. Hunt conceded that Cowley's conceits were a "fault," but emphasized that they failed to touch the "heart of his writing." George L. Craik maintained that a deeper insight into Donne's poetry revealed "the sunniest and most delicate fancy, and the truest tenderness and depth of feeling." [18]

The third step was scarcely more than a half step, but was important in preparing the way for the great stride of the fourth. It was simply a growing feeling that the metaphysicals' concern with analogies was very interesting in itself, although inappropriate to sincere personal lyric expression. One critic granted that there was "frequently a good effect" in "images and illustrations of a sentiment being farfetched," but added that "if the sentiment itself has any appearance of being so, we doubt the truth of it immediately" and are unsympathetic. Coupled with this view was a perceiving, though distorted, comprehension of the seventeenth-century concern with correspondences. It was explained that the metaphysicals "did not know the real and intrinsic value of any object, whether moral or physical; but only in what manner it might be connected with any other object, so as to be made subservient to their particular views of the moment." [19] The critics realized the importance of a system of analogies for the writers as metaphysical poets, but did not grasp its significance for them as Renaissance men.

The fourth step extended into the twentieth century. It was taken when it came to be believed that conceits did not ruin natural feelings any more than natural feelings compensated for conceits, but that conceits actually aided in the expression of feelings and — it was believed later — merged with them. This view gained popularity as sincerity came to be considered as a matter of complexity rather than of simplicity. Coleridge and Lamb defended the use of conceits in the expression of feeling and Landor explained that they were the natural product of passion. Taking issue with Addison, Hartley Coleridge approved of conceits and contended that "the mind in certain states finds comfort in playing with occult or casual resemblances, and dallying with the echo of a sound." [20]

Wit and ambiguity, too, were only gradually acclimated during the nineteenth century. Hazlitt asserted that "the slightest want of unity of impression" was fatal to serious poetry and "an infallible ground to rest the ludicrous upon." Other critics thought mixing wit with religion was almost sinful and found even Herbert's wit and humor shocking and incomprehensible. However, Coleridge and Hunt defended puns, and *The Retrospective Review* maintained that some of Donne's poems combining wit with "beauties" were valuable "partly on account of that very union of opposite qualities." Craik's statement that Marvell's "To His Coy Mistress" is "remarkable for the union of grace and force" suggests Eliot's reference to Marvell's "tough reasonableness beneath the slight lyric grace." Craik also wrote that Donne harmonized "the graceful and the grotesque, the grave and the gay, the pious and the profane." Macdonald realized that puns could be serious and found that Herbert's "graceful humor" added much to his charm, while Samuel Brown, examining Herbert's "Anagram of the Virgin Marie," was prompted to exclaim, "How sublime a prank." [21]

This reconciliation of conceits and wit with feeling helped prepare for the modern conception of the close relationship between thought and feeling in metaphysical poetry. However, as some of the old opposition remained, writers often experienced a strong tension probably not felt by seventeenth-century literary men who saw no contradiction *per se* in the mingling of passion and wit.

DELLA CRUSCANS AND "THE CHRISTIAN YEAR"

New approaches to the metaphysical style were devised as critics compared recent poets to Donne and his followers and as poets worked with a metaphysical style. Most significant were the comparisons drawn between the metaphysicals and the Della Cruscans and later between Herbert's *The Temple* and John Keble's *The Christian Year*, a cycle of devotional poems following the church calendar.

The Della Cruscan group, consisting of Robert Merry, William Parsons, Bertie Greathead, and Mrs. Hester Piozzi, flourished during the 1780's and published two collections of verse, *The Florence Miscellany* and *The British Album*. One critic found "no slight resemblance" between the metaphysicals and Della Cruscans "in as much as both are purely artificial and are dependent for their effects on a particular manner of treating their subject." He distinguished between the artificiality of the metaphysicals, which involved thoughts and images, and that of the Della Cruscans, which was based chiefly on words.[22]

But there are also figures and a playful logic reminiscent of seventeenth-century Caroline and metaphysical poetry. A conceit somewhat ill at ease in its Della Cruscan dress can be detected in "To Mrs. Piozzi":

> As the ore must for ever obedient be found
> By the load-stone attracted along,
> So in England you drew all the Poets around
> By the magical force of your song:
> The same power on Arno's fair side you retain,
> Your talents with wonder we see:
> And we hope from your converse those talents to gain,
> Though like magnets — in smaller degree.

Almost precisely the same figure occurs in Edward Herbert's "The First Meeting," but an influence is unlikely. In "Song" Mira, who appears passionate but is really cold, is compared to the "rich summer fruits and wreaths of spring" which Swiss youths each year bring into a glacier, while Julia, who appears cold but is really passionate, is like a snow-capped volcano in which her lover will perish. Another pretty piece of paradoxical praise asserts that Stella's art, her painted flowers, is more beautiful than nature, but that her nature, the flowers in her cheeks, is more lovely than her art.[23] Although there is no conclusive evidence of metaphysical influence upon the Della Cruscans, their work certainly indicates a familiarity with earlier seventeenth-century poetry.

More deeply rooted was the conviction continuing to the end of the nineteenth century that George Herbert and John Keble had much in common both as men and as poets. It was pointed out that both *The Temple* and *The Christian Year* were written without thought of publication and passed among close friends, but that both became best-sellers when finally published. Both men were known for their amicable disposition, preference for country pastoral work, and devotion to the usages and ceremonies of the Anglican Church. "Why are not *Sonnets* made of thee," Herbert had inquired of God, while Keble was saddened that Shelley and Byron did not devote their talents to the service of the church. Keble had a sympathetic understanding of Herbert's poetry and was in some measure influenced by it. He recognized Herbert as one of a class of poets who "trifle with and play around their dearest delights" in order "to maintain the true dignity of poetic reserve, and to protect their inmost thoughts and enthusiasms and emotions from being exposed to the full daylight." [24]

Even before it was known that Keble was the author of *The Christian Year* (1827), *The Temple* was compared with the popular new devotional work. There was the same interest in pastoral duties and the ceremonies of the Anglican Church and "the same love of paradox in language." Critics often found Herbert the more personal of the two, but if Herbert, as Keble said, hid his deep love of God and inmost emotions "behind a cloud of precious conceits," Keble hid his own thoughts and feelings beneath ecclesiastical forms and descriptions of external nature. Those who found the influence of Herbert "very perceptive throughout *The Christian Year* — here and there in the very words of it" [25] — were correct, as these passages from Keble and Herbert show:

> These are Thy wonders, hourly wrought,
>   Thou Lord of time and thought,
> Lifting and lowering souls at will,
>   Crowding a world of good or ill
> Into a moment's vision.

> These are thy wonders, Lord of power,
> Killing and quickning, bring down to hell
>   And up to heaven in an houre;
> Making a chiming of a passing-bell.[26]

Although Keble rarely employed conceits, he depended on a system of correspondences related to that of the Renaissance, but suffused with the new romantic sensitivity to external nature. For Keble the sun was like the Light of the World, the moon

like the Christian Church which reflected its rays; the trees and
flowers might represent saints and hermits and the dew and winds
might suggest divine grace and the Holy Spirit. However, Keble's
analogies were frequently closer to those of Marvell and Vaughan
than to Herbert's. Although he avoided extensive use of some of
the metaphysicals' favorite devices, such as the conceit and most
forms of wit, he resembled them in his use of a system of correspondences, in his references to subtle theological problems,
and in his reliance on an underlying logical structure. These qualities combined to give *The Christian Year* a certain obscurity,
which prompted at least one reader to refer to it as his "Sunday
puzzle" and which probably moved a number of others to think
it all the more like Herbert and the metaphysicals.

BEDDOES AND HOOD

During the earlier nineteenth century a new "metaphysical"
poetry also appeared in the works of Beddoes and Hood. It was
an interesting new product, grafted on to a romantic aesthetic,
and it occasionally attained the same heights and sometimes sank
to the same depths as the metaphysical poetry of the seventeenth
century.

Beddoes was dubbed "The Last Elizabethan" by Lytton Stra-
chey, but through temperament and cultivation his spirit was of
the seventeenth century. Cowley introduced him to the metaphysical style. "I am, alas, a little partial," he wrote, "for Cowley
was the first poetical writer whom I learned to understand." He
apparently learned the metaphysical style from Cowley and occasionally borrowed from him. He also absorbed much of the
flavor of the earlier seventeenth century — with its intellectualism,
melancholy, and grotesquerie — from Webster, Middleton, Massinger, and Sir Kenelm Digby. It is not certain how familiar he
was with Donne, but Beddoes and Donne were in some ways
strikingly similar. Beddoes probably approached Donne's concern
with the material aspects of death more closely than any other
English poet since Donne. It would have been "in character" for
Beddoes to pose in his shroud — as did Donne — or for Donne to

seek the secret of the soul in a study of skeletons – as did Beddoes. Beddoes committed suicide; the reader of *Biathanatos* and Donne's letters is convinced that Donne on many occasions almost did.[27]

In his poetry Beddoes wove together the metaphysical style and English and German romanticism. He held these together through his interest in a romanticized system of correspondences and his belief in the supremacy of the gothic style, with its ornamentation and "wild fancy." His theory of the gothic was supported by his conception of correspondences, for "the choice and method of combining" materials in a gothic form "arise from that disposition to interpret the phenomena of nature as types in reference to humanity, which is so strikingly expressed in modern poetry and philosophy." [28]

Beddoes' quatorzain "To My Lyre" illustrates his merging of the metaphysical style with romantic techniques:

> My Lyre! thou art the bower of my senses,
> Where they may sleep in tuneful visions bound;
> These troubling chords shall be their breeze-kissed
>   fences,
> Which are the music's tendrils warmly wound,
> As with some creeping shrub, which sweets dispenses,
> And on each quivering stalk blossoms a sound.

As in Shelley's *Defence of Poetry*, the poet is conceived of as a lyre upon which some invisible influence, like an inconstant wind, can play. This first section is metaphysical in treating the lyre not only as a symbol of creativity, but more concretely as a haven that actually protects and confines. The pun on "chords" had been employed by Marvell. In the second section the creative spirit is represented as imprisoned in the lyre until it is released through actual creative activity, and there is a companion pun on "bars." The consideration of a psychological experience through an extended metaphor is metaphysical, but the experience described is romantic. The use of wit in a serious poem is metaphysical, but the sense of animated nature and the use of synaesthesia, as in "tuneful visions," are romantic. A similar mixture

46

of metaphysical and romantic techniques is found in "A Fantastic Simile," which represents a lover as a "glowing urn" on beauty's shrine and his heart as passion-lit incense from which arises smoke thought of as sighs that mingle with his mistress's whisperings to produce tears. In "Life a Glass Window" man is portrayed as leaning against "that glassy interval," gazing on the "frost-work hopes" of his own breath, until death "knuckles the pane."

In "Dirge" there is a mixture of wit and solemnity reminiscent of the seventeenth century:

> Let dew the flowers fill;
> No need of fell despair,
> Though to the grave you bear
> One still of soul – but now too still,
> Since the still soul has fled –
> One fair – but now too fair,
> The lily being dead.–

In "Resurrection Song," as in Donne's "The Autumnall" and Herbert's "Dooms-day," wit and humor merge with the grotesque:

> Heart and artery merrily shake
> And eyelid go up, for we're going to wake.
> His eye must be brighter – one more rub!
> And pull up the nostrils! His nose was snub.

Beddoes' intellectualism, his feeling for the conceit and for wit indulged in under the aegis of romantic irony, and what one biographer has called his "skeleton complex" all blended fortuitously to make Beddoes the first significant poet in the modern metaphysical tradition. In combining metaphysical and romantic styles he anticipated a number of later metaphysical poets.

Hood, like Beddoes, could juggle Renaissance and romantic styles, sometimes with a confusing skill. However, if Beddoes had a superabundance of seventeenth-century melancholy, Hood had a virtually inexhaustible supply of seventeenth-century wit. Beddoes became a metaphysical poet largely through an academic analysis of style and a meticulous craftsmanship. But one feels it was a happy accident – a fortunate conjunction of almost unrelated literary talents – that enabled Hood to write in the metaphysical vein. In the work of Beddoes the serious strand and the witty strand are usually intertwined; in the poems of Hood the two are more often like parallel lines. Hood's knowledge of Renaissance and romantic poetry, his touch of sentimental melancholy, and his genius as a punster produced an uneasy and uneven amalgam that frequently hovers around the edges of the metaphysical style and sometimes achieves a balance of wit and gravity.

Hood apparently imitated one of Donne's lyrics. His "A Valentine" and Donne's "The Apparition" deal similarly with the visit of a ghost to the bedside of a mistress who has killed the poet through her cruelty, and both poems stress her agonized fright and repentance. Both poems also mention foreboding tapers, and Hood's reference to eyes growing "dropsical" also suggests Donne. Hood's version, however, is garnished with the obvious pun on "sprightly" and a forced one on "treble" screaming.

Although Hood was pre-eminently the pundit of the pun, he often employed conceits. Some of the passages from his "Hero and Leander" would not appear out of place amid the metaphysical portions of Chapman's version of the same story. Hood, for instance, wrote of the lovers' parting:

> O for a type of parting! Love to love
> Is like the fond attraction of two spheres,
> Which need a godlike effort to remove,
> And then sink down their sunny atmospheres,
> In rain and darkness on each ruin'd heart,
> Nor yet their melodies will sound apart.[29]

In "The Sick Bed" the patient's troubled breathing is like the wave of life "heaving to and fro" and the silent, motionless friends seem to have lent her half their powers to "eke her living out." The dominant themes and attitudes of both poems, however, are romantic. In Hood's "Hero and Leander," which is more pathos than passion, the sea-god's storm of the Marlowe-Chapman version is replaced by the story of a siren who falls in love with Leander and unwittingly kills him. The difference between the sentimentality of "The Sick Bed" and the confident logic of Donne's "Hymne to God My God, in My Sicknesse" is striking and revealing.

Paronomasia, however, was Hood's favorite medium of wit. Although he avoided puns in his most highly serious works, he apparently found no contradiction between wit and sincerity. A seemingly sincere sentiment is sometimes overlaid with word-play of which a modern television comedian would be ashamed. In a poem on death's universality, he noted that the laundress would receive her "last linen" and that "e'en the stable boy will find this life no stable thing." In a punning conceit he compared his head to a top spun by thoughts. Sometimes a more personal quality lends added emotional appeal, as in an allusion to "a son-shine in a shady place" and in some lines addressed to an absent friend:

> So angels walked unknown on earth,
> But when they flew were recognized.[30]

Hood's poetry testifies to the nineteenth century's gradual acceptance of ambiguity. Beddoes and Hood together adumbrated most of the tendencies of the metaphysical poetry of the later nineteenth and earlier twentieth centuries. The metaphysical revival was to be carried on by a poet who was an admirer of Beddoes and a friend-in-need of Hood — Robert Browning.

＊§ I I I §＊

John Donne
and Robert Browning

EW today would link Browning, the "Victorian," with
Donne, the herald of the modern sensibility. Browning's
poetry is certainly in many important ways very different
from Donne's. Yet the intellectual kinship between the two poets
was very close and was recognized by some of Browning's critics.
Despite the vital differences in their philosophical ideas and in
their aesthetic theories and practices, there were also important
similarities. Coleridge and others associated with the Elizabethan
revival started the metaphysical revival, but Browning gave it an
added impetus that did much to carry it into the twentieth century.

BROWNING'S CRITICS AND THE REVIVAL

Many of Browning's contemporaries and early critics pointed
out similarities in the work of Donne and Browning. The reputations of both poets rose about 1870 as a growing approval of
the intellectual in poetry gradually crystallized. The names of the
two poets were frequently linked and Donne profited through
association with Browning's increasing prestige. Browning and
his critics played a significant role in the metaphysical revival
until about the beginning of the First World War, when interest
in the Victorian poet began to wane while Donne became increasingly popular.

The linking of the names of Donne and Browning apparently
began in 1872 when Alexander Grosart dedicated his edition of

50

Donne's poems to Browning, "the poet of the century for thinkers," and assured prospective readers that Browning "has a wealth of admiration for Donne." At the turn of the century Edmund Gosse wrote that "the modern appreciation of Donne seems to begin with Robert Browning." He explained that "the stamp of the Dean's peculiar intensity of feeling can be traced in many of Browning's lyrics; his famous 'obscurity' is closely analogous to Donne's." A few years later Stephen Gwynn commented on the relationship between Browning and Donne, "a man of very similar qualities and defects."[1] In the United States Felix E. Schelling pointed out as early as 1890 that the "arabesque," defined as an elaborate type of ornamentation, was used similarly by Browning and the metaphysicals. In their biographies of Browning, Stopford Brooke and C. H. Herford mentioned his affinity with Donne and the metaphysicals, and W. Hall Griffin asserted that Donne's poetry was "a potent literary influence" on Browning — then dropped the subject.[2]

"YOUR DONNE"

Browning's interest in Donne began during his early youth and continued to the end of his life. Mrs. Sutherland Orr, a close friend in later life, credited him with setting to music and singing Donne's "Go and catch a falling star" before he was twenty-one. Moreover, Browning has indicated that he was familiar with Donne before writing "Paracelsus" when he was twenty-three. He wrote to Julia Wedgwood about thirty years later that during a "bad sore throat right before writing *Paracelsus* I remember I was a little light-headed one night and fancied I had to go through a complete version of the Psalms by Donne, Psalm by Psalm!"[3] Browning perhaps had read Donne's version of "The Lamentations of Jeremy" and knew of Donne's partiality for the Psalms.

The clearest evidence of Browning's interest in Donne, however, is in the consistent allusions to Donne in the correspondence between Browning and Elizabeth Barrett in 1845 and 1846. The letters reveal that not only Browning, but also his future wife, had a minute knowledge of Donne's poetry. Referring in one letter to a conversation with Thomas Carlyle on music, Browning wrote that "he is not mechanically 'musical,' he meant, and the music is the poetry, he holds, and should enwrap the thought as Donne says 'an amber drop enwraps a bee.'" In another letter, alluding to his desire for Elizabeth Barrett to go to Italy, Browning wrote, "Why, 'lean and harken after it,' as Donne says . . ." Again, speaking of his rapidly accumulating collection of love letters, he noted that "like Donne's bride" he made a jeweled "constellation of them all!" On another occasion he inquired if Miss Barrett recalled "Donne's pretty lines about seals" and quoted the passage in its Latin and English versions. Miss Barrett's remarks about Donne are equally revealing. In her letters to Browning she wrote of "your Donne." Once she asked, "Did you ever hear that I was one of 'those schismatiques of Amsterdam' whom your Dr. Donne would have put into the dykes?" Again she told Browning that a friend "meant to stay here [London] for a time . . . 'hating it perfectly,' like your Donne." [4]

Browning maintained his familiarity with Donne's poetry. Writing later in life to F. J. Furnivall, he compared the unpleasantness of his early unfavorable reviews to the "loud perfume" of Donne's "The Perfume." Moreover, William Rossetti noted in his diary in January 1869, that Browning "speaks with great enthusiasm of a poem by Donne named *Metempsychosis*," while Sidney Colvin wrote in his memoirs that he recalled Browning's "coming out once with a long, crabbedly fine screed from John Donne" — the "Elegy on Mistress Boulstred." [5]

But Browning proclaimed his admiration for Donne more publicly — in his poetry. The most significant reference to Donne is in "The Two Poets of Croisic":

> *He's greatest now and to de-struc-ti-on*
> *Nearest.* Attend the solemn word I quote,
> O Paul! *There's no pause at per-fec-ti-on.*
> Thus knolls thy knell the Doctor's bronzed
>   throat!
> *Greatness a period hath, no sta-ti-on.*

John Donne and Robert Browning

> Better and truer verse none ever wrote
> (Despite the antique outstretched a-i-on)
> Than thou, reverend and magisterial Donne!

The stanza described the position of an eighteenth-century Croisic poet, Paul Desforges-Maillard, who ironically attained the height of his fame when his beautiful sister posed as the writer of his poetry and who found his work neglected again when he revealed himself as the true author. The italicized lines, taken from Donne's unfinished epic, "The Progresse of the Soule," sound a tribute to Donne – a tribute inspired by much the same spirit that prompted Schubert to quote musically from Beethoven's Ninth Symphony in his own Great C Major. Once again in his half-humorous "Epps" Browning commended Donne as a poet both brave and rare.[6]

Browning's interest in Donne probably lay in a kinship he felt with Donne both as poet and as man. Both writers were seized early with "an immoderate hydroptique desire for human learning" and both during their early youth broke sharply with tradition in writing poetry that was metrically rugged and intellectually complex. Browning may have felt an increasing personal sympathy with Donne as he too flouted an irate father-in-law to make a secret marriage inspired by a deep love, saw the marriage flower despite hardship and sickness, and then lost his wife just when real success seemed assured. Moreover, some fundamental attitudes of the two poets were similar. Browning's examination of conflicting religious attitudes in "Christmas Eve and Easter Morn" is reminiscent of Donne's third satire and eighteenth "holy sonnet" ("Show me deare Christ, thy Spouse, so bright and clear"). One of Donne's verse letters suggests Browning in protesting against a life "like a paire of beads" that "makes the Past, a patterne for next yeare" and explains that despite the body's decay, the soul "strives to urge upward and her fortune raise."[7] One wonders if Browning thought of Donne when near the end of "La Saisiaz" he wrote of himself as "wielding, with Wit's bauble, Learning's rod."

AN INTELLECTUAL KINSHIP

Browning's references to Donne make it clear that he regarded him not just as a metaphysical stylist, but as a poet of vast and varied powers. He apparently realized there were ways in which their basic aesthetic theories were similar and perhaps exaggerated the similarity. He no doubt felt a particular sympathy for Donne's dependence on a system of analogies linking the spiritual and physical, his emphasis upon intellectual matter over musical manner, his thought-revealing style and psychological perception, his willingness to employ both ugliness and wit, and his experiments in dramatic structure, stanzaic form, metrics, and language.

Browning's interest in correspondences probably owed something to his knowledge of Renaissance writers, including Donne, something to his knowledge of romantic writers like Shelley, and a great deal to his own talent for perceiving analogies between the various realms of being. Browning declared that poetry should reveal "the correspondency of the universe to Deity, of the natural to the spiritual, and of the actual to the ideal." Like Renaissance writers, he often thought in terms of a correspondence between the earth and man. This conception runs through Browning's work. "Paracelsus" alludes to the earth's "bare and skeleton framework" and compares the "convulsive throes" with which the hero's deeds are born to "the sheet of winding subterraneous fire" which sends up huge islands. Both Sordello and Prince Hohenstiel-Schwangau compare themselves at some length to the earth.[8]

There were, however, profound differences between Browning's attitudes[9] and those of the Renaissance. Central to Browning's system of correspondences was his belief in a transcendent God who was nevertheless partially revealed in all things as power, knowledge, and love. Although Browning's framework of relationships in part comprehended the Renaissance system of correspondences, it placed more emphasis upon the temporal and dynamic, the complete inadequacy of the material and finite, and the need for a reconciliation of opposites. He apparently thought that the infinite impinged on the finite and in a sense interpenetrated it, but that the two remained essentially distinct. Browning probably regarded poetic images and figures as striving to express what they could only hint at. Although Donne was also aware of the inadequacy of symbols and referred to circles as only "poor types of God," there is a difference in emphasis between the Renaissance and earlier nineteenth-century attitudes. Donne found the finite dignified through its relation to the infinite and took pleasure in the relationship for its own sake. Browning was impressed by the imperfection of the finite in its relation to the infinite and considered the relationship chiefly as a ladder helpful to one seeking to mount from the material to higher and higher spheres of the spiritual. While Browning's approach to analogies was more logical than that of many of the earlier nineteenth-century poets, it was characteristically more subjective and intuitive than that of the seventeenth-century metaphysicals. He probably regarded the Renaissance system of correspondences as an interesting conception, not as objective truth. He believed that man's discovery of himself in nature was essentially empathic.

Browning's view of the finite-infinite relationship supplied him with a theory of romantic irony that regarded aesthetic creations as a kind of ironic play for which the artist could not be held fully accountable since his vision was too sublime for expression through material media. Aesthetic theories different from those of the metaphysicals thus led Browning to employ a kind of metaphysical wit. Although he sometimes maintained that the artist should make his works as expressive of his imaginative conception as possible, he frequently introduced various kinds of wordplay, Hudibrastic rhymes, and other witty devices into his serious poetry.

Browning seems to have believed that life for the individual should always be an increasing freedom within limitations and that the artist best expressed life and fulfilled his own destiny of self-expression in voicing increasingly transcendent truths for which the media were increasingly inadequate. This central theory of the importance of the individual personality and of the importance of matter over manner, which probably served Browning both as a philosophy and as a rationalization, supplied the aesthetic basis for many of the characteristics which Browning's poetry shares with Donne's. It justified his concern with the intellectual, his effort to reveal the whole truth, his use of wit, and his personality-revealing style that sometimes resulted in obscurity and harshness — and it also justified that lack of polish that sometimes makes Browning's works read like mediocre translations of very great poems.

Donne referred to his verse as "harsh" and Browning admitted that he himself brewed "stiff drink." [10] Browning probably thought that his theories of structure and meter were similar to those of Donne and that the earlier poet's description of his "words masculine perswasive force" and the seventeenth century's praise of "strong lines" were applicable to his own work. Certainly in the work of both Donne and Browning "style is the man."

Browning's own aesthetic theories, perhaps themselves partly a product of his familiarity with Donne, thus enabled him to maintain a particular interest in Donne and to be sympathetic to the stimulus of his poetry. Some of Browning's figures and techniques apparently reflect the direct influence of Donne. Many others, similar to Donne's, may owe much also to his poetic predilections and general knowledge of older poetry. However, since many of Browning's techniques resemble those of Donne more closely than those of any other poet and since Browning was intensely interested in Donne throughout his writing career, it seems probable that many of the similarities between his and Donne's use of the dramatic monologue, metrics, and various metaphysical devices are the produce of his thorough absorption and understanding adaptation of Donne's style.

Browning's very original dramatic monologues probably owe something to Donne's poems in a similar form. Donne's "The Good-Morrow," "Breake of Day," "The Dreame," "The Flea," "Apparition," and the last part of "The Extasie" are essentially dramatic monologues. One of the best examples of Donne's work in this genre is "The Canonization," in which the speaker justifies the religion of love to an unamorous layman who cannot really understand. Many of Donne's dramatic pieces, like Browning's, begin *in medias res*, so to speak, frequently with an exclamation, provide a vivid sense of a setting and listener, proceed with a mixture of logic and erudition tempered with colloquialism, and reveal a great deal about the personality and thought processes of the speaker. Browning's shorter dramatic lyrics, such as "Two in the Campagna" or "The Laboratory," resemble Donne's work much more than his longer monologues. Most of Browning's monologues afford a more comprehensive portrayal of the speaker and give a more forceful impression of a past impinging on the present. Although the first impression is that Donne's dramatic lyrics reflect a personal point of view much more than those of Browning, their respective poems perhaps contain less of Donne the man and more of Browning the man than has often been supposed.

Both poets experimented extensively in irregular metrics and rhythms and created many new stanzaic forms, including a number that were both relatively long and complex. But the poems of both frequently take their life from the over-all rhythm rather than from any external forms. There is an unmistakable similarity in subject matter, mood, rhythm, and general structure in these two similes from Browning and Donne:

> As when a sick man very near to death
>   Seems dead indeed, and feels begin and end
>   The tears and takes the farewell of each friend,
> And hears one bid the other go, draw breath
> Freelier outside, ("since all is o'er," he saith,
>   "And the blow fallen no grieving can amend;")

> As virtuous men passe mildly away,
>   And whisper to their soules, to goe,
> Whilst some of their sad friends doe say,
>   The breath goes now, and some say, no: [11]

Browning, however, was most like Donne where Donne was most metaphysical — in his examination of the psychological and emotional in terms of logic, metaphor, and wit. In the work of both there is a kind of casuistry, a half-serious and half-playful attempt to use the specular stone of logic to convert old sins into new virtues or at least to contrive new excuses for them. Donne's casuistical vein is clearly evident in his "Paradoxes and Problemes" and one can almost imagine Browning's "hitching into verse" Donne's *Biathanatos* as the monologue of a suicide. A tinge of casuistry occurs in many of Donne's love poems, such as "Communitie," "Womans Constancy," "Lovers Infiniteness," and "Negative Love," and occasionally in the devotional lyrics, as in the thirteenth "holy sonnet," in which the poet depicts himself as losing his fears of Judgment Day because Christ's "beauteous forme assures a pitious minde." A casuistical argument for seduction is put forth playfully in "The Flea." Many of Browning's characters are primarily concerned with rationalizing a situation which either they or others find difficult to accept. Their rationalizations range from the spontaneous reactions of the disappointed lover of "The Last Ride Together" to the contrived casuistry of Bishop Blougram, Sludge, and Prince Hohenstiel-Schwangau.

Browning's "Fifine at the Fair," which treats Don Juan's attempt to justify his infidelities to his wife, is similar to several poems by Donne. It resembles "The Extasie" in its use of Platonic doctrines to support physical love and is similar to several of the so-called "libertine" lyrics in its defense of promiscuity. It is most similar, however, to Donne's two elegies "Change" and "Variety," particularly the latter. Don Juan is willing to twist any argument to make a "case" for himself. He argues that the attractive body of the gypsy temptress Fifine must reflect a beautiful mind, that one cannot know good apart from evil and that he will appreciate his wife more because of his experience with Fifine, and that one can rise through the less pure element to the else unattainable pure element. Donne's "Change" seeks to justify promiscuity in proving that change is the nursery "of musicke, joy, life, and eternity" and his "Variety" maintains that change should be the law of love as it is everywhere the law of nature. However, both "Fifine at the Fair" and "Variety" conclude that the many women must be found in the one rather than the one in the many. Both Browning and Donne had a limited faith in reason, but took pleasure in setting forth ingenious arguments to which they partly subscribed — but which they completely transcended.

Many of Browning's metaphors, like the most characteristically metaphysical figures of Donne, are logical, extended, organic, de-animizing, dynamic, spatial, and conceptual. The similarity between the conceits of the two poets is probably not due so much to any direct imitation as to Browning's interest in correspondences, his love of ingenious analogies for their own sake, and his ability to incorporate Donne's general techniques into his own style. Browning's most typical metaphysical metaphors are in his longer poems and are often more extended, more prolix, and less precise than Donne's. Only rarely, as in "Love in a Life," "Natural Magic," "Magical Nature," and a few other poems, did he elaborate a figure in a short lyric. Although much of Browning's and Donne's imagery is similar, Browning employed some images peculiar to the post-Newtonian world, such as the prism and steam engine, and others reflecting his individual interests, such as those from music and painting.

"Can't we look through the crimson and trace lines?" inquired one of Browning's characters after the bloodshed of "The Ring and the Book." Browning's numerous geometrical figures reveal his constant tendency to "trace lines" in treating characters and situations. Donne's most famous circle figure is that of the geometer's compass in "A Valediction: Forbidding Mourning," in which the "fixt foot" represents the woman who "leanes, and hearkens after" her absent lover. As the poet explains to his mistress:

> Thy firmnes drawes my circle just,
> And makes me end, where I begunne.

One of Browning's figures similarly concerns two parting lovers and depicts the woman as the center of a circle about which the man moves:

> I know you; give me time,
> Let me be proud and think you shall know me.

59

> My soul is slower; in a life I roll
> The minute out whereto you condense yours —
> The whole slow circle round you I must move,
> To be just you.[12]

This figure from "In a Balcony" is less precise than Donne's, but describes a subtler psychological relationship. It treats time in spatial terms in indicating the relative ability of two persons to reveal their souls to each other.

Browning's "Numpholeptos" also is based on an extended center-circumference figure. The center again represents the woman, an ideal creature of an alien sphere, who is also apparently envisioned as a diamond from whose white brilliance are rayed out many hues that color and sometimes stain the lover who must travel back and forth along her rays, "from centre to circumference."

Some of the circle figures of both Donne and Browning show the relationship of abstract concepts. One of Donne's verse letters ("Honour is so sublime perfection") compares the Countess of Bedford's noble life to a circle permeated by rays from its center, religion. His elegy on Prince Henry treats the close relationship between faith and reason in terms of superimposed circles. Browning explained that "truth displayed i' the point, flashes forth everywhere" within the soul's circle, but is "hid from sense." [13] A figure in "La Saisiaz" treats the relationship of intuition and reason:

> Thus have we come back full circle: fancy's
>   footsteps one by one
> Go their round conducting reason to the
>   point where they begun.[14]

Browning, like Donne, regarded the circle as a symbol of perfection. "Good you are and wise, full circle: what to me were more outside?" one of Browning's characters declares. Browning also referred to music "perfect from centre to circumference." [15]

Browning was as fond of spheres as he was of circles. In one of his metaphors two touching spheres illustrate the relation of Francesco Romanelli to Beatrice Signorini, a more transcendent personality. The two attain a limited union only through their art:

> Her sphery self was whole —
> Might only touch his orbit at art's sole point.
> Suppose he could persuade her to enjoint
> Her life — past, present, future — all in his
> At art's sole point by some explosive kiss
> Of love through lips, would love's success defeat
> Artistry's haunting curse — the Incomplete?
> Artists no doubt they both were — what besides
> Was she? who, long had felt heart, soul spread wide
> On either side Art's narrow space where fell
> Reflection from his own speck: but the germ
> Of individual genius — what we term
> The very self, the God-gift whence had grown
> Heart's life and soul's life — how make that his own?
> Vainly his Art, reflected, smiled in small
> On art's one facet of her ampler ball;
> The rest, touch-free, took in, gave back heaven, earth,
> All where he was not.[16]

Some of the ways in which Browning's technique differs from that of Donne are apparent in this passage. The idea is not expressed entirely through the metaphor, as in Donne's most characteristic figures, since there is a running commentary on the metaphor. The problem of the reflections is relevant, though not worked out clearly, and there is considerable repetition. A similar metaphor explains that Christopher Smart's poetry touches in one respect the greatness of Milton and Keats as a sphere touches one point of an adjacent cube. Browning's "Cleon" considers the relation of the ancients to modern Christians in terms of a hollow sphere filled first with water and then with air.[17]

Much of Browning's sphere imagery is distinctly different from Donne's in its involved, shifting, and imprecise character. In many of his longer poems, such as "Sordello," metaphors weave in and out and become submerged only, like Arethusa, to burst forth again tauntingly in a changed context. The sphere imagery in "Sordello" is astrological rather than purely geometrical and often not very concrete or fully realized. The poem represents both

Sordello and Palma as spheres which need the influence of another sphere, an "out-soul." Sordello is later identified with the sea that must have some moon's control or else be wasted in foam. Donne sometimes used similar imagery, but more precisely and compactly. His "A Valediction: Of Weeping" examines an amorous relationship in terms of spheres and of the moon's influence on the sea, and his epithalamium on "The Lady Elizabeth" refers to a "shee Sun" and "hee Moon." But Browning, particularly in his longer poems, handled geometrical imagery with more freedom than did Donne.

In his mixing of geometry and poetry Browning, like Donne, also brought into service points and lines. In "Paracelsus" the figure of the "point where all those scattered rays should meet" illustrates the convergence of all other forms of life in the faculties of man.[18] Donne had described the point as "much entirer than a million," and Browning apparently had very much the same idea:

> Could life begin anew. His problem posed aright
> Was — "From the given point evolve the infinite!"
> Not — "Spend thyself in space, endeavoring to joint
> Together, and so make infinite, point and point:
> Fix into one Elvire a Fair-ful of Fifines!"

For Browning, as for Donne, the straight line suggested mortal perfection. One poem explains that man's earthly deeds determine his life hereafter just as points determine straight, inclined, or crooked lines. Like Marvell, Browning could delineate a personal relationship with two lines — but this time the "Same lines of liking, loving run" so close together that they converge at a third person.[19]

Browning's unflagging desire to "trace lines" reached a grand climax in his most complex geometrical jigsaw, the much-maligned "Prince Hohenstiel-Schwangau," a thinly veiled attempt to reveal what Browning regarded as the machinations and rationalizations of the recently fallen Louis Napoleon. Although the poem is virtually devoid of lyrical graces, the structure and technique are extremely interesting and probably unique. The exiled prince is represented as explaining his life to a feminine companion in a cheap London *café*. He takes a piece of paper and draws between two blots a line "five inches long and tolerably straight." Only through the diagram, he says, can his companion understand his actions which puzzled all of Europe:

> Understand one, you comprehend the rest.
> Rays from all round converge to any point:
> Study the point then ere you track the rays!
> The size o' the circle's nothing.

In lieu of someone inspired to change the circle to a square, the prince continues,

>   I profess to trace
> The broken circle of society,
> Dim actual order, I can redescribe
> Not only when some segment silver-true
> Stays clear, but where the breaks of black commence
> Baffling you all who want the eye to probe —

Continuing the use of geometrical figures, the prince recommends living out one's life in the world with the chance

>   of learning how set foot
> Decidedly on some one path to Heaven,
> Touch segment in the circle where all lines
> Lead to the centre equally, red lines
> Or black lines, so they but produce themselves — [20]

The blots apparently represent the prince's own endowments and circumstances — in any case two "givens." The line he draws to connect them illustrates both his life and his philosophy of action. He prefers to link them rather than to leave them and to use what is at hand rather than to strive for novelty. The actual act of drawing is a kind of microcosm of which all the actions of his past life are the macrocosm. Variations are built around the basic figure of the line between two blots. It is considered first as the retraced circle of society and then as the radius of a circle whose center is heaven. There is nothing in Donne's work quite equivalent to Browning's procedure here. However, the poem suggests Donne's "A Valediction: Of My Name in the Window," in which the poet indulges in geometrical elaborations on the name he has just carved, and his description of court life as "a line discontinued, and a number of small wretched points, uselesse, because they concurre not." [21]

Browning also drew figures from arithmetic, the physical and biological sciences, mechanics, and the arts. Apropos of the futility of inquiring into the complex causes of different faiths, Browning also wrote that to "Substitute thing meant for thing expressed" was as difficult as to reduce a number "to zero, then bring zero back/To value of supreme preponderance." Donne used arithmetical imagery in "The Primrose," "Negative Love," and a few other poems. In another of Browning's poems deafness is compared to a prism that enables the "vexed Love" to shine more beautifully on the face, and the old pope of "The Ring and the Book" thinks of man's mind as a convex glass which gathers "scattered points" from the "immensity of sky." In "Red Cotton Night-Cap Country" Lucie Muhlhausen's revelation of her impure past to Leonce Miranada, her lover, is treated in a chemical or alchemical figure. The "very truth" makes "the tardy mixture crystallize" into new love. At the beginning of "The Ring and the Book" Browning explained his aesthetic theory of the re-creation of history by the analogy of the chemical process used in the making of a rare ring. As the artificer mixes gold and alloy to form a ring, so the poet combines his imagination with facts to shape a work of art. A figure from "The Inn Album" gives a new mechanical twist to a Renaissance convention:

> I had felt
> Ice in me grow steam, drive to effect
> Any or all the fancies sluggish here
> I' the head that needs the hand she would not take
> And I shall never lift now . . .
> . . . .
> The steam congeals once more.[22]

Metaphors derived from the arts probably assume a more important role in the poetry of Browning than in that of any other poet using a metaphysical style. A figure weaving in and out of his "Master Hughes of Saxe-Gotha" compares a complicated fugue, the weaving of a fabric, and the course of human life and thought. In a passage of synaesthetic rhetoric Browning's Don Juan compares his perception of his wife Elvire to his reaction to music which moves him emotionally even while he analyzes technically the modulation, enharmonic change, and resolution that provide its power. Commenting again on changing subjective perceptions, Don Juan asserts, "What was my Rafael turns my Michelagnolo." [23]

Donne's direct and specific influence is probably reflected in a few of Browning's figures. In "A Grammarian's Funeral," for example, Browning wrote:

> He (soul-hydroptic with a sacred thirst)
> Sucked at the flagon.

Not only was "hydroptic" one of Donne's favorite words, but the source of Browning's conception was very possibly this passage from Donne's "The Second Anniversary":

> Thirst for that time, O my insatiate soule,
> And serve thy thirst with Gods safe-sealing Bowle.
> Be thirstie still, and drinke still till thou goe
> To th' only Health, to be Hydroptique so. [24]

A line from Donne, "When my Soule was in her owne body sheath'd," may have suggested to Browning the figure of the body as the sheath of the soul, an image which he employed at least eight times with only slight variations in poems from "Sordello" to "La Saisiaz." These examples are typical:

> In short, the soul in its body sunk
> Like a blade sent home to its scabbard.

> What if a certain soul
>   Which early slipped its sheath,
>   And has for its home the whole
> Of heaven . . . [25]

Browning was like Donne in his consistent concern with elaborate analogies linking unlike spheres and in his use of specialized knowledge for the interpretation of various personal relationships.

The Revival of Metaphysical Poetry

In some poems, such as "Numpholeptos" and "Beatrice Signorini," the emotional potentialities of a psychological relationship are realized through the metaphor, but Browning's figures more frequently than Donne's interpret abstractions in terms of other abstractions or describe the material in terms of the material. Although Browning's figures probably reflect in some measure his belief in a correspondence between the material and spiritual, they apparently are not a product of the poet's perception and conception of the universe to the extent that Donne's are. His metaphors probably depend more on sheer ingenuity — and less on belief — than those of Donne. Browning's use and development of the metaphysical metaphor also shows a break with Donne. In many of Donne's best poems the metaphors *are* the poem. Most of Browning's metaphysical metaphors, however, are only a relatively small part of the poem and are themselves often broken into several parts and loaded with material extraneous to their logical development. Sometimes too they are combined with a system of symbols and *leitmotifs*.

Besides the conceits, a wide variety of witty devices are scattered through Browning's poetry. However, as much of this wittiness is spoken by Browning's characters, it is difficult to know in a particular case if the wit reflects an aesthetic theory or functions merely as a kind of "humors" tag. "Deaf and Dumb, A Group by Woolner" develops a paradox in the seventeenth-century fashion:

> Only by Deafness may the vexed Love wreak
> Its insuppressive sense on brow and cheek,
> Only by Dumbness adequately speak
> As favored mouth could never, through the eyes.

"A Death in the Desert" explains that man, finding love in himself, denies Christ as Love, and so rejects Christ through very need of him.

Sometimes Browning's word-play serves the cause of drama or concentration. There is Count Guido's cry:

> You have my last word, — innocent am I
> As Innocent my Pope and murderer. . . .

66

Prince Hohenstiel-Schwangau, imagining how history will treat him, puns on the dozen volumes of his life that will "lie." The title of Browning's "Cenciaja," a kind of footnote to Shelley's "The Cenci," is a pun which carries a reference to Shelley's play and yet by addition of the depreciative suffix dismisses Browning's own efforts as a mere bundle of rags.[26]

Several poems by Browning have traces of the mixture of wit and grotesquerie characteristic of Donne and the metaphysicals. For instance, Count Guido compares all the attendant circumstances preliminary to his beheading, this "grooming for the next world," to the grooming and general preparations of a horse for a race. In "Confessions" a sick man exultingly identifies the medicine bottles on a nearby table with a house, wall, and garden where he had secret meetings with an early love. A similar witty grotesquerie marks the long disquisition on night-caps near the beginning of "Red Cotton Night-Cap Country." The title is a blood-tinted version of "white cotton night-cap country," the name Browning's friend Mrs. Thackeray gave to the section of Normandy in which took place the sanguinary events treated in the poem. Certainly this strange philosophical discourse of several hundred lines approaches very serious play when, in biblical terms, the poet explains, "Though sins are scarlet they shall be as wool," and later adds,

> Oh there, or nowhere else,
> Will I establish that a Night-cap gleams
> Of visionary Red, not White for once!
> "Heaven," saith the sage, "is with us, here inside
> Each man:" "Hell also," simpleness subjoins,
> By White and Red describing human flesh." [27]

Browning lacked Donne's lightness of touch. Consequently the witty and grotesque are often not well assimilated into his poetry. There are a few poems whose ambiguity seems to reflect a complex state of mind, but the line between the serious and witty is in general much sharper in the work of Browning than in that of Donne.

The most significant influences are those that supplement and reinforce a writer's natural talents and predilections. Insofar as Donne influenced Browning, the influence was chiefly of this general, yet fundamental nature. Although in a few cases Browning apparently borrowed directly from Donne, he more frequently received from the earlier poet broad suggestions for his poetic structures, techniques, and imagery. Browning probably was in some measure influenced by Donne in his development of the dramatic monologue, in his experimentation with conversational metrics and idiom, and in his use of metaphysical logic, conceits, and wit. Browning undoubtedly had a distinct style of his own; however, except for the Shelleyan flavor of "Pauline" and "Paracelsus," his style resembles Donne's more closely than that of any of his other predecessors.

IV

The Beginnings
of the Revival in America

I N T H E United States, as in England, the seventeenth-century metaphysical poets, generally neglected during the eighteenth century, were revived, re-evaluated, and imitated during the nineteenth century. The revival was relatively free of English influence. American critics generally appreciated the metaphysicals' transcendental qualities, their hard core of thought, and the union of body, mind, and soul reflected in their poetry.

Many American writers read and enjoyed the metaphysicals. Edgar Allan Poe maintained that the writings of the metaphysicals "sprang immediately from the soul — and partook intensely of that soul's nature." He remarked on the "simplicity and single-heartedness" of Cowley and lauded the beauty, pathos, and "most exquisitely delicate imagination" of some of Marvell's poetry. Henry Wadsworth Longfellow, after visiting James Russell Lowell one morning, wrote: "Read Donne's poems while he went down to feed his hens and chickens." Commenting on Cowley, Longfellow later noted, "I like this half-forgotten, much-neglected bard." In the back of a case book, Oliver Wendell Holmes once jotted down: "Attempting to write poetry like Herbert's or Donne's." Holmes particularly admired the "purity of holy George Herbert" and visited Herbert's old home in Bemerton.[1]

Lowell regarded Donne as his favorite poet. With Charles Eliot Norton, he edited an edition of Donne that appeared in 1895 and became one of the landmarks of the revival. Lowell asserted that

Donne "wrote more profound verses than any other English poet save one only," and praised the vistas of imagination opened up by Donne's "self-irradiating mind." "One needs to brace oneself with a strong dose of Dr. Donne's," he once wrote to Norton. He declared that Donne's poetry was full of "thoughts that first tease us like charades and then delight us with the felicity of their solution." Like Browning, he could quote a passage from Donne appropriate to almost any occasion. But he also found the "good arguments" of "that fine old poet Herbert" to be "the more pleasing for their quaintness" and lamented that the "divine Cowley" was not better known.[2]

American critics, like the English ones, disputed about metaphysical conceits and wit. Lowell was completely undaunted by complex metaphysical figures, and John Greenleaf Whittier asserted that "Appleton House," which contains some of Marvell's most farfetched metaphors, had "many not unpleasing conceits." However, William Cullen Bryant criticized the metaphysicals for neglecting beauty, grandeur, and "earnestness of feeling" in their dependence on "surprise at quaint and strange resemblances." One of the most perceptive treatments of the problem of wit and ambiguity occurs in Margaret Fuller's imaginary dialogue between Edward Herbert and George Herbert. Edward raises the oft-repeated objection of earlier nineteenth-century critics: "In your likenesses, you sometimes appear to quibble in a way unworthy the subject." And George replies: "It is the nature of some minds, brother, to play with what they love best."[3]

Nineteenth-century American poets were sometimes compared with various seventeenth-century metaphysical poets. Norton wrote that some of the poems of Jones Very, Emerson's eccentric "brave saint," "are as if written by a George Herbert who had studied Shakespeare, read Wordsworth, and lived in America." Although a few of Very's figures are faintly reminiscent of Herbert and the seventeenth century, the resemblance today does not seem very striking. With more insight, Lowell grouped Henry Thoreau with Donne and Browne, while Bronson Alcott declared that Thoreau's poems were as "vigorous and rugged" and as

"sound and seasonable" as Donne's. Thoreau himself concluded:
"Donne was not a poet, but a man of strong sense, a sturdy English thinker full of conceits and whimsicalities, hammering away at his subject . . . with an occasional fine distinction or poetic phrase." [4]

HENRY THOREAU

If "American" is read for "English," Thoreau's description of Donne might apply to Thoreau himself as a poet. Thoreau resembled Donne chiefly in his idiom, rhythm, and metrics, but the thought and figures of the two poets are sometimes similar. He shared, for instance, Donne's delight in astronomical figures and his feeling for an almost mystic union in love:

> We two that planets erst had been
> Are now a double star,
> And in the heavens may be seen,
> Where that we fixed are.

The planets "evermore with spheral song/Revolve about one centre." The "two solitary stars" of another lyric are through their "conscious light . . . determined to one pole," and in another poem the lovers are completely united as "two summer days in one,/Two Sundays come together," and two rays making one sun.[5] Again, probably depending on his knowledge of the New England woods, Thoreau described himself as a "parcel of vain strivings tied/By a chance bond together":

> A bunch of violets without their roots,
> And sorrel intermixed,
> Encircled by a wisp of straw
> Once coiled about their shoots,
> The law
> By which I'm fixed.

In another poem friendship is considered as a legal partnership whose "true wealth is made/For current stock and not for dividends." [6]

"Truth is always paradoxical," Thoreau once asserted, and he based several of his poems on paradoxical truths. Donne is here

71

suggested not only in the use of paradox, but in the language, rhythm, and tone:

> Let such pure hate still underprope
> Our love, that we may be
> Each other's conscience,
> And have our sympathy
> Mainly from thence.

He also explained that the ship of state was "ballasted with hate" and that "Every Congress that we hold/Means the union is dissolved." [7]

RALPH WALDO EMERSON

The nineteenth-century American poet most frequently compared with the seventeenth-century metaphysical poets was Emerson. The poet's early biographer George Willis Cooke asserted that Emerson's language and style showed his "native affiliations" with George Herbert, Marvell, and other poets of their era. Holmes pointed out Emerson's relation to Herbert and maintained that Marvell's influence "is plain to every reader in some of Emerson's poems." [8]

Emerson himself wrote that for Herbert, Marvell, and some of their contemporaries "I have an affectionate admiration I have for nothing else. They set me on speculations . . . They suggest the great endowment of the spiritual man. They open glimpses of the heaven that is in the intellect." His favorite books included the works of Donne, Herbert, and Browne, and he read selections from the metaphysical poets in his lectures and sometimes quoted and borrowed from them in his essays. Herbert was Emerson's favorite metaphysical poet. One of his early commonplace books, presumably belonging to school days, contains some lines by Herbert written in Emerson's hand, and in his first recorded reference to him (in a letter to William Emerson, February 20, 1829) he wrote: "I dearly love Geo. Herbert's Poems." He praised Herbert's "exquisite refinement of thought," and declared that "his thought has that heat as actually to fuse the words." Emerson thought Donne and Cowley were rich in philosophical insight, but lacking in the appreciation and presentation of beauty. Crashaw's "Sospetto d'Herode," he felt, contained "masterly verse."[9] Thus he clearly avowed his interest in these earlier poets.

Because of his own philosophy of transcendentalism, Emerson could be sympathetic to the seventeenth-century faith in correspondences between God, the earth, and man. Like the metaphysicals, he believed in an organic universe characterized by an elaborate network of analogies and was interested in "signatures" and in the circle and other "types." "Secret analogies tie together the remotest parts of Nature," he asserted, and quoted from Herbert's "Man" in illustration. But, like most nineteenth-century thinkers, he did not believe in a system of correspondences as literal, all-embracing, and hierarchical as that of the seventeenth century. He was interested chiefly in the correspondence of nature and its laws with the human mind and its laws. "The whole of nature is a metaphor of the human mind," he wrote. Behind both nature and mind was the over-soul. The imagination was the interpreter of nature's symbols.[10]

Emerson was also sympathetic to the "new criticism" conceptions of ambiguity and of the unified sensibility. He praised the marriage of wit and piety in Herbert, emphasizing that both were genuine, and explained that Donne and Cowley "like life afford the chance of richest instruction amid frivolous and familiar objects; the loose and the grand, religion and mirth stand in surprising neighborhood, and like the words of great men, without cant." The close relationship that Donne attributed to the mind and body of Elizabeth Drury in "The Second Anniversary" was approved by Emerson. "Passion beholds its object as a perfect unit," he observed. "The soul is wholly embodied and the body is wholly ensouled." He also praised the "fine and acute" relationship between Thoreau's body and soul.[11]

Through symbols that hint at correspondences, a transcendent spiritual world shines radiantly through the physical world in Emerson. An analogy, as in "May-Day," may be very general:

> Under gentle types, my Spring
> Masks the might of Nature's King . . .

In "Monadnoc" the mountain's rugged crag is a "type of permanence!/Firm ensign of the fatal Being." In "The Daemonic Love" the relationship between the macrocosm of the universe and the microcosm of man is the basis of a comparison of man's teeming "unwonted thoughts" to a shower of meteors. However, "The World Soul" employs a traditional incarnational symbolism suggesting Crashaw:

> Over the winter glaciers
> I see the summer glow,
> And through the wild-pild snow-drift
> The warm rosebuds below.

Another similar figure in "Monadnoc" asserts that a line of mountain peaks "But beads are of a rosary/On prayer and music strung."

Emerson's figures approached most closely the style of Herbert. William Henry Channing made a very natural mistake when he presumed that Herbert was the author of Emerson's "Grace":

> How much, preventing God, how much I owe
> To the defences thou has round me set;
> Example, custom, fear, occasion slow,—
> These scorned bondsmen were my parapet.
> I dare not peep over this parapet
> To gauge with glance the roaring gulf below
> The depths of sin to which I had descended,
> Had not these against myself defended.[12]

The poem expresses the desire for restriction and protection typical of Herbert and closely resembles his "Sinne" (I) — "Lord, with what care has thou begirt us round!" But while Emerson's poem tends to be abstract, Herbert's mentions parents, schoolmasters, "Bibles laid open" and other guardians. Emerson's "Terminus" is also similar to some of Herbert's dialogue lyrics and employs a tent figure symbolizing smallness and restraint very much as in Herbert's "Content." Emerson's description of the sage who "in large thoughts . . . /Shall string Monadnoc like a bead" seems derived from the "fleet Astronomer" of Herbert's "Vanitie" (I) who could "thred the spheres with his quickpiercing minde." A number of homely figures express the greatness

74

of the universe in the manner of Herbert. Emerson referred to "roomy Eternity" and to the "stairway of surprise" leading to the many "compartments of the floors" in paradise. The lightning "must to school and learn his verb and noun."[13] In "The Waterfall" an extended metaphor makes apt use of more recent scientific knowledge:

> The tremulous battery Earth
> Responds to the touch of man;
> It thrills to the antipodes,
> From Boston to Japan.

A number of Emerson's geometrical metaphors resemble those of Donne and Browning. Emerson rarely analyzed personal relationships, but in "Celestial Love" he examined the highly spiritual relationships of two lovers in sphere imagery:

> And the point is paradise,
> Where their glances meet:
> Their reach shall yet be more profound,
> And a vision without bound:
> The axis of those eyes sun-clear
> Be the axis of the sphere:
> So shall the lights ye pour amain
> Go, without check or intervals,
> Through from the empyrean walls
> Unto the same again!

The poet whose imagination grasps the symbols of the universe is described as "a crystal soul/Sphered and concentric with the whole." Frequently Emerson employed geometrical imagery to express abstract truths. In "Circles" Emerson treated fundamental conceptions of nature in sphere figures, and in "Uriel" he adapted circle imagery to present his own doctrine of eternal return and compensation by which good may proceed from evil. The young deities addressed by Uriel see only the circle, not the spiral that is return combined with advance.

Marvell was apparently the direct source of one of Emerson's conceits:

> He looketh seldom in their face,
> His eyes explore the ground, —

> The green grass is a looking-glass
> Whereon their traits are found.

Marvell's mower had sung:

> My mind was once the true survey
> Of all these meadows fresh and gay,
> And in the greenness of the grass
> Did see its hopes as in a glass . . .

Almost the same figure occurs in Marvell's "Upon Appleton House." Emerson's treatment of nature in crisp tetrameters is frequently in the style of Marvell even when there is no striking similarity in the use of figures. His work also suggests Marvell in an occasional phrase such as "green silence." [14]

Many of Emerson's figures showing his own adaptation of the metaphysical style reflect his constant study of nature as the greatest metaphor. In a conceit worked out with considerable detail and precision the poet's words are compared to "water-haunting birds" that dive and dip before a jeering crowd and then "new-bathed, new-trimmed" soar to heaven. Some other figures are salted with just a dash of homely humor:

> They love me as I love a cloud
> Sailing falsely in the sphere,
> Hated mist if it come near.

> Friends to me are frozen wine;
> I wait the sun on them should shine.[15]

Wit and ambiguity are at a minimum. Emerson was essentially apart from the tradition that sanctioned play on the paradoxes and metamorphoses in the fundamental Christian mysteries. He was more concerned with the one in the many than with the many in the one. However, his interest in compensation led him at times to develop paradoxes, as in "Spiritual Laws," which had the ring of a seventeenth-century lyric. There is a slight ambiguity in the lines Emerson wrote for a well dedicated to war martyrs:

> Fall, stream, from Heaven to bless; return as well;
> So did our sons; Heaven met them as they fell.

A pun on "well" is possible. An amusing ambiguity that was perhaps unintentional occurs as nature is compared to an "infinite paroquet" repeating one note.[16]

Because of his transcendental interests, Emerson was sympathetic to the metaphysical poets' habit of perceiving analogies between the physical and supersensible worlds. He was probably somewhat influenced by most of the metaphysicals, but felt a particular affinity with Herbert's fusion of thought and piety and Marvell's metaphysical nature poetry. His philosophy, his wonderment, his humanity, and his humor stamp Emerson's own metaphysical poetry.

EMILY DICKINSON

The poetry of Emily Dickinson provides the best example of poetic work which, though apparently not directly influenced by the metaphysical poets, is strikingly illuminated when examined in terms of metaphysical techniques. Although several critics have compared her with the seventeenth-century metaphysical poets, there is no real internal or external evidence to indicate that she was familiar with them or influenced by them. In fact, the only bits of real evidence show only that she was acquainted with one poem by George Herbert and with one by Vaughan. Eight lines of Herbert's "Mattens" copied in her own handwriting were found after her death and mistakenly printed in *Bolts of Melody*. As "Mattens" appeared in the October 28, 1876, edition of *The Springfield Daily Republican*, a paper she saw regularly, this almost certainly was her source. In a letter to her literary adviser, Colonel Higginson, probably written in August 1880, she quoted briefly from Vaughan's "Friends in Paradise," which she could have read in Palgrave's *The Golden Treasury*.[17] The evidence is too little and too late — the flood-tide of creation was over by 1865 — to reveal an influence. Although she could have found the metaphysicals represented in various anthologies and seen references to them in the writings of Emerson, there is no indication that she felt she was working with problems or techniques similar to theirs. There is no reason to doubt her when she asserts, "I . . . never consciously touch a paint mixed by another person,"[18] but to study and enjoy her own paints in the light of our knowledge of the metaphysicals provides some new insight into her original and distinctive achievements.

A comparison of Miss Dickinson with the metaphysicals calls attention at once to her habit of transposing an experience into new terms in a different realm of being and to her witty, mischievous, or naïve tone in a serious context. These characteristics of her work link her with the metaphysicals, but her creative use of these techniques reveals a fresh poetic imagination. Although she apparently had little theoretical interest in correspondences and did not perceive the universe through any single system, she regarded the three realms of man, nature, and God as distinct and separate, but as partly open to each other. She evidently shared also the traditional view that part of man's duty was to study God's single plan of the world through analyzing the world's diversity. This view of the world provided her with a system of metaphors that she felt carried with them simultaneously both the power to stun and the art to veil. "The thought beneath so slight a film–/Is more distinctly seen–" she concluded, and again advised: "Tell all the truth, but tell it slant." [19]

Miss Dickinson had an essentially new way of analyzing her poetic material by transposing it into a new framework. She frequently liked to interpret experience as a physicist or semanticist. In many poems she defined the psychological in terms of a mechanical universe of measurable time and space. But to eternity and infinity she added bliss and agony. These four words — "infinity," "eternity," "bliss," and "agony" — were much overused by Miss Dickinson, but this was because they formed the ultimates in her kind of five-dimensional universe where these conceptions were closely associated in essentially mathematical relationships. Agony and bliss are measured in units of space and time, but the universe of space and time is experienced and understood through agony and bliss. "I measure every Grief I meet/ With analytic eyes," she once explained. She perhaps acquired her scientific vision through her study of astronomy, chemistry, physiology, and mathematics at Amherst College, which during her enrollment was devoted to scientific pursuits.[20] Although in reducing ideas and feelings to bare abstractions she approached the geometrical figures of Donne and Marvell, she went much further, and maintained a detached scientific view more consistently. Much of her poetry could have been written only by one who took the post-Newtonian universe for granted.

Complementing this view was her persistent study of her favorite book — the dictionary — which enabled her to marshal the few exact words necessary to define the most subtle and complex feelings. This practice of raising an experience to its highest level of abstraction by reducing it to its lowest verbal terms became equivalent to projecting it into another corresponding realm. "The poet probed philology," she confessed in a poem on composition, but in another poem asserted, "I found the words to every thought/I ever had — but One." [21] Her poetic statements, often definitions, are exact, concise, logical, and often mathematical.

Many of Miss Dickinson's best and best-known lyrics show her attempt, as scientist and semanticist, to transfer an experience into a new realm. Every word counts as renunciation, usually regarded as a central experience in Miss Dickinson's life, is analyzed with a cool mathematical detachment:

> Renunciation — is the Choosing
> Against itself —
> Itself to justify
> Unto itself —
> When larger function —
> Make that appear —
> Smaller — that Covered Vision — Here —

In this and in a number of other poems she apparently analyzed her own experience to write clipped, precise, and universally applicable definitions of words describing psychological states. She defined experience as "the Angled Road/Preferred against the Mind/By — Paradox." [22] "Expectation — is Contentment —" she explained; any gain was satiety since there must be "an Austere trait in Pleasure."

79

Miss Dickinson's way of transposing life, color, and feeling into the abstractions of a mechanical world is almost frighteningly clear in a passage on the flight of a bird:

> At Half-past Seven, Element
> Nor Implement, be seen —
> And Place was where the Presence was —
> Circumference between.[23]

Again in an extended figure she applied the law of the conservation of matter to the spiritual:

> The Chemical conviction
> That Nought be lost
> Enable in Disaster
> My fractured Trust —
>
> The Faces of the Atoms
> If I shall see,
> How more the Finished Creatures
> Departed me!

Bliss and agony and other feelings are analyzed as though they were elements in a scientific problem. Crisis is atomistically defined as only "a Hair/Toward which forces creep/Past which forces retrograde"; a hesitating atom may deflect the hair separating one from eternity. She sometimes thought in terms of ratios and equations. She discovered that one "must an anguish pay/In keen and quivering ratio" for "each ecstatic instant." Miss Dickinson defined delight as in a ratio to flight. She also referred to the "fading ratio" of the dead to the living and, reasoning that life was short and "Anguish absolute," she hoped for a "new Equation" in heaven. She "dissected" the play of the "Reflex Holiday"; it would have been "Thanksgiving Day" if there had been "no sharp Subtraction/From the early Sum." [24] Many feelings are measured and defined quantitatively. Some could be expressed only as absolute negation. Pain's infinite has "an Element of Blank." "From Blank to Blank" she "pushed Mechanic feet." Again she described a face as "Infinites of Nought," and more playfully she felt "Zero at the Bone" upon seeing a snake. She and her lover felt like "Hesitating Fractions" surveying infinity.

She referred to "an instant's Width of Warmth," to "Murder by degrees," and to being stunned by degrees. "Suspense — is Hostiler than Death," she explained, because it can increase.[25] It is as though all human life could be measured on a slide rule.

Time as well as quantity and feeling played an important part in her five-dimensional universe. She was particularly concerned with the relativity of time:

> Two Lengths has every Day —
> Its absolute extent —
> And Area superior
> By hope or Horror lent.

For her the "second half of joy" was "shorter than the first." "Softened by Time's consummate plush," childhood's bleak griefs in later life seemed sleek and insignificant. Pain, she learned, paradoxically both expands and contracts time: it seems that "Ages coil within" the brain, but again eternities seem as nothing.[26]

Miss Dickinson, who once boasted of making a perfect score on an examination on Euclid,[27] sometimes employed geometrical figures to define the mysteries of experience. She examined lives in relation to circles:

> Except the smaller size
> No lives are round —
> These hurry to a sphere
> And show, and end —

Man carries in his mind "a circumference/In which I have no part," she remarked. She felt that her "little Circuit would have shamed" the "new Circumference" if her love had been consummated. Like seventeenth-century writers she found it natural to think of God as a great circle. She felt that through the vast circumference of space God prepared us gradually for "the stupendous Vision/of his Diameters." The circle was also used in describing feelings. "Circumscription — enables Wo," she said, but "No Man can compass a Despair."[28] A poem apparently on the death of a friend uses lines in the manner of Marvell:

> Might He know
> How Conscious Consciousness — could grow —

> Till Love that was — and Love too blest to be —
> Meet — and the Junction be Eternity.

In another poem Miss Dickinson described herself as "bisected" by grief.[29] In such figures geometry and poetry merge to reveal the richness in bareness.

Other sciences also, such as astronomy, optics, and mechanics, supplied her with instruments for her detached analysis of thoughts and feelings. She compared faith to the knowledge that the sun was setting on the other side of the earth, but was sometimes more erudite:

> Enchantment's Perihelion
> Mistaken oft has been
> For the Authentic orbit
> Of its Anterior Sun.[30]

In an elaborated conceit she regarded the idea of death as a concave and convex glass enabling one both to look forward toward God and the infinite and back toward time and the finite. In another extended figure she asserted that a poet lights a lamp whose illumination each age disseminates as a lens, and again conceived of God as a telescope. She compared her love to a prism, but also thought of transport as "Prism born" since its "decomposition" follows immediately. Reason was seen as a revolving mechanism whose cogs would clog and whose "esoteric belt/Protects our sanity," while "Ideals are the Fairy Oil" and "help the Wheel." [31]

In contrast to her scientific approach, Miss Dickinson's second controlling interpretation of her material was rooted in traditional Christian symbols and correspondences. Her affinities with the metaphysicals would suggest this incarnational and sacramental approach, and it occurs boldly enough — but with her own distinctive flavor. Once the birds seemed to her to be celebrating an "unobtrusive Mass." Again she felt she could partake of God through summer days as through the communion:

> Oh Sacrament of summer days,
> Oh Last Communion in the Haze —
> Permit a child to join.
>
> Thy sacred emblems to partake —

Thy consecrated bread to take
And thine immortal wine! [32]

But it was apparently the reddening leaves of Indian summer that reminded her most of the Eucharist. Summer's folding of its miracle suggested a priest's putting away the bread and wine. More playfully, she compared the bee, the butterfly, and the breeze to the holy Trinity, robins to angels, and the mushroom to Judas Iscariot.[33] Symbols of paradise appeared to her throughout nature.

In bolder moods she felt that everything, particularly herself and her beloved, partook of Christ's passion. She found as many Calvarys as persons and thought Gethsemane "but a Province — in the Being's Centre." Several times she alluded to herself as queen or empress of Calvary and spoke of being crowned with thorns. On another occasion she compared herself to Christ and her lover to the forgetful Peter.[34] She also regarded her lover as Christ and as "the Sacrament of Him":

Perceiving thee is evidence
That we are of the sky
Partaking thee a guaranty
Of immortality.

She compared her banishment from him to his from "the Savior's face," and mourned that absolute deity had removed the relative Deity.[35]

She differed from her metaphysical predecessors in her readiness to use the language and concepts of puritanism. For instance, again considering herself in the role of deity, she proclaimed:

Of all the souls that stand create —
I have elected — One —

She claimed her love by the "White Election" and was "Justified/ Through Calvaries of Love." She was

Baptized, before, without the choice,
But this time, consciously, of Grace
Unto supremest name — . . .[36]

She also alluded to the "saved" and the "lost" and to the "new life" — often satirically.

Besides the scientific and religious systems that supplied her with controlling metaphors, the vast reservoir of the ordinary provided Miss Dickinson, as it had Herbert, with many characteristic figures. Circuses, guns, clothing, and household affairs became charged with meaning in her poetry. It is not surprising that Miss Dickinson, who would sit up all night to watch a circus parade gaily into town in the dim dawn, liked to use metaphors based on circuses and similar spectacles in her poetry. She lamented that many saw in the forests and hills only the "Tents to Nature's Show" and failed to gain "admission" as a child. She referred to the "fair Theatricals of Day" applauded by the universe and particularly by God. Sometimes she thought the real show to be "they that go," and observed "Menagerie to me/My neighbor be." [37] But a gun suggested one of her most elaborate figures:

> My life had stood a — Loaded Gun —
> In Corners — till a Day
> The Owner passed — identified —
> And carried Me away —

After four more stanzas she concluded that she had "but the power to kill/Without — the power to die."

A distinctly feminine world is reflected in another group of metaphors. When she felt a "split" in her mind, she tried to match the thoughts "Seam by Seam," but they "ravelled out of Sound/Like Balls — upon a Floor." She found that stormy weather scared "Muslin souls" away and that "broadcloth Hearts" were firmer than those of organdy. Outgrown love was compared to old costumes put away in drawers.[38] In another figure she returned to the central experience of her poetry:

> He put the Belt around my life —
> I heard the Buckle snap —
> And turned away, imperial,
> My Lifetime folding up —

A comparison of Miss Dickinson with Herbert and other metaphysicals also brings into focus her quick and surprising juxtaposition of the familiar with the mysterious, the sensate with the supersensible. However, in her work these compressed conceits are more frequent, and their contrasts sharper. She referred to a scalped soul and to "a Cobweb on the Soul," to the "eclat of Death," "the underside of his Divinity" (adapted from Browne), "Mortality's Ground Floor," the "Table Land of immortality," "Fate's Telegram," and to the picking of "Eternity's vast pocket." Her personifications endow the natural and the supernatural with very human characteristics. She mentioned a "Nervous Star," the "Caprices of the Atmosphere," "industrious Angels," dimpled saints, and homesick dead. This kind of juxtaposition of course sometimes gives an ambiguous tone to her work.[39]

Some of Miss Dickinson's techniques are basically metaphysical, but in their pronounced subjectivity anticipate the twentieth century. Her figures usually define precisely a state of mind; however, one elaborated dream-like metaphor suggests vividly — but only suggests:

> I felt a Funeral, in my brain,
> And Mourners to and fro
> Kept treading — treading — till it seemed
> That Sense was breaking through —

There was a "Service like a Drum," a box creaked across her soul, and "Space — began to toll" as though "all the Heavens were a Bell" and "Being, but an Ear." The poet found herself as completely overwhelmed as a speck of silence in a universe of ever increasing sound. To compare this with the logical and rhetorical figures of the seventeenth century is to measure Miss Dickinson's original achievement in presenting this nameless feeling almost wholly in terms of sound.

Her use of paradox, like that of the metaphysicals, shows another aspect of her incisive, sometimes mischievous analysis of the human situation. She apologized to God for "thine own Duplicity," and in another poem with a similar paradoxical twist she asked that she might intercede for Christ. She was fascinated with time's paradoxical relationships with pain and love. One poem seems almost a study in paradox and antithesis. She explained not only that she "rose" when her lover "sank," but that she had "thought it would be opposite." However, "when his power bent,"

85

her "Soul stood straight," and she "told him Best — must pass/ Through this low Arch of Flesh." She learned also that "A Death blow is a Life blow to Some" and that "We lose — because we win." Almost her only resemblance to Crashaw was in her use of oxymoron. She referred to a "Gay, Ghastly Holiday," an "Etherial Blow," a "piercing Virtue" and a "piercing Comfort," and to a "Bliss like Murder" and a "Bliss to cauterize." [40]

The wittiness that was part of a cultivated, fashionable style in the seventeenth century was apparently completely natural for Miss Dickinson. At college she wrote a "comic column," and a friend in later life, Mrs. Thomas Eliot, explained she was "possessed of a keen sense of humor, which sometimes betrayed itself in grotesque play upon words, and always in the queerest, quaintest turns of expression." The disillusionment that followed her intimacy with her sister-in-law Sue Dickinson was compressed into a reference to her "pseudo-sister." She wrote of the death of her crippled mother: "It never occurred to us that though she had not Limbs, she had *Wings* . . . we hope that our Sparrow has ceased to fall." Again she hoped that a friend's "Walk on the Water" (to avoid seasickness aboard ship) was a success.[41] However, she realized clearly that her wit could be essentially serious:

> The truth I do not dare to know
> I muffle with a jest.[42]

A kind of *chiaroscuro* results from her mixing of wit with tragedy and passion. One four-line elegy with the hard clarity of a cameo mourns for "one Defaulting Face/Behind a Pall." Once Miss Dickinson imagined that anguish had strung the beads of sweat upon the forehead of a dying friend. The merest touch of satiric humor softens the elegies on the "odd old man" with the "stated Hat" and on the "Indolent Housewife" whose home is now dirty and cobwebby. There is also some ambiguity in poems given their tone by understatement, such as "All but Death, can be Adjusted," and those written from a child's point of view, such as "We do not play on Graves." Miss Dickinson made a punning allusion to the undertaker as of the "Appalling Trade." Probably her most serious puns were the several references to herself as queen and empress of Calvary. These suggest her amorous sacrifice and also apparently contain a hidden allusion to the Reverend Charles Wadsworth, minister of Calvary Church in San Francisco and evidently the lover spoken of in some of her poems.[43]

Only a trace of the witty grotesquerie of the seventeenth-century metaphysicals appears in Miss Dickinson's poetry. She treated the dead a little jauntily more often than naturalistically. The tone of Donne's "The Relique" is suggested in the sharp contrast of butterflies and "Sunset's Yellow play" with "eyelids in the Sepulchre." Another poem explains that tickets to the grave admit but two — the bearer and the borne — and seat only one. The resurrection of the dead, sometimes treated lightly by Donne and Herbert, was described in a similar spirit by Miss Dickinson, who on other occasions, however, felt an "Omen in the Bone/Of Death's tremendous nearness —." [44]

Despite the naïve tone of some of her work, Miss Dickinson's poetry is seldom really simple. Its complexity, like that of most metaphysical poetry, comes from her playing one sphere of knowledge and experience against a very different one and from her simultaneously holding quite different attitudes toward a subject. The comparison, then, of her work with that of the seventeenth-century metaphysical poets discloses some of her most fundamental ways of experiencing her world and some of her poetic habits that give her poetry its distinctive flavor. Most important, her conceits reveal the two basic systems she employed in transposing and interpreting experience: she measured and analyzed the gamut of emotions from bliss to agony with scientific detachment and philological precision, or she brought man, nature, and God together through living Christian symbols. Her commitment to either of these systems was apparently highly qualified. There was a much deeper cleavage in her ways of looking at the world than in, for instance, Donne's. This is seen, too, in the incongruous juxtapositions of her condensed conceits and in the audacity of some of her religious metaphors and paradoxes.

She touched most of her themes with her own metaphysical wit (often a little naïve and mischievous), but she also often resorted to it to "muffle with a jest" the mysteries of God and death and other subjects toward which her attitude was essentially ambiguous. Although Miss Dickinson was evidently not influenced directly by the seventeenth-century metaphysicals, there is a metaphysical approach at the heart of her work that reveals much about her deepest inner life and thus, too, much about the original and distinctive poetry that sprang from this.

V

The Catholic Revival and
the Metaphysicals

URING the nineteenth century the metaphysical style was
allied with a Catholic and Anglo-Catholic point of view
much as it had been during the seventeenth century. The
metaphysical revival and the Catholic revival cross-fertilized each
other. Though the Catholic revival was God-centered in a way
that the romantic revival was not, both the Catholic revival and
the metaphysical revival apparently owed something to the romantic movement. Cardinal Newman pointed out that Sir Walter
Scott had turned men's minds toward the medieval period and
hence toward the Catholic Church and asserted that Coleridge
had indirectly "made trial of his age, and succeeded in interesting its genius in the cause of Catholic truth." Wordsworth and
Southey, he added, "carried forward their readers in the same
direction." There was a close relation between the Oxford Movement, whose leaders returned with pleasure to a study of the high
tide of Anglicanism in the seventeenth century, and the Catholic
revival, which inspired an imposing list of conversions and restored the Catholic hierarchy to England. Many, such as Newman, who were active in the Anglican movement, later played
significant roles as England's "second spring" of Roman Catholicism flowered. Francis Thompson asserted late in the century that
all the Catholics then writing were "indirectly the children of
the Oxford Movement." [1]

The movement toward Catholicism was rich in the raw mate-

rial of poetry. Newman referred to it as "not so much a movement as a spirit afloat," and Gerard Manley Hopkins, alluding to
a group of converts, wrote: "All our minds were ready to go at
a touch." [2] Thompson, sharing this mood, began his early essay
on Shelley by calling upon the church to take poetry back into
the fold. It was natural that English Catholicism should turn to
metaphysical poetry, with its frequent dependence on incarnational and sacramental symbolism.

Catholic-revival writers gladly accepted the unifying power of
correspondences. Newman rejoiced in the "idea of an analogy
between the separate works of God," and Thompson felt that
man could not "stir a flower/Without troubling of a star." But
the system of correspondences embraced by Catholic-revival
poets was more exclusively theistical than the generally accepted
Renaissance system. It was more concerned with the relation of
everything to God and less concerned with the manifold relationships of all things, under God, to each other. Hopkins and
others felt God's presence very directly, particularly in out-of-
door beauties. "This world then is word, expression, news, of
God," Hopkins asserted. Thompson believed that the poet's chief
job was to present the divine idea of things, a kind of Platonic
"Primal Beauty" that he tended to identify with God, through
images drawn from a corresponding earthly beauty. He regarded
the relationships between the mind of man and the mind of God
as most significant and believed that the poetic imagination perceived the "secret subterranean passages," the identities "rooted
in the hidden nature of things." [3]

A changing attitude toward wit also enabled Catholics to read
metaphysical devotional poetry sympathetically. "Suffer her [po-
etry] to wanton, suffer her to play, so she play round the foot
of the Cross," wrote Thompson, while Lionel Johnson defended
conceits, familiarity, and "the very foolishness and madness of
devotion" and praised the "devout audacity" of devotional poets
from Southwell to Thompson. [4]

Both Catholics and Anglo-Catholics frequently found the English religious literature of the earlier seventeenth century con-

genial. In an essay on Thompson, Mrs. Alice Meynell wrote: "There is a call to our time from the noble seventeenth century; and this purely English poet cried *Adsum*! to the resounding summons." Newman, Johnson, Edward Dowden, and Archbishop Trench also answered the call. However, Thompson was representative in his sympathy for "the religious movement which had Laud for its militant apostle," Donne for its first poet, and "Herbert for its most representative singer." Herbert and Marvell were admired by Catholics despite their attacks on the Roman Catholicism of their day, and Dean Alford, in an early poem expressing dissatisfaction with the Anglican Church, linked together the names of Herbert and Crashaw as reminders of the great promise shown in the earlier seventeenth century.[5] This affinity with the earlier seventeenth century was reflected in much of both the poetry and criticism of the Catholic revival. In Hopkins' close-packed experiments, in Thompson's flood of lyrical imagery, and in Mrs. Meynell's brittle grace — in the work of three poets so similar and yet so distinctive — the Catholic revival's reinterpretation of the metaphysical style can be seen clearly.

GERARD MANLEY HOPKINS

Hopkins knew something of the work of some of the seventeenth-century metaphysical poets. He admired George Herbert and he had read a little of Marvell and Vaughan. He also knew Southwell, who sometimes wrote in the metaphysical manner. Hopkins' admiration for Herbert was attested by his intimate Oxford companion William Addis and by his lifelong friend Robert Bridges. "George Herbert was his strongest tie to the English Church," Addis said in later life. Hopkins thought Vaughan had "more glow and freedom than Herbert but less fragrant sweetness." "Still," he added, "I do not think him Herbert's equal." He described Marvell, whom he had read only in extracts, as a "most rich and nervous poet."[6]

Hopkins had a deep understanding of the significance and function of analogy, metaphor, and wit. In his work Catholic dogma and symbols take on a life and meaning that had gradually disappeared from English poetry after Henry VIII's break with Rome. Hopkins once more expressed the feeling of Christ's real presence in the Eucharist, in history, and in each mortal thing. Like Donne, he delighted in finding relationships between abstract thought and sensuous experience. Probably only a truly metaphysical mind, with a romantic background, could have been reminded of Scotus's philosophy whenever he caught sight of any attractive pattern of sky or sea. Often he used "farfetched or exquisite" as virtually synonymous terms. He wanted the feeling to "flush and fuse the language," but insisted that metaphors be logical and even scientifically true to nature. He had what he himself called "an over-perspectiveness of mind." He also approved of antithesis and paradox as means of awakening the reader's attention. Bridges felt that many of Hopkins' rhymes had a comic quality and intimated that his friend prided himself upon his ingenuity. But Hopkins' replies to Bridges' objections indicate he was so involved in his own elaborate and extremely serious technical experiments in rhyme that he never fully understood his friend's point of view. In the seventeenth century a poem sometimes existed for the sake of the wit; Hopkins always thought of wit as existing for the sake of the poem and as being a completely organic part of the poem. Although he believed in an almost impassable barrier between the strictly serious and the strictly funny, he apparently had virtually no suspicion of an inappropriateness in a mixture of wit and religious seriousness.[7]

Hopkins approached the seventeenth-century conceit a little more closely than did any other nineteenth-century poet. Many of his most characteristic metaphors depend on an incarnational and sacramental view of reality and on a knowledge of traditional Christian trope and symbol. Hopkins' "Barnfloor and Winepress" resembles Herbert's "The Bunch of Grapes"; but the sense of real analogical union is greater in Hopkins than in most seventeenth-century writing. In Hopkins' poem the historical Christ, the Eucharist, and the living church are one in sacrifice as Christ's passion is compared to the various steps in the harvesting of grain and grapes and in the making of bread and wine. It is only a short step from this kind of figure to those in Hopkins' two shipwreck poems, in which the fatal storms are viewed paradoxically as a kind of divine harvest. "Does tempest carry the grain for thee?" the poet asked of God in "The Wreck of the Deutschland." And in "The Loss of the Eurydice" he asserted: "One stroke/Felled and furled them, the hearts of oak!"[8] These events, suggesting the discovery of eternal life through death and of divine love through destruction, become analogues of Christ's crucifixion. They are a kind of incarnation of the eternal union between God and man continually realized through the Eucharist.

"The Blessed Virgin compared to the Air we Breathe" is Hopkins' most metaphysical poem. Mary is compared to the air that "girdles" each eyelash and penetrates the "fleeciest, frailest-fixed snow-flakes." The comparison is significant since it treats Mary as omnipresent rather than as a historical figure; the assumptions are Catholic rather than Anglican. Each physical service of air to the earth is matched by a spiritual service of Mary to man. As air, that "nursing element" and "meal at every wink," nourishes us physically, so does Mary spiritually. As the air transmits the glories of the universe, so Mary "lets through" God's glory, dispenses his providence through her prayers, and is herself both almoner and alms. And as air protects the earth from the dazzling force of the sun and makes its appearance more pleasant and welcome to the human eye, so Mary shields man and presents God more appealingly to the human soul:

> Through her we may see him
> Made sweeter, not made dim,
> And her hand leaves his light
> Sifted to suit our sight.

The conceit is similar to one in Donne's "The Extasie":

> On man heavens influence workes not so,
>   But that it first imprints the ayre,
> So soule into the soule may flow,
>   Though it to body first repaire.

The same basic idea is expressed by the same figure in both poems: in Hopkins' poem the air represents the human Mary in her relation to deity and in Donne's the air represents the body in its relation to the soul. In Donne's "Aire and Angels" a similar relationship between a grosser and a finer substance is treated in a similar figure. Another conceit resembling that of Hopkins occurs in a poem attributed to Donne. Both Donne and Hopkins credited the air with a motherly love for the earth.[9]

Hopkins is also reminiscent of the metaphysicals, particularly Donne, in his ability to define a complex psychological state in terms of a conceit. In an early fragment of Hopkins' projected drama *Floris in Italy*, the hero reasons in defense of his not returning Giulia's love. He considers her beauty:

> Allow at least it has one term and part
> Beyond, and one within the looker's eye;
> And I must have the centre in my heart
> To spread the compass on the all-starr'd sky: [10]

Donne's mixture of passion and scholasticism was never more abstruse than Hopkins' attempt here to consider love in terms of epistemological and aesthetic theories of beauty. Floris says, in effect, that he cannot love Giulia for her beauty unless this beauty depends in part on his own subjective perception of her. Hopkins' figure resembles Donne's celebrated compass conceit in "A Valediction: Forbidding Mourning," in which the "fixt foot" represents the woman who "leanes, and hearkens after" her absent lover. Donne's "The Extasie" and "A Valediction: Forbidding Mourning" are certainly possible sources for Hopkins' figures in these poems, since if he read Donne at all, even in an anthology, he probably would have read these two poems.

A more mature type of psychological conceit gives a distinctive power and coloring to "The Wreck of the Deutschland":

> I am soft sift
> In an hourglass — at the wall
> Fast, but mined with a motion, a drift,
> And it crowds and it combs to the fall;
> I steady as water in a well, to a poise, to a pane,
> But roped with, always, all the way down from
> the tall
> Fells or flanks of the voel, a vein

Of the gospel proffer, a pressure, a principle, Christ's
gift.[11]

These metaphysical conceits, depicting the see-saw relationship
between physical degeneration and spiritual regeneration, are
based on opposing paradoxes. Both images represent a stability
which is only apparent; but in the first, that of the hourglass, the
actual movement is an undermining while in the second, that of
the well, it is a building up. Thus the transition between the two
is logically grounded, but somewhat more abrupt than in most
seventeenth-century metaphysical poetry. Hopkins' comparison
of himself to an hourglass is almost paralleled by a passage from
Herbert's "Church-monuments." The series of short metaphors
at the end of the stanza suggests the close of Herbert's "Prayer"
(I):

Church-bels beyond the starres heard, the souls bloud,
The land of spices; something understood.

Possibly Hopkins had this passage in mind, for at the end of the
next stanza he wrote that he blessed God when he understood.

A group of figures in which spiritual life is treated in a homely,
everyday manner are typically Herbertian. In fact, Hopkins apparently took the title of his early "Heaven-Haven" and an allusion at the close of "The Wreck of the Deutschland" from
"heav'n the haven" in Herbert's "The Size" and his reference to
"mankind's medley" in "The Loss of the Eurydice" from Herbert's "Mans Medley." Herbert compared thoughts to thorns
and to knives, and Hopkins found them equally prickly. Hopkins alluded to "thick/Thousands of thorns, thoughts" and to
thoughts, "sheathe — and shelterless," that grind against each
other. Both poets also asked that they might be a part of the
world's music glorifying God. In other Herbert-like metaphors,
comparing the greater with the lesser and the all-important with
the trivial, Hopkins spoke of a youth's first communion as a
"treat" fetched from a cupboard and of his unanswered cries to
God as "dead letters sent/To dearest him" that lives away. In one
of his most philosophically metaphysical poems Hopkins consid-

ered man as the "clearest-selved spark" of "million-fueled, nature's bonfire." [12]

One of Hopkins' figures in "Rosa Mystica" closely resembles some of Crashaw's. Hopkins wrote:

> What was the colour of that Blossom bright?
> White to begin with, immaculate white,
> But what a wild flush on the flakes of it stood,
> When the Rose ran in crimsoning down the Cross-wood.

The handling of the imagery approaches passages such as this from Crashaw's "The Weeper":

> Such the maiden gemme
> By the purpling vine put on,
> Peeps from her parent stemme
> And blushes at the bridegroome sun.
> This watry Blossom of thy eyn,
> Ripe, will make the richer wine.

The passages are basically very similar. In both a blossom changes its color to red and then changes from a solid to a liquid. As Austin Warren has pointed out, this constant symbolic flow from white to red and from solid to liquid, and vice versa, is one of the most significant characteristics of Crashaw's poetry. Hopkins' stanza depicts the white of purity stained by the red of sacrifice. A similar story is told by the imagery of numerous poems by Crashaw.

Hopkins invented many metaphysical figures very different from those of the seventeenth century. The majority of these were probably derived from out-of-door nature, but others seem tossed up from the inner depths of his own soul. While Donne mourned "how lame a cripple this world is," Hopkins found the world "charged with the grandeur of God." "Thrush's eggs look little low heavens," and a starlit sky suggests a heavenly farm and a "piece-bright paling" shutting in Christ and his saints. A lark's song bursts forth like skeins from a "wild winch." In another poem Hopkins declared that man's soul would be no more encumbered by his risen body than meadow-down is by "a rainbow footing it." But some of the probing figures of the late sonnets

96

make it painfully clear that Hopkins did not find it so easy to dismiss the conflicts between the body and the soul in this life. "I am gall, I am heartburn," he cried. "Self-yeast of spirit a dull dough sours." In another poem he pictured the "Sheer, no-man fathomed" cliffs of the mind that only he "who ne'er hung there" could hold cheap.[18] One is reminded that in Marvell's "A Dialogue between the Soul and Body" the body claims that the soul has forced it to become its "own precipice."

Hopkins' use of paradox, pun, and other witty devices is often similar to that of the seventeenth-century metaphysicals. His "New Readings," which is rooted in a paradox, suggests Herbert in its soft-spoken conversational tone and parable structure:

> Although the letter said
> On thistles that men look not grapes to gather,
> I read the story rather
> How soldiers platting thorns round CHRIST'S HEAD
> Grew grapes and drops of wine were shed.

In "The Half-way House" Hopkins declared, "To see thee I must see thee, to love, love," possibly recalling Herbert's "Let me not love thee, if I love thee not." Hopkins' penchant for paradox is reflected in his humorous " 'The child is father to the man,' " but is pre-eminently apparent in "The Wreck of the Deutschland," which derives most of its power from its spirit of passionate paradox. "Thou art lightning and love, I found it, a winter and warm," Hopkins called to God. He found God, "fondler of heart thou has wrung," most merciful in his "dark descending." [14] Some lines from Crashaw function almost as a commentary on Hopkins' "a winter and warm," explaining the significance of the paradox by putting it in its traditional Christian context:

> Summer in Winter! Day in Night!
> Heaven in Earth! And God in Man!

Both Hopkins' idea of a divine union of love and force and the steady clenched blows of his idiom were sometimes anticipated by Donne:

> That I may rise, and stand, o'erthrow mee, 'and bend
> Your force, to breake, blowe, burn and make mee new.

Although the rhetoric and spiritual abandon of "The Wreck of the Deutschland" suggest Crashaw and Donne, Hopkins could also have found the seeds of most of these paradoxes in the work of Herbert. Conceiving of himself as a tree in paradise, Herbert called for God's pruning knife. "Such sharpness shows the sweetest Frend," Herbert explained.[15] Herbert's "Bitter-sweet," addressed to "my deare angrie Lord," is a kind of muted epitome of the dominant themes and attitudes of "The Wreck of the Deutschland."

There is a whirl of word-play and number-play in Hopkins' poetry. This wit produces more intellectual concentration than that of the seventeenth century, but it seldom suggests an expanded range of attitudes. While the seventeenth-century metaphysicals apparently felt that such wit made their work more effective because more pleasant, Hopkins probably intended his wit to be an unobtrusive framework or buttress to the design of the poem. Often his puns are pins to peg together the various themes of a poem. The most famous of Hopkins' puns is that on "buckle" in "The Windhover." It has been interpreted by various critics to mean virtually everything that "buckle" or any of its variants could mean under any circumstances. A touch of paradox lends piquancy to this pun as well as to those on "mind" ("out of mind" and "Christ minds") in "The Lantern out of Doors" and on "piecemeal peace" and "plumed" (adorned and stripped) in "Peace." A faint sparkle of levity reminiscent of the seventeenth century darts through the play on "silver" (hair and anniversary) in "The Silver Jubilee" and on "magnify" in "The May Magnificat."

In his number-play Hopkins was able to probe deeply and to symbolize significantly. His explanation in "Rosa Mystica" that the rose symbolic of the Virgin Mary has five leaves, "Five like the senses and numbers of men," suggests the relation worked out in Donne's "The Primrose" between the perfect rose's five petals and five as the number-symbol of woman. More seriously, Hopkins wrote:

> Five! the finding and sake
> And cipher of suffering Christ.
> Mark, the mark is of man's make
> And the word of it Sacrificed.
> But he scores it in scarlet himself on his own
> bespoken,
> Before-time-taken, dearest prizèd and priced —
> Stigma, signal, cinquefoil token
> In lettering of the lamb's fleece, ruddying of
> the rose-flake.[16]

Since the five nuns killed in the wreck of the *Deutschland* were followers of St. Francis, who was believed to have received the stigmata of Christ's wounds, they were compared to the five wounds of Christ. The effect of this kind of wit, which at first might seem fanciful and arbitrary, is to equate the sufferings and sacrifice of the nuns with those of Christ and to symbolize the sacrificial union of Christ and his church. Hopkins probably also recalled that five is the number of the cross (it takes five points to designate one) and of the sphere, a symbol of God.

Hopkins also resembled the seventeenth-century metaphysicals in his use of the witty grotesque, but primarily in the early and unfinished poems. His prize poem on the Escorial compared St. Lawrence collapsing on the gridiron to "a wreck that flames not billows beat." In "Easter Communion" Hopkins blandly suggested that the welts resulting from self-inflicted ascetic flagellation might be pieced together to form "crosses meant for Jesus." Hopkins compared St. Winefred's tumbling head, "lapped in shining hair," to a waterfall; it "flashed and fell and ran like water away." The figure, with its juxtaposition of sensuous brightness and death, suggests Donne's "The Relique" and Edward Herbert's description of the "bright hair," "Threds of life," of his mistress, Death, in "To His Mistress for her True Picture." He explained that Margaret Clitheroe was "crushed out flat" since her "will was bent at God." In sewing her own shroud, "She mends the way she means to go."[17] However, the only clear mixture of the somber and witty in Hopkins' mature work is in the reference to "the residuary worm" in "That Nature is a Heraclitean Fire."

To what extent, then, did Hopkins depend on various seventeenth-century metaphysicals and in what ways did he work out his own interpretation of the metaphysical style? Herbert's influence seems clearly evident in the whole texture of many of the early poems, such as "New Readings," "The Half-way House," "Barnfloor and Winepress," and "Heaven-Haven." Scattered through Hopkins' later work are Herbertian figures presenting the great Christian mysteries in familiar household terms.

Hopkins' work resembles that of Donne and Crashaw in several ways. While Hopkins could have discovered some of their techniques independently or in Herbert, Southwell, or the Catholic tradition generally, it seems probable that he knew some of Donne's and Crashaw's poetry. Although there is no clear evidence of direct imitation, some of the resemblances are teasingly close. He was associated with the Oxford Movement and the Catholic revival at a time when both Anglo-Catholics and Catholics found the English religious literature of the earlier seventeenth century particularly congenial. Donne and Crashaw were grouped with Herbert, whom Hopkins knew well, not only by literary critics, but also by religious writers. Hopkins also had a good background in English literature and read several literary journals fairly regularly. It is particularly difficult to believe that so staunch an Englishman and so ardent a Catholic as Hopkins did not know at least a little about the work of the foremost English Catholic devotional poet of the past.

The absence of recorded references to Donne and Crashaw is an undependable guide to Hopkins' knowledge of their work. Most of the allusions to poets in his letters are topical and incidental and frequently in references to his friends' poetry. The notebooks and journal, even for the periods covered, do not appear to give a complete account of Hopkins' reading. Furthermore, this silence may reflect his lack of sympathy with much in the work of these poets. W. H. Gardner and other critics have been puzzled by his failure to comment on Donne and Crashaw because they have assumed that he would have admired them and felt an affinity with them if he had known their work. It is very possible, however, that Hopkins knew the poetry of Donne and Crashaw and that on the whole he did not like it. Despite the significant similarities between his work and theirs, he might very easily have parted with them because of the dissimilarities.

Like many other Victorians, Hopkins objected to a lack of propriety in poetry. He disapproved of Vaughan's "licentious" early sonnets, Blake's "ribaldry," and the coarseness of Browning's "The Ring and the Book." [18] He was possibly disgusted by the franker portions of Donne's amorous poems and perhaps agreed with Ben Jonson that the exalted praise given to Elizabeth Drury in the "Anniversaries" was due only to the Virgin Mary. Nor is it likely that his opinion of Donne was raised by any knowledge he may have had of Donne's anti-Popish *Pseudo-Martyr* or of his anti-Jesuitical *Ignatius His Conclave*. In Hopkins' eyes Donne might well have appeared as a renegade who deserted the Catholic and Jesuit tradition of his family in the hope of secular advancement.

Hopkins, who favored a masculine Anglo-Saxon idiom and a concentrated structure, perhaps disliked Crashaw's soft Latinisms and Italianisms and his languorous expansiveness. Furthermore Hopkins, who always censured logical discrepancies in other poets, possibly objected to some of Crashaw's tangled figures.

Hopkins, then, in keeping with his religious position and poetic taste, probably sampled the work of Donne and Crashaw, set it aside when he found much of it unpalatable, but nevertheless received some stimulating suggestions from a few figures and techniques that were in harmony with his own interests and style. He very possibly depended on figures in Donne's "The Extasie" and "A Valediction: Forbidding Mourning" in his own "The Blessed Virgin compared to the Air we Breathe" and *Floris in Italy*. Hopkins' late "terrible" sonnets perhaps reflect his absorption of some of Donne's "Holy Sonnets." A passage in "Rosa Mystica" and possibly some in "The Wreck of the Deutschland" indicate a sampling of Crashaw. A knowledge of Donne and Crashaw is apparently reflected in a very general way in the technique of some other poems.

Although the differences that separate Hopkins and the seventeenth-century metaphysicals and their respective "worlds" are probably more numerous than the similarities that link them, Hopkins' fundamental kinship with the metaphysicals is an important and distinctive element in his poetry. Hopkins' originality in employing metaphysical techniques — not simply the techniques themselves — contributed immeasurably to the freshness and significance of his poetry. He somehow fused the sensuousness of Keats and the dynamism of Donne. He drew into taut metaphysical structures the Wordsworthian nature symbolism that Keble had employed in the incarnational and sacramental figures of *The Christian Year*. Hopkins' concern with Scotist philosophy gave him an overwhelming sense of the significance of the distinctive features of "each mortal thing," including himself. After the tentative experiments of Beddoes, Hopkins was the first to combine successfully a revived metaphysical technique and the new romantic stress on the particular, the personal, and the subjective. This union was brought to its ripest and maturest nineteenth-century fruition in Hopkins' poetry, and partly through his poetry this fusion was to be richly seminal for the twentieth century.

FRANCIS THOMPSON

Thompson knew the seventeenth-century metaphysicals better than Hopkins and — in his own diaphanous way — probably depended on them more. As a critic he contributed to the metaphysical revival with his essays on Herbert, Crashaw, Cowley, and Marvell, while as a poet he carried on the metaphysical tradition and was classed with the metaphysicals by several of his contemporaries.

Although Thompson has often been compared with Crashaw, he was like Hopkins in according higher praise to Herbert than to any of the other seventeenth-century metaphysicals. He asserted that Herbert leavened "daily bread with mysticism" and blended "the subtleties of spiritualities with a homely practicality, a Teutonic common sense." He rejoiced that "a germ of the seventeenth-century fancy, in all its unexpectedness," had fallen into Herbert's poetry. Thompson felt that the poetry of Herbert had a "human and sympathetic element" because its writer was not "a saint completed at a stroke." His enthusiasm for Herbert was attested by Katherine Tynan, who recalled how he exclaimed, "It is beautiful, beautiful," when she called to his attention a passage in *The Temple*.[19]

Thompson viewed Crashaw with mixed feelings. He regarded him as a precursor of Shelley and praised him for the fecundity and "rapturous ethereality" of his imagery and the "ardorous abandonment" of his odes, but he found the ardor cooled by too many "frigid" conceits and verbal gymnastics generally. Thompson found Donne "pregnant," "pungent," and "clever" — but little more. He considered Cowley too frequently cold and prosaic "despite his graceful fancy and gay sense of humor, his enormous erudition, and his command of a really original poetic style." Thompson did not read Marvell until comparatively late in life and regarded him then as a good eclectic mixture of Donne, Vaughan, and Herrick. He protested vigorously against a tendency to dismiss the seventeenth-century metaphysicals as a product of decadence. He thought that the metaphysicals' concern with underlying analogies foreshadowed Coleridge and Shelley and that metaphysical poetry was "an unfulfilled but fruitful experiment which showed the direction that English poetry would ultimately take to its triumphant gain." [20]

Virtually all possible combinations of relations resulting from the correspondence between God, the earth, and man are given a metaphysical expression in Thompson's poetry. In his odes on the rising and setting sun Thompson used sacramental imagery. He apparently depended somewhat on Crashaw and possibly on Donne. Day, "a dedicated priest," lifts the "orbed sacrament" from its "Orient tabernacle" in the "sanctuaried East" and then finally sets it in "the flaming monstrance of the West." He also explains that an inner sun, "in glad twinkling advent," dwells within our body as within a tabernacle. The setting sun, hanging "in dreadful pomp of blood" upon its "Western rood," is regarded as a "type memorial" of Christ, for it too will rise again. As he watches the sunset, however, the poet's "sun of Song" also sets.[21] These odes suggest Crashaw's Epiphany hymn. Both Thompson and Crashaw worked out analogies between the sun, the Son, and an inner light, but Thompson regarded this inner sun as his poetic talent. Thompson's "Ode to the Setting Sun" resembles Donne's "Good Friday, 1613. Riding Westward" in that in both poems a cross is actually envisioned in conjunction with the sun. Thompson also saw things as related to religious adjuncts. The earth was like a censer swung by the sun, a graceful woman's "lucid body" like a "silver thurible" and — in the most metaphysical use of that image — an anguished heart was like a fuming censer, "fed with oozed gums of precious pain," and swung by unrest.[22]

Thompson's "Any Saint" explains man's role as an image of God and as a link between spirit and sense in the great chain of being. The poem suggests Herbert's "Man" and "Mans Medley" in its theme and suggests his style in its use of a string of short metaphysical figures to express a single idea. Man is described as "secret metaphor," "cosmic metonymy," and "Trope that itself not scans/ Its huge significance." In a similar seventeenth-century fashion Thompson referred to "man's self, the little world" and to "my little-worlded self." [23]

Many of Thompson's figures suggest those of one or another of the metaphysicals. A Donne-like geometrical conceit occurs in a passage addressed to flesh:

> Epitomized in thee
> Was the mystery
> Which makes the spheres conjoint —
> God focussed to a point.[24]

Thompson, like Donne, also employed quaint old beliefs or stimulating new discoveries to express psychological relationships. Music and metempsychosis were combined in one figure. After imagining woe set against woe in antiphon, the poet explained that "grief's soul transmigrates" and that old pangs are reincarnated in new ones. Again he concluded that no stone, with "its inter-particled vibration," could be idler than he.[25] In another poem he used a complex spectrum image:

The very loves that belt thee must prevent
My love, I know, with their legitimacy:
As the metallic vapors, that are swept
Athwart the sun, in his light intercept
                    The very hues
Which their conflagrant elements effuse.[26]

This figure depends on the theory accounting for the shadowy bars falling across the colors in spectrum analysis. The metaphor develops the idea that love is like light not only in its many-hued radiance, but also in its tendency to prevent (both anticipate and hinder) itself.

A wide chasm separates the controlled, contained calm of Herbert's lyrics and the precipitate prodigality of Thompson's odes. While Herbert was satisfied with a star, Thompson wanted a sky-rocket. Yet when Thompson's metaphysical figures are not distinctly his own, they are most frequently like those of Herbert. Many of Thompson's metaphors have Herbert's way of interpreting great spiritual things in terms of lowly earthly ones and of employing the inanimate to express the most deeply vital. He asked his friends to look for him after death "in the nurseries of Heaven," and in another poem thought of his soul as "clinging Heaven by the hems." He pictured the man in contemplation who hears the stars shout to one another "from the peaks of space" as though they were mountaineers.[27] Again he wrote:

Designer infinite! —
Ah! must Thou char the wood ere Thou
                    canst limn with it?

There is no expeditious road
To pack and label men for God,
To save them by the barrel-load.[28]

Thompson also resembled Herbert in his use of a series of compact metaphors strung along a single theme. The images are mixed, the abstract and abstruse with the sensate and homely, so that the whole passage is like a string of pearls that is the more beautiful for not being perfectly matched. For Thompson, man is:

> Primer where the angels all
> God's grammar spell in small,
>   Nor spell
> The highest too well.
>
> Point for the great descants
> Of starry disputants;
>   Equation
> Of creation.

Man is also "cosmic metonymy," a "world-unshuttering key," and the "narrow bed" in which are wed the worlds of spirit and sense. Thompson's description of man as a "swinging wicker" set between the seen and the unseen suggests Herbert's description of man as a "wonder tortur'd in the space/Betwixt this world and that of grace." [29]

Thompson sometimes combined the metaphysical manner with his own preference for a burst of emotionally connotative imagery. He made a show of logical development, but the logic does not stand close examination:

> And now my heart is as a broken fount,
> Wherein tear-drippings stagnate, spilt
>   down ever
> From the dank thoughts that shiver
> Upon the sighful branches of my mind.[30]

An idea of sentimental desolation is expressed by the highly connotational images; the slightly logical framework upon which they are limply hung is of secondary importance.

He also liked to represent the earth and sometimes the entire solar system as something very small and almost trivial. The earth is described as "a trinket at my wrist," as a censer swung by the sun, and as one circling fish among "gold schools of ponderous orbs." [31] These references, together with the sense of infinite time and space suggested in "The Hound of Heaven" and other poems, indicate Thompson's efforts to present the scientist's vast reaches of space as both familiar and meaningful.

In Thompson's poetry, more than in that of Hopkins, there is an amicable partnership between the serious and the witty. In his use of antithesis and paradox Thompson approached the style of

Crashaw. The "Sweetnesse so sad, sadnesse so sweet" of Crashaw's "The Weeper" apparently suggested Thompson's "all the sadness in the sweet" and "sweetness in the sad." Thompson's "immortal mortal," "passionless passion," "wild tranquillities," and "pallid-dark" are similar to Crashaw's "unconsum'd consumption" and similar expressions; however, much of Thompson's paradox is even more exclusively verbal than Crashaw's. Thompson's description of the "cold like heat" and the scorching "cold-white purities" of chastity resembles paradoxes of Crashaw and Hopkins, and other writers in a Jesuit poetic tradition.[32]

Some of Thompson's early notebooks, filled with chains of imagery well mixed with puns,[33] reflect his metaphysical habit of mind. All kinds of analogies, ranging from the most sacred to the most trivial, interested him. In his "Desiderium Indesideratum" his empty, searching arms, when clasped athwart his breast, are discovered to form the august embraces of the cross. This symbol-play is very similar to that in a passage which Thompson copied into an early notebook from Donne's "The Crosse." Thompson punned in the midst of seriousness. As his friend and biographer, Everard Meynell, observed, he was witty "not so much to laugh, as to be distracted in the exercise."[34] Thompson praised Crashaw's "adroit yet reticent use of turn" in an elegy, and achieved a similarly well-mannered wittiness in his own elegy on Stephen Parry, a Jesuit astronomer:

> Starry amorist, starward gone,
> Thou art — what thou didst gaze upon!
> Passed through thy golden garden's bars,
> Thou seest the Gardener of the Stars.

The poet envisioned the deceased astronomer as dropping his tube upon discovering "the fairest Star of all." "I meant the thing merely for a pretty, gracefully turned fancy," Thompson explained; "what the Elizabethans would have called an excellent conceit."[35]

Mrs. Meynell recalled that Thompson's more famous elegy on Cardinal Manning, in which he wrote chiefly of his own premonition of approaching death, was composed "in the grief and terror" of one of his "days of deep depression." Yet, as she noted, some of the poem's tragic verses are "poignantly witty":

> Life is a coquetry
> Of Death, which wearies me,
>   Too sure
> Of the amour;
>
> A tiring-room where I
> Death's garments try,
>   Till fit
> Some fashion sit.[36]

The poet felt that life was too long a rehearsal for death's mean and single scene. A comparison of his veins to an hourglass is reminiscent of similar figures in Herbert and Hopkins. Thompson conceived of death as both destroyer and deliverer. It purifies the "muddy wine of life" and flushes the "cumbered gutters of humanity."[37]

There is a sharp juxtaposition of the witty and the grotesque in a poem supposedly addressed to Jane Williams by Shelley's spirit while his body is tossing on the waters of the Spezzia. Shelley's spirit explains that his "good-night draught" cannot be wiped from his lips, for "it was Death/Damped my lips that has dried my breath." Nor did Thompson apparently see any irreverence in the familiarity, conceits, and wit employed in his treatment of the sufferings of the English martyrs, whom he pictured as wedding "high and reverend Death" upon the "scaffold's bed" and as welcoming sweetly the "unrelenting cord" as the "bridegroom's arm." Punning on Thomas More's name (Latin "morus" means fool) and on his reputation for wit and foolery, Thompson referred to the English saint as a "happy Fool of Christ" and as a "Jester in the Courts of God," who jested death out of gravity in his "laughing martyrdom."[38]

In his attempt to bring God and the Catholic tradition into the center of the romantics' web of mysterious relationships, Thompson employed a style similar to that of the seventeenth-century metaphysicals. He often interpreted the spiritual or personal in terms of the abstract or physical, but seldom explored a personal relationship through an extended conceit in the manner of Donne and Marvell. However, in the lightness and grace of his wit and his well-tempered modulations between a major and a minor key Thompson was more like the seventeenth-century metaphysicals than was any other nineteenth-century poet. Browning was too heavy-handed and Hopkins was too earnest. But like Hopkins, Thompson differed from the metaphysicals in his emphasis on external nature, his greater sensuousness, and his increased subjectivism. His metaphysical style enabled him to unite a traditional Catholicism and a fresh romanticism in a new sacred poetry.

ALICE MEYNELL

Twentieth-century devotees of the seventeenth century might well enshrine Mrs. Meynell as a patron saint. She carried on a quiet but fervent crusade for the distinctive qualities of the seventeenth century when it was not yet popular to champion the era. She praised writers of this period in her unsigned column, "The Wares of Autolycus," which appeared regularly in *The Pall Mall Gazette*, and distilled much of the spirit of the seventeenth century into her own poems. She never tired of praising that time when "England had but to speak in order to say something exquisite." "Indeed, I am in love with the seventeenth century," she observed, "when I see how purely it could recall the age gone past, and with what majesty it could forebode the age to come." For her the period had rapture, nature, spirituality, and light, and its end was like the "closing of a shutter and a sudden exclusion of sky." [39]

Mrs. Meynell contended that the seventeenth-century writers "had a taste extraordinarily liberal, generous, and elastic, but not essentially lax." She explained that "the conceits are almost all perfectly poetical, rapturous in spite of artifice." She apparently approved of the paradox and "holy facetiousness" of much devotional poetry and of the many seventeenth century lyrics "which brought poetry and sanctity to meet." [40]

Mrs. Meynell showed a particular interest in the works of the seventeenth-century metaphysical poets, especially their devotional poetry. She wrote of the "beauty, the wit, the tenderness and intimacy that never failed Herbert," that "wit and worshipper." She held that Crashaw's reference to "fair and flagrant things" described his own poetry, but insisted that many of his "flagrant" things "were not flagrant, but just buoyant, balanced, zephyr-gentle, spring-fresh, impulsive, frolic, and free." [41] However, the secular line of metaphysical poetry drew from her a less enthusiastic response. She praised Donne's "fine onsets," but found some of his poetry of uneven quality. "Cowley the cold," she charged, "wrote in a gay language, but contributed nothing to its gaiety." She was entranced by the "wild civility" (her "wild" was highly complimentary) of some of Marvell's garden poems. She felt that Marvell at his best was very good indeed, and explained that "this poet two or three times did meet a Muse he had hardly looked for among the trodden paths" and came away from the "divine ambush a wilder and a simpler man." [42]

Mrs. Meynell tended to base a poem on a carefully constructed logical relationship, preferably a paradox. She liked to turn an old idea around, to view it upside down and from behind, and then to give it a surprising logical twist. She probably owed her penchant for paradox to her familiarity with the metaphysicals and to her absorbing interest in the great paradoxes of Catholic thought. She not only thought that the world expressed the underlying paradox of God, but felt that the expression itself was paradoxical. Her "To a Daisy" suggests how the flower both reveals and conceals the supersensible world. She delighted in transposing conventional religious attitudes. In "Veni Creator" man, instead of asking forgiveness of God, asks God to come and be forgiven for "the mournful world" he decreed. In "Veneration of Images" she insisted that flesh, like spirit, should be enshrined and knelt to as a "rood of every day," while in "Free Will" she protested that she treasured most her "trespasses" and "proved iniquities," for without them she could not hate, love, weep, hope, and grope for lowliness.

She was fascinated by the way in which she could seem both younger and older than antiquity, than Shakespeare, than her father, and than herself. She portrayed antiquity as a babe. Having lived through the tercentenary anniversaries of Shakespeare's birth and death, she thought of herself paradoxically as an "ignoble clasp" around Shakespeare's "infinite between." [43] In "Time's Reversals" she compared her own relation to her deceased father to Johnson's relation to the wife, twenty years his senior, whom he outlived by thirty years. Time that gave Johnson a younger wife in "late lone years" will soon give the poet "A daughter's riper mind, a child's seniority." Both her juggling of paradoxical relationships and her characteristic touch of sentimentality occur in "A Letter from a Girl to Her Own Old Age":

> The one who now thy faded features guesses,
> With filial fingers thy grey hair caresses,
> With morning tears thy mournful twilight blesses.

Mrs. Meynell's metaphors are fundamentally simple, but apparently sometimes show the influence of seventeenth-century metaphysical poems. In "The Shepherdess" she wrote:

> She walks — the lady of my delight —
> A shepherdess of sheep.
> Her flocks are thoughts. She keeps them white;
> She guards them from the steep;

The conceit appears to be a development of a figure in Herbert's "Christmas":

> My soul's a shepherd too; a flock it feeds
> Of thoughts, and words, and deeds.

A simple figure in "I Am the Way" is also in the style of Herbert:

> Thou art the Way.
> Hadst Thou been nothing but the goal,
> I cannot say
> If Thou hadst ever met my soul.

In "The Crucifixion" Mrs. Meynell portrayed Christ as disproving the seeming unfathomable infinity of sorrow and pain by touching the floor of this sea. The figure is similar to one in Cowley's "Christ's Passion." The comparison in "To the Beloved Dead" of her memory of a loved one to "a tune that idle fingers/

Play on a window pane" resembles Carew's comparison, in "Mr. Carew to His Frind," of the continual running of the poet's thoughts on his absent Celia to the hand of one playing by memory.

"Reflexions" is Mrs. Meynell's most distinctive achievement in metaphysical metaphor. She herself believed the poem embodied the highest "intellectual passion" of which she was capable.[44] A series of complex ideas grow out of a single conceit. The figure, that of facing mirrors, first suggests the growing internal dissension in Ireland, then the relationship between Othello and Desdemona, and finally, in the section "In Two Poets," the relationship between two writers:

> A MIRROR faced a mirror: O thy word
>   Thou lord of images, did lodge in me,
> Locked to my heart, homing from home, a bird,
>   A carrier, bound for thee.
>
> Thy migratory greatness, greater far
>   For that return, returns; now grow divine
> By endlessness my visiting thoughts, that are
>   Those visiting thoughts of thine.

Mrs. Meynell's figures were confined to a narrow range of the familiar. Her greatest gift was for binding sensitive insights and delicate feelings into a taut framework of unbending logic, especially a paradox.

VI

The Metaphysical Revival
1872–1912

I T H A S been generally assumed that the contemporary revival
of Donne and other seventeenth-century metaphysicals began
with the publication of Sir Herbert Grierson's edition of
Donne in 1912 and that the recent critical theories about the
sensibility reflected in metaphysical poetry were first presented
in some essays by Eliot that appeared in the early 1920's. In reality,
however, Grierson's edition marked the end of the first stage of
the metaphysical revival. His edition was in part the cause of the
renewed interest in Donne which reached a scholarly climax in
1931 with the observance of the tercentenary of his death. It was
also the result of the increased interest in Donne that began during
the later decades of the nineteenth century. Similarly, Eliot's
essays were not so much a new note as a sensitive formulation of
ideas that had become familiar by 1912.

FROM GROSART TO GRIERSON

During the earlier nineteenth century there was a gradually
broadening acceptance of the metaphysicals both in Great Britain
and in the United States. Then from the 1870's until 1912 there
was a steady quickening in the tempo of the revival. This later
phase of the revival may be dated from the appearance of Alexander Grosart's edition of Donne's poems in 1872, despite the
editor's timid praise and apologetic assertion that "those whom
these volumes may be assumed to reach are 'strong' enough to use
them for literary purposes unhurt." During the 1870's and 1880's

Grosart also published editions of the poems of George Herbert, Crashaw, Marvell, and Cowley. In spite of his formidable "memorial introductions" and his wayward scholarship, his successful efforts — sometimes at his own expense — to "get these glorious old fellows into appreciative hands and hearts"[1] were a significant contribution to the metaphysical revival. He was the first of the three G's — Grosart, Gosse, and Grierson — who dominated this stage of the revival. Edmund Gosse's biography of Donne, published in 1899, climaxed a decade of excitement about the poet-preacher. During the 1890's there appeared editions of his poems by the Grolier Club and the Muses' Library, Augustus Jessopp's biography of Donne as a religious leader, and numerous articles. Frank L. Babbott edited a bowdlerized American edition of Donne's poems in 1905. Wightman Fletcher Melton announced in 1906 that he was preparing a new edition of Donne's poems, but the work was never completed.[2]

During the late nineteenth century Francis Thompson and several American critics noted the increased interest in Donne and the other metaphysicals.[3] Grierson has recalled that he was interested in the textual problems of Donne's poetry as early as the 1890's.[4] Shortly after the turn of the century W. J. Courthope explained that "the revival of mediaeval sentiment, which has coloured English taste during the last three generations, has naturally awakened fresh interest in the poems of Donne, and there is perhaps in our own day a tendency to exaggerate his merits."[5]

Almost all the reviews of the Grierson edition referred to the Donne revival as a *fait accompli*. E. K. Chambers remarked that Donne's reputation "stands now higher than ever it did since a new manner of writing first displaced his," and credited the revival to "men of letters, caught by the essential poetry in Donne, and literary historians, discerning his unique influence upon the fashioning of Caroline verse." In a similar vein *The Spectator* critic asserted that "for the last fifteen years there has probably been more genuine interest taken in his poetry by lovers of English literature than during the whole preceding period since the days of Dryden." In another review Rupert Brooke rejoiced that

"Donne's glory is ever increasing." Apparently already weighing the effect of the long-awaited Grierson edition, another critic announced that Donne had "suddenly become to many readers and lecturers the most exciting poet of his century." [6]

THE REINTERPRETATION OF DONNE THE MAN

The increased interest in Donne was due not only to an awakened appreciation of his work, but also to a growing concern with his personality. Many critics echoed Campbell's early declaration that the life of Donne was more interesting than his poetry. William Minto even maintained that "the admiration which Donne's contemporaries expressed for him as a writer was doubtless largely influenced by the impression which he made upon them as a man." [7] From the mass of Donne criticism there emerged three closely related conceptions of the man: Donne the rebel, Donne the mystery, and Donne the unique individual. These conceptions of the man are basic to the recent critical accent on the originality, complexity, and psychological realism of his poetry.

To regard Donne as a rebel was not unreasonable. Thomas Carew in his elegy on Donne had credited him with purging the muses' garden and with planting "fresh invention." Most of the earlier writers associated with the metaphysical revival failed to notice, however, that Donne's distinctive qualities were well grounded in Renaissance tradition. They pictured him as an isolated, morose hero, coldly and deliberately attempting to change the course of English poetry. Frederic Carpenter portrayed Donne as a "thoroughly original spirit and a great innovator . . . thoughtful, indirect, and strange," who "nurses his fancies, lives with them, and broods over them so much that they are still modern in all their distinction and ardour in spite of the strangeness of their apparel." [8]

Gosse's conception of Donne the rebel was both the most extreme and the most influential. Gosse attributed to Donne "the scornful indifference of the innovator, the temperament of the man born to inaugurate a new order of taste." He referred to "his austere and contemptuous silence" in regard to the other poets of the Countess of Bedford's circle and to the attraction of "the severe and repellent Donne" for Jonson. He also elaborated upon the idea that Donne "intentionally essayed to introduce a revolution into English versification." Reviewers of Gosse's biography embroidered the growing myth of Donne the tortured, tragic literary rebel. Arthur Symons, dwelling on Donne's "morbid state of body and brain and nerves" and the neurotic "preying upon itself of the brain," concluded that his strange personality led Donne to seek to "correct" English poetry and to "make a clean sweep of tradition." H. M. Sanders characterized Donne as an "intentional innovator" with an "iconoclastic impulse." Grierson helped to perpetuate the idea by pointing out Donne's scoffing challenge of the style of Petrarch and his emancipated and critical attitude toward religious problems.[9] American critics pictured Donne as a great rebel, but as a less romantic one. Paul Elmer More declared that Donne was like Socrates in arousing men from their apathy and that his originality was responsible for "one of the few real turning points in our literature." Melton investigated Donne's innovations in the use of the same words and sounds in arsis and in thesis and concluded that "while the verses of other poets rime in the middle or at the end, Donne's rime everywhere." John Chadwick alluded to Donne's "stiff-necked individuality" and William Vaughn Moody and Robert Morss Lovett stressed his strong new note.[10]

Donne's contemporaries did not regard him as a mystery. The seventeenth century had fitted him conveniently into the ready-made Augustinian mold of the convert, as Izaak Walton's biography and many of the elegies show. But the later nineteenth century was fascinated by the seeming paradox between Jack Donne, the gay libertine, and Dr. John Donne, the somber dean of St. Paul's. Francis Palgrave expressed a common attitude in asserting that Donne was "almost equally fascinating and repellent." Another critic wondered whether Donne did not leave his own character as one of the riddles which he wished posterity to solve. However, the cult of Donne the mystery attained an almost mystic expression when Gosse described the poet as "this enigmatical and subterranean master, this veiled Isis whose utterances outweigh the oracles of all the visible gods." Symons referred to Donne as "a fascinating and puzzling creature whom each of us may try to understand after his own fashion." [11] Leslie Stephen mourned that "the real Donne . . . has disappeared, and just enough is revealed to make us ask for more." American critics were similarly enchanted with Donne the mystery. Chadwick, for instance, characterized Donne himself as "the one riddle surpassing all those connected with his life," while another writer declared that "Donne drew around him a cloudy something which keeps him forever to himself." [12]

The emphasis upon the unfathomable mystery of Donne's personality led almost inevitably to a comparison with Hamlet. As early as 1880 Minto compared Donne, weak-willed, contemplative, and despondent, to Shakespeare's puzzling hero. Sanders declared that as W. E. Henley had written of Robert Louis Stevenson, there was in Donne "much Antony, of Hamlet most of all." Rupert Brooke later observed that "Hamlet, with his bitter flashes, his humor, his metaphysical inquisitiveness, and his passion, continually has the very accent of the secular Donne, but that he is an avenger, not a lover. To Ophelia he must have been Donne himself." [13]

The conception of a mysterious Donne was closely bound up with the idea of Donne the unique individual. This idea involved a questionable faith in the confessional character and psychological realism of his writings. The seventeenth century did not share the nineteenth and twentieth centuries' high regard for uniqueness *per se*, and even the most flattering elegies on Donne did not represent him as a unique personality. Grosart, however, insisted that Donne was "an absolute and unique genius," and most later nineteenth- and earlier twentieth-century critics agreed that he was a most uncommon man. One reviewer complained that in Clyde Furst's discussion of Donne in *A Group of Old Authors* "one misses those picturesque details with regard to Donne's personal peculiarities," indicating that no treatment of the poet was complete without the familiar emphasis upon his marked individuality. Stephen referred to Donne as a "strange complex human being" who had "extraordinary talents at the service of a most peculiar idiosyncrasy." [14] Rupert Brooke helped to bridge the gap between the romantic criticism which dramatized Donne's eccentricities and the more recent tendency to distinguish sharply between the ordinary man and the man with a unified sensibility. In the United States F. E. Schelling contended that Donne "shone and glowed with a strange light all his own" and interpreted his rugged metrics in terms of his "strange personality." Martin G. Brumbaugh tried to explain Donne's "real self," and concluded that "his personality was immeasurably precious." [15]

THE BACKGROUND OF ELIOT'S CRITICISM

While earlier critics were dramatizing the personality of Donne, they were also engaged — although less consciously — in another important phase of the revival. They were forging new instruments for evaluating, interpreting, and enjoying metaphysical poetry, especially Donne's. These ideas, which were to attain their most significant formulation in some of T. S. Eliot's essays of the 1920's, were gradually developed and refined. The criticism of the late nineteenth and early twentieth centuries reveals the development of the conceptions of the merging of thought and feeling, psychological realism, and the modernity of the metaphysical poets. These ideas had become familiar before the publication of Grierson's edition of Donne's poems; since its appearance they have become increasingly popular. They were crystallized in Eliot's "The Metaphysical Poets," "Andrew Marvell," and "John Donne." In these essays Eliot held that much seventeenth-century metaphysical poetry reflected a unified sensibility that could relate disparate experience. He also explained that metaphysical poetry often expressed the truth of human experience in all its flux, complexity, and ambiguity, and declared that this earlier poetry was similar to much modern poetry.

The development of the idea of the close relationship between hard thinking and deep feeling in metaphysical poetry would have been impossible if the nineteenth century had not gradually dismissed the idea that conceits and other displays of intellect were inimical to feeling. Criticism made a complete right-about-face and held that intellectual devices could play a significant role in the expression of sincere personal feeling. Grosart maintained that Marvell's conceits "sprung out of a vital thought or emotion or fancy." George Herbert Palmer defended Herbert's conceits as "cases of condensed imagination," and another earlier twentieth-century American critic asserted that the "cunning of the intellect is as necessary in verse as the display of emotions or sensibility." [16]

Grosart was one of the first to stress the quick transitions between thought and feeling in the work of the metaphysicals. To illustrate the thought-feeling relationship in Crashaw's poetry, he turned to the familiar description of Elizabeth Drury:

> . . . her pure and eloquent blood
> Spoke in her cheekes, and so distinctly wrought,
> That one might almost say, her body thought;

"I have much the same conception of Crashaw's thinking," Grosart wrote. "It was so emotional as almost always to tremble into feeling." He pointed out that in Donne's poetry "the light of his imagination lies goldenly over his thinking." Praising Cowley's combination of "high thought" with "high imagination," he asserted that in his poetry "the thought is not only illumined with imagination, but made to pulsate with feeling, whenever and wherever the emotional is touched." [17] Grosart was one of the first critics to discover in metaphysical poetry a dynamic process in which thought and feeling were merging into one another. He denied the contention of many earlier critics that thought clogged the flow of feeling, and began to investigate the way in which thought and feeling fused and formed a new whole.

The idea of a vital interaction between thought and feeling in metaphysical poetry was gradually developed and defined. Symons wrote of Donne: "This lover loves with his whole nature, and so collectedly because reason in him is not in conflict with passion, but passion's ally." He added that in Donne's elegies "his senses speak with unparalleled directness." These observations anticipated Eliot's remarks about the desirability of a poet's looking into the cerebral cortex and nervous system before writing. Stephen believed that metaphysical poetry took its peculiar flavor from its "odd combination of syllogism and sentiment" resulting from the cramming of passionate outbursts into logical frameworks. Grierson similarly referred to the "intimate wedding of passion and argument which is the essential quality of the metaphysical lyric." [18] Meanwhile American critics were thinking along similar lines. Lowell praised Donne's ability to "open vistas for the imagination through the blind wall of the senses." In the 1890's Schelling called attention to Donne's contributions to the development of "intellectualized emotion" in the English lyric, and later Edward Bliss Reed supposed that Donne's mind, when deeply moved, transformed thoughts and feelings into apt conceits which were arrived at instinctively. Thompson anticipated recent custom in finding this metaphysical blend of thought and feeling in the poets of his own time. Even in his own psyche he perceived a "sensoriness instinct with mind" and a "blended twilight of intellect and sensation." He asserted that Patmore was "like Crashaw for his power of fusing translucent abstractions by a white flame of passion" and that the essence of Mrs. Meynell's poetry was "feeling oozed through the pores of thought." [19]

Some of Rupert Brooke's critical essays strikingly suggest those of Eliot in their sensitive insight, style, and treatment of similar ideas. In his "John Donne" and "John Donne the Elizabethan," both inspired by the Grierson edition, he gave a preliminary formulation to ideas which Eliot was to treat more definitively in the 1920's. These essays, together with the Grierson edition, mark the end of one stage of the metaphysical revival and the beginning of another. Like Eliot, Brooke stressed the relationship of the metaphysicals to the sensibility that pervaded much English Renaissance drama. He declared that "Donne applied the same spirit the dramatists applied to the whole world, almost solely to love." [20] Eliot later discovered the same kind of sensuous thought in both Chapman's plays and Donne's lyrics. Both poet-critics distinguished sharply between the ordinary man and the man with a particular type of sensibility. Brooke wrote of Donne:

The whole composition of the man was made up of brain, soul, and heart in a different proportion from the ordinary prescription. This does not mean that he felt less keenly than others; but when passion shook him, and his being ached for utterance, to relieve the stress, expression came through the intellect. Under the storm of emotion, it is common to seek for relief by twisting some strong stuff. Donne, as Coleridge said, turns intellectual pokers into love-knots. An ordinary poet, whose feelings find far stronger expression than a common man's, but an expression according to the same prescription, praises his mistress with some idea, intensely felt . . . Donne, equally moved and equally sincere, would compare her to a perfect equilateral triangle, or to the solar system. His intellect must find satisfaction.[21]

Eliot similarly explained that, while "the ordinary man's experience is chaotic, irregular, fragmentary," the poet with a unified sensibility is always forming new wholes, even from such disparate experiences as falling in love, reading Spinoza, hearing the typewriter, and smelling the cooking.[22]

Both Brooke and Eliot pointed out that the metaphysicals were frequently able to view an experience both emotionally and intellectually at the same time. Brooke wrote: "And as Donne saw everything through his intellect, it follows in some degree that he could see everything humorously. He could see it the other way, too . . . But while his passion enabled him to see the face of love, his humor allowed him to look at it from the other side. So we behold his affairs in the round." Eliot, discussing seventeenth-century wit as an "intellectual quality" often confused with erudition and cynicism, declared that it involved "a recognition, implicit in the expression of every experience, of other kinds of experience which are possible." Brooke's statement that Donne "could combine either the light or grave aspects of love with this lack of solemnity that does but heighten the sharpness of the seriousness" resembles Eliot's allusion to an "alliance of levity and seriousness (by which the seriousness is intensified)." Brooke also said of Donne that "it must not appear that his humor, or his wit, and his passion alternated." In other words, he was the exact opposite of some of the post-metaphysical poets of whom Eliot wrote: "They thought and felt by fits, unbalanced; they re-flected." [23]

Brooke's and Eliot's conceptions of a metaphysical sensibility involve important similarities and differences. Both considered Donne as an intellectual poet because of the quality of his view, not because of intellectual subject matter, and both devoted considerable attention to the interaction of the intellectual and emotional elements in his poetry. Although Brooke's theories were never completely defined, he apparently perceived in Donne's poetry a conversion of the emotional into the intellectual. "The pageant of the outer world of matter and the mid-region of the passions came to Donne through the brain," he explained. Eliot, however, found in metaphysical poetry primarily a conversion of the intellectual into the emotional. [24]

Very closely associated with the idea of a dynamic thought-feeling relationship was an increased emphasis on the metaphysical poets' psychological realism, their fidelity to psychological processes and to the flux and flow of complex experience. This conception of the expression of the whole truth of human experience, only dimly envisioned by the seventeenth century, was associated with the confessional temper of the romantic era and the nineteenth century's gradual acceptance of ambiguity. It received one of its most significant formulations in Eliot's criticism. This growing interest in psychological realism during the later nineteenth and early twentieth centuries was accompanied by an increased sympathy for a mixture of wit and seriousness. Grosart assured readers that there was nothing irreverent in Herbert's "serious punning" nor in the alleged "levity" of Crashaw's "The Weeper." Minto defended Donne's "quick shifting between jest and earnest," but regarded his wit as unconscious and sincere rather than as deliberate and playful. [25]

A full-blown theory of psychological realism, however, did not appear until the 1890's; it was concerned chiefly with the poetry of Donne and was of course closely bound up with the fabulous interpretations of Donne the man. Pointing out the particularity, complexity, and "abundance of mental movement" in Donne's poetry, Gosse asserted that the poet was, "in a totally new and unprecedented sense, a realist," and concluded that he was the "forerunner of modern Naturalism in English poetry." Finding the "incongruities of an age of transition and revolution" reflected in "the Fantastic Poets," Arthur Clutton-Brock characterized Donne as "a realist not so much of facts as of the imagination," who expressed the truth as he saw it with seriousness and honesty.[26]

Several critics noted Donne's faithful expression of the flow of experience. Saintsbury held that "for those who have experienced, or who at least understand, the ups-and-downs, the ins-and-outs of human temperament," the alteration of moods, "there is no poet and hardly any writer like Donne." Symons maintained that no one else "has ever rendered so exactly and with such elaborate subtlety every mood of the actual passion." He explained that Donne "forgot beauty, preferring to it every form of truth." Grierson developed more fully this contrast between a poetry of static beauty, which records an ideal passion recalled in tranquillity, and Donne's "strain of vivid realism," which "utters the very movement and moment of passion itself." Brooke further stressed Donne's psychological realism, his faithful recording of "all the pitched battles, alarms, treaties, sieges, and fanfares of that extraordinary triangular warfare" of the body, the soul, and the mind. "Donne," he wrote, "was true to the reality of his own heart." Chadwick found that Donne's poems "give an impression of profound reality."[27]

Critical opinion slowly reversed itself. During the earlier nineteenth century critics had often held that complexity, obscurity, and harshness prevented sincere personal expression. By the first decade of the twentieth century, however, it was granted that these qualities reflected a fidelity to the truth of experience. With a penetrating insight into the change that was taking place at the turn of the century, Palmer wrote: "Indeed, I believe it will be found that the most lucid poets of our language are the least sincere, and that writers peculiarly intricate are often at the same time peculiarly sweet, tender, and veracious. What startling insights into reality has Donne! And how inevitably we distrust the lucidity of Pope! These metaphysical poets often seem artificial because they observe profoundly and speak individually." Defending Donne's knotty structure as evidence of his sincerity, Barrett Wendell declared that his lack of conventional grace made his poems seem astonishingly genuine. He observed that "they seem to express not fancy, but fact, and in a temper very like that of the art which modern cant calls realistic." [28]

While seventeenth-century metaphysical poetry was being interpreted in the light of more recent aesthetic ideas, Donne and his followers were coming more and more to be considered as among the foremost representatives of the modern temper. While turning back to the seventeenth-century poets with whom they had an affinity, poets and critics of the late nineteenth and early twentieth centuries insisted that the metaphysical poets were moderns — much more "modern" than most nineteenth-century poets. This movement began with the comparison of Keble with Herbert and of Keats and Shelley with Crashaw, and it was bolstered by the persistent comparison of Browning with Donne. The tendency was probably climaxed by Eliot's consideration of metaphysical poetry as closely akin to French symbolist poetry and as a desirable influence on contemporary English poetry. In 1900 one critic with considerable insight perceived significant similarities between literary movements at the beginning of the Jacobean period and at the beginning of the twentieth century.[29] These similarities were later to be increasingly stressed.

Among the first recent poets to be compared with the metaphysicals was Thompson. Patmore credited him with qualities that would put him "in the permanent ranks of fame with Cowley and with Crashaw." Geoffrey Bliss found similarities in the work of Thompson and Crashaw, and Mrs. Meynell noted that Thompson enthusiastically responded to the cry to his time from the seventeenth century. Symons later emphasized Thompson's relation to Donne and to Crashaw and regarded Marvell's ode on Cromwell as a model for Thompson's "To the Dead Cardinal of Westminster." [30]

However, it was Donne's modernity which was stressed. Stephen, for instance, wrote:

In one way he has partly become obsolete because he belongs so completely to the dying age. But on the other side, Donne's depth of feeling, whether tortured into short lyrics or expanding into voluble rhetoric, has a charm which perhaps gains a new charm from modern sentimentalists. His morbid or neurotic constitution has a real affinity for latter-day pessimists. If they talk philosophy where he had to be content with scholastic theology, the substance is pretty much the same. He has the characteristic love for getting pungency at any price; for dwelling upon the horrible till we cannot say whether it attracts or repels him; and we can love the "intense" and super-sublimated as much as if he were skilled in all the latest aesthetic canons.[31]

Another impetus to this tendency to associate Donne with contemporary poets was given by members of a little group of Georgian poet-critics, including Rupert Brooke, John Drinkwater, and Walter De La Mare. Brooke remarked that it was fitting that Donne "should be read in an age when poetry is beginning to go back from nature, romance, the great world, and other fine hunting places of the Romantics, by devious ways and *ambages*, to that wider home which Donne knew better than any of the great English poets, the human heart." [32]

De La Mare pictured Brooke himself as a kind of twentieth-century John Donne. He compared his era to the Jacobean era and elaborated upon Donne's influence on Brooke's poetry. He considered Brooke, like Donne, to be "more self-centered than the rest, more analytical, and intellectual," more defiant toward tradition, and closer to actual experience. After Brooke's death he said that "in his metaphysical turns, his waywardness, his contradictoriness, his quick revulsions of feeling, he reminds us not less — he reminded even himself (in a moment of exultation) — of the younger Donne." [33]

A few other poets were compared with Donne. Gosse suggested that Robert Bridges' "irregular lyrics" and Donne's new poetic forms were the products of similar aesthetic attitudes. Another critic declared that Bridges was the hierophant of "a tendency, which reminds us of Donne, to vary metrics, to study balance, and the use of resolved feet." As the interpretation of Donne continued, it was to be expected that an American critic would eventually compare him with a distinctly American poet. Citing his "riot of the senses," Chadwick regarded Donne as "a Whitman born in Shakespeare's time." [34]

Before 1912 there was also the beginning of a tendency to compare the seventeenth-century metaphysicals with the nineteenth-century French symbolist poets. Gosse suggested that the symbolists' "endless experiments" would shed light on Donne's aesthetic aims, and Grierson maintained that both Donne and Baudelaire were "naturally artificial; for them simplicity would be affectation." No great emphasis was given to the resemblance until the 1920's, when Eliot found in the symbolists "a method curiously similar to that of the metaphysical poets." [35] Although the relationship was dimly perceived and inadequately defined, several critics were interested in both metaphysical and symbolist poetry and the two styles tended to stimulate interest in each other. This cross-fertilization was natural since there were basic similarities between the metaphysical and symbolist aesthetics, since both depended on a system of underlying analogies.[36]

GOSSE, SYMONS, AND BROOKE

Gosse, Symons, and Brooke anticipated Eliot in making their poetic practices a reflection of their critical theories of the metaphysicals. Only Brooke, however, seems to have identified himself with Donne and to have been regarded as a metaphysical poet by his contemporaries.

Gosse only occasionally struck a metaphysical note in his poetry, despite his absorption in Donne during the 1890's. In several poems he used extended metaphors of some complexity. In "The Tide of Love" he compared his reunion with God to a returning tide, guided by the moon of destiny, which flooded all the dry creeks of his soul. In an expanded figure in "Circling Fancies" he compared the insects continuously circling around the scented acacia to his own hopes and fancies which, powerless either to desert the circle or to approach the center, wheel even in sleep around his desires:

> Clasped by a chain that makes no sign
> My hopes and wheeling fancies live;
> Desires, like odours, still confine
> The heart that else were fugitive.[37]

Some of Symons' poems have much more of the subtlety, complexity, abstraction, and sometimes even the idiom of Donne. The beginning of one poem, "For God's sake, let me love you," is suggestive of the "For Godsake hold your tongue, and let me love" of Donne's "The Canonization." Again Symons referred to the body as the "image of the world." Like Donne, he was interested in the relationships between the soul and the body — in what he once called "the spirit of your sense." [38] In some other poems he employed the kind of amorous casuistry typical of Donne. In "Madrigal" he justified by a show of logic the relationship of two lovers, each of whom was also in love with someone else. Although their delights would be either the double or only a fraction of those who loved only one, they would still paradoxically have been both spare and prodigal to love only each other. In "The Rapture" he reasoned that he possessed all of his mistress in the same way that a small lake possessed all of the moon's reflections or as each angel had all of heaven, and contended that "supreme delight" was one and infinite. Donne's mixture of theology and love is suggested in "Liber Amoris" where unsatisfied desire is viewed as paradise, poised between heaven and hell. In an elaborated Donne-like figure in "The Alchemy" Symons treated two would-be lovers whom the despairing alchemist had not yet united:

> No, we are strangers yet;
> The divine alchemy
> Not yet, or vainly, has set
> Our longing currents free.
>
> We meet, what loving goes,
> Who vainly would combine
> Cross virtues, that dispose
> The draught to be divine.

Symons approached the delicate irony of Marvell's poetic dialogues in his own dialogue between the soul, the senses, and the seven deadly sins. The senses charge that the soul provides spiritual eyes and mind only that they may perceive sin and err more craftily. Symons also imitated the French symbolists and at times combined metaphysical and symbolist techniques. Something of the sad aestheticism and so-called decadence of the later nineteenth century was reflected in some of the poems Symons wrote in a metaphysical manner. He employed an extended figure to compare Salome to a young tree, found his heart in possession of all the qualities of rubies, and compared his soul at length to a "cloudy, flaming opal ring," since both were constant in their varying.[39]

Symons' interest in the way in which Donne expressed personality and merged thought and feeling was reflected in his own work. Like Donne, he mastered the art of dramatic conversation and of effective modulation from casuistical protest to the quiet depths of passion. Like Donne also, he loved analogies; but he apparently took more delight in shocking the fair sex with unsavory figures than in puzzling them with scholastical quiddities. He frequently achieved an ambiguity of tone by introducing humor or irony into a serious poem, but he made comparatively little use of paradox or verbal wit.

Brooke's most metaphysical poem is "Thoughts on the Shape of the Human Body." The poem resembles Donne's "The Extasie" in its urgent probing of the relation of the body and soul in love; but the poet discovered not with satisfaction (as in Donne's poem), but with horror, that the body was the soul's book. Like seventeenth-century writers, he was concerned with the symbolic implications of the structure of the human body, but he found it a monstrosity, grotesque and extravagant, analogous to human fevers and perversions rather than to the macrocosm of the universe:

> How can love triumph, how can solace be,
> Where fever turns toward fever, knee toward knee?
> Could we but fill to harmony, and dwell

Simple as our thought and as perfectible,
Rise disentangled from humanity
Strange whole and new into simplicity,
Grow to a radiant round love, and bear
Unfluctuant passion for some perfect sphere . . .[40]

Although the geometrical contrast between the body and the soul
is in the metaphysical style, the juxtaposition of the perfection of
the sphere and the irregularity of the human body probably
would never have occurred to Donne.

A mixture of passion and grotesquerie similar to that in Donne's
"The Funerall" and "The Relique" seems seasoned with a touch
of Baudelaire in Brooke's "Dust":

When your swift hair is quiet in death,
And through the lips corruption thrust
Has stilled the labour of my breath —[41]

The tone of "Dead Men's Love" is similar, and "The Life Beyond," which compares an awakening after the death of love with
an actual rising from death, also recalls the seventeenth-century
metaphysical style. "Jealousy" has all of the passionate, indelicate
vehemence of Donne's elegy on the same theme and is similar to
it in its rhythms and idiom. The manner of Marvell is suggested
in the crisp pentameters of "Heaven," a satiric fish's view of the
"Almighty Fin" and "Eternal Brook." In a homelier vein Brooke
compared love to "a breach in the walls, a broken gate" and again
to a scrap of paper "tossed down dusty pavements by the wind."[42]

These poet-critics, together with Hopkins, Thompson, Mrs.
Meynell, and a number of other critics, had by 1912 brought to
a fruitful maturity the metaphysical revival that began with the
Elizabethan revival and with Browning. The publication of Hopkins' poems in 1918, which had been prepared for in part by the
metaphysical revival, in turn eventually gave an added impetus to
the growing interest in metaphysical poetry. With the metaphysical poetry of Yeats and Eliot the revival reached full tide.

Yeats, Donne
and the Metaphysicals

MATURING as a poet with the metaphysical revival as a part of his intellectual milieu, W. B. Yeats made a place for himself in the metaphysical tradition because of a passionate lifelong desire to weld the world together through his poetry. During the seventeenth century an increased emphasis on correspondences and analogy had helped to hold together a universe threatened by the new science. Yeats similarly tried to recapture the unity, harmony, and vitality of a world that he felt modern science was transforming from a living organism to a complex of opposing forces and abstract theories. Always aware of the warring forces symbolized by the whirling gyres, Yeats nevertheless envisioned a realm beyond change in which matter and spirit, body and soul, desire and knowledge would meet in harmony. Yeats found the seventeenth-century metaphysical poets only one of many influences that contributed to his poetic development; but he gradually fashioned his own metaphysical poetry, partly through a direct knowledge of Donne and his followers and a cultivation of interests and aims similar to theirs.

METAPHYSICAL AFFINITIES

Yeats apparently knew something of Donne and the metaphysicals as early as the 1890's. He has recalled that the Jacobean lyrists were imitated by the Rhymers, with whom he was associated during the early part of his career. During the 1890's he was friendly with Arthur Symons and Lionel Johnson, both of whom wrote about Donne. Then in 1906 he met Grierson and, in fact, stayed with him overnight while he was lecturing at Aberdeen. The two met again during the First World War and, later, in New York in 1932. Grierson has recalled that "to Yeats Donne had always been a source of interest," but when he sent Yeats a copy of his new edition of Donne, the poet replied: "I have been using it constantly and find that at last I can understand Donne." Whatever Yeats had thought of Donne previously, he was now enthusiastic and ready to explain why. "I notice," he continued, "that the more precise and learned the thought the greater the beauty, the passion; the intricacies and subtleties of his imagination are the length and depths of the furrow made by his passion. His pendantry and his obscenity — the rock and loam of his Eden — but made me the more certain that one who is but a man like us all has seen God." In 1926 he wrote to Grierson, "I have been reading your Donne again." Yeats was particularly fascinated by Donne's "A Nocturnall upon S. Lucies Day," which he described as "intoxicating" and a "poem of great passion." Something of Yeats's approach to Donne is revealed in his conviction that Donne was really the lover of the Countess of Bedford and was not merely offering the Platonic devotion due a patron. Yeats also praised Donne's avoidance of sentimental sensualism, but felt he provided an example for poets who needed to explore long forbidden subjects "out of sheer mischief, or sheer delight in that play of the mind." "Donne," he said, "could be as metaphysical as he pleased and yet never seemed inhuman and hysterical as Shelley often does because he could be as physical as he pleased." But Yeats found an element of "spiritual torture" in Donne and felt that he, along with El Greco and Spinoza, was part of a great imaginative wave.[1] Perhaps it was Donne's mixture of thought and passion, pedantry and frankness, that led Yeats in 1918 to write:

> And I may dine at journey's end
> With Landor and with Donne.[2]

Yeats knew some other poets writing in a metaphysical style, both of the seventeenth century and later periods. In *A Vision* he placed George Herbert in Phase 25 among poets who "are always stirred to an imaginative intensity by some form of propaganda" and who may have "great eloquence, a mastery of all concrete imagery." Yeats described Crashaw's hymn to St. Teresa as "the most impersonal of ecstasies." He recognized Browning's use of correspondences, but regarded him as a dangerous influence. He was apparently familiar with the work of another later metaphysical, Francis Thompson. He of course came to know the work of some of his metaphysical contemporaries, such as Eliot, Edith Sitwell, and Elinor Wylie.[3]

Yeats, like Donne, was an intellectual who read increasingly widely in philosophical and pseudo-philosophical writings, enjoyed engaging in philosophical arguments, and sometimes made his learning an integral part of his poetry. The word "thought," Dorothy Wellesley said, was "continually on his lips. For ever he craves for philosophical 'thought.'" He read widely in the mystical and philosophical writings of both East and West. He ranged from Plato and Plotinus to Nicholas of Cusa, Vico, Kant, Berkeley, and Whitehead. He did not share Donne's fascination with science. He read Huxley and Tyndall, but grew to detest science with a "monkish hate." However, he was willing and able to tangle with thorny opponents in defending his own idealism and the mind's autonomy. During the middle 1920's he carried on a long controversy by correspondence with Sturge Moore, who frequently consulted his brother, the philosopher G. E. Moore, before replying.[4] Probably Yeats's long-nurtured *A Vision* is the best evidence of his wide reading and persistent need to frame an all-embracing philosophical system on which he could rely in his thinking and writing.

Much of Yeats's thought was devoted to a drive toward wholeness which comprehended his continued concern both with correspondences and with "unity of being." Both of these interests helped draw him into the metaphysical tradition. Yeats became steeped in various conceptions of correspondence and had even thumbed through Paracelsus, whose notions continually appear in Donne's work. He read such seventeenth-century writers as More and Cudworth and shared many of their ideas of correspondences and a world soul. Two important early sources for his ideas were Madame Blavatsky's *The Secret Doctrine*, allegedly depending on the oldest manuscript in the world and describing seven corresponding periods, continents, elements, races, etc., and her *Isis Unveiled*, carrying from the Smaragdine Tablet the message at the core of all systems of correspondence: "What is below is like that which is above." His study of Swedenborg and his work as co-editor of Blake also contributed to his knowledge of correspondences. Believing that the Irish with their spirit-seeing faculties were particularly well qualified to demonstrate the relationship between the physical world and the spiritual world, Yeats continually affirmed this relationship himself. In a vein reminiscent of the seventeenth century, Yeats observed, "Every organ of the body has its correspondence in the heavens: and the seven principles which made the human soul and body correspond to the seven colours and the seven planets and the notes of the musical scale." Again he recalled that he found at Lady Gregory's estate at Coole what he had always sought, a place "where all outward things were the image of an inward life." Yeats, like Donne, frequently thought of man as "a little world made cunningly of elements," and constructed some of his early poetic characters like Hanrahan and Robartes in accordance with the mixture in them of the traditional four elements.[5] Yeats's mind dwelt of course at various times on many different theories of correspondence. But in general, though he sometimes spoke of "transcendence" and "incarnation," he was closer to the seventeenth century than to the Catholic revival poets in regarding the different corresponding orders as intimately related but discrete.

In his search for "unity of being" Yeats arrived more self-consciously and by a different route at a realm of experience suggestive of Donne's. While he was more insistent than Donne about the importance of a personal expression of feeling, he knew also that thought was an important part of this expression and that an experience must be approached from more than one emotional perspective. In his *Autobiographies* Yeats explained that he tried "to write out of my emotions exactly as they came to me in life," and again expressed a desire to make his work "convincing with a speech so natural and dramatic that the hearer would feel the presence of a man thinking and feeling." But Yeats never wanted a mere boiling over of emotions. Rather he felt, as he told Dorothy Wellesley, that all passion "depends on the completeness of the holding down." Ellmann has explained that Yeats at first expressed moods and then "affirmations," but that these always included ideas and thought and had to satisfy the whole man. Yeats early developed a preference for symbols that were intellectual as well as emotional, and in *A Vision* explained that "love is created and preserved by intellectual analysis." His poetry became more whole and rounded as he "drifted" toward his theory of the mask, which demanded that he approach experience as though he were also his opposite. He insisted that poetry should be simultaneously "passionate" and "cold." Yeats was familiar with Castiglione, who was well known in the earlier seventeenth century for his approval of wit in poetry, and seconded his praise of nonchalance in poetry.[6] Altogether, in his attempt to restore the unity of mind and being that he felt had existed until the seventeenth century, Yeats desired something comparable to Eliot's "unification of sensibility."

THE METAPHYSICAL POETRY OF YEATS

Although Yeats apparently felt an affinity with the seventeenth-century metaphysicals primarily because of his quest for wholeness and his own interest in certain metaphysical techniques, he evidently depended more directly in a few poems on Donne and George Herbert. In Donne's "The Extasie" and Yeats's "A Memory of Youth" the setting, dramatic situation, mood, metrics, and some of the phrasing are similar. Donne wrote:

> We like sepulchrall statues lay;
> All day, the same our postures were,
> And wee said nothing, all the day.

And Yeats:

> We sat as silent as a stone,
> We knew, though she'd not said a word . . .

The lock of his mistress's hair that Donne imagined was buried with him in "The Funerall" and "The Relique" must have fascinated Yeats. Donne had thought that this might lead the lovers' souls to meet after death. In Yeats's "Crazy Jane and Jack the Journeyman" love is a skein that will bind the lovers "ghost to ghost." In "Her Dream" the speaker thinks she has shorn her locks away and "laid them on Love's lettered tomb," only to see "nailed upon the night/Berenice's burning hair." The image is striking in much the same way as Donne's "bracelet of bright haire about the bone." In Yeats's "His Bargain," as in "The Relique," the hair is the means to a union that transcends the grave:

> I made, and may not break it
> When the last thread has run
> A bargain with that hair . . .

Donne's "Twicknam Garden" contrasts the world before and after the fall of man and mentions a "spider love"; Yeats's "Solomon and the Witch" has the same contrast and a reference to love's "spider eye." In "The Gyres" Yeats's description of a "dark betwixt the polecat and the owl,/Or any rich, dark nothing" suggests Donne's witty discussion of different degrees of nothingness in his "Nocturnall." References to "household spies" occur in the comparable little lovers' dramas enacted in Donne's "At His Mistress's Departure" and Yeats's "Parting." Perhaps, too, Yeats's "Heavens in my womb" in "The Mother of God" owes something to Donne's description of the Virgin Mary's womb as a "strange heav'n" in "The Litanie."

Some influence of Herbert also seems evident in Yeats. In "A Friend's Illness" Yeats wrote:

> Why should I be dismayed
> Though flame had burned the whole
> World, as it were a coal,
> Now I have seen it weighed
> Against a soul?

This must have been suggested by Herbert's "Vertue":

> Onely a sweet and vertuous soul,
> Like season'd timber, never gives;
> But though the whole world turn to coal,
>   Then chiefly lives.

"In Memory of Major Robert Gregory," IX, has a similar figure. Both Yeats's "Veronica's Napkin" and Herbert's "Sunday" use a string of appositive metaphors and some very similar imagery. Veronica's napkin is the "Tent-pole of Eden; the tent's drapery." Herbert's "Sundaies the pillars are,/On which heav'ns palace arched lies," and his "Content" depicts a soul as draped from the world's tent-poles. The beginning of Yeats's "Father and Child" ("She hears me strike the board and say") seems clearly derived from the opening of Herbert's "The Collar" ("I struck the board, and cry'd, No more").

Of more importance than such borrowings is the way a broader subject matter, a greater range and depth, and a sophisticated mixture of learning, grace, and wit brought Yeats increasingly within the metaphysical tradition after his study of Donne in the Grierson edition. As in many of Donne's poems, some abstruse philosophical conception that is perhaps only half believed may become the bedrock of a graceful and airy lyric. Sometimes this basis of hard thought suggests a hierarchical or analogical world view. Ellmann has discussed the many poems, including the well-known "The Lake Isle of Innisfree," employing the symbolism of the four elements.[7] The great circles, gyres, and spheres, in terms of which the world is presented in Yeats's philosophy, carry over into the poetry. In "Coole Park and Ballylee, 1931" both water and sky are hailed as emblems of the soul in different states, and in a very different spirit Yeats finds correspondences more than abstract speculation:

> That I may hear if we should kiss
> A contrapuntal serpent hiss,
> You, should hand explore a thigh,
> All the labouring heavens sigh.

More particularly Yeats resembled Donne in attributing an

external, transcendent quality to a person or a relationship like love so that the subject became a kind of Platonic idea or assumed divinity. Donne, for instance, never spared erudition or witty logic in addressing the Countess of Bedford:

> If good and lovely were not one, of both
> You were the transcript and originall,
> The Elements, the Parent, and the Growth,
> And every piece of you, is both their All.

Again he told her that by faith and reason "we reach divinity — that's you." Donne subtly attributed divinity also to a more profane mistress because she knew his thoughts "beyond an Angel's art," and thought again of the whole world begging from above a "patterne" of his and his mistress's love.[8] Yeats dealt with similar conceptions in a number of poems. In "Quarrel in Old Age" he apparently thought of Maude Gonne as a kind of Platonic idea:

> Old sages were not deceived:
> Somewhere beyond the curtain
> Of distorting days
> Lives that lonely thing
> That shone before these eyes
> Targeted, trod like Spring.

In "Young Man's Song" there is the old eye-heart conflict, with the heart affirming: "No withered crone I saw/Before the world was made." The love of a night is really eternal, says "Crazy Jane on God," for "All things remain in God." A light, sophisticated wit tempers the philosophy in "Before the World Was Made":

> If I make the lashes dark
> And the eyes more bright
> And the lips more scarlet
> Or ask if all be right
>
> From mirror after mirror,
> No vanity's displayed:
> I'm looking for the face I had
> Before the world was made.

Yeats, like Donne, could raid more than one philosophy for imagery. In "A Bronze Head" he turned to Aristotelian-scholastic thought like that used by Donne in his "Nocturnall" and other poems. The entire poem, characterized by a Donne-like dialectic, shows Yeats pondering the Maude Gonne enigma:

> Which of her forms has shown her substance right?
> Or maybe substance can be composite,
> Profound McTaggart thought so, and in a breath
> A mouthful held the extreme of life and death.

There is, then, in Yeats the same kind of half-serious, half-playful casuistical logic that abounds in Donne. The ideas are poetically exploited rather than philosophically explored. The chief difference is that in Donne there is a great show of twisted, knotted logical thinking, while in Yeats the philosophy lurks just beneath a deceptively smooth and colloquial surface.

Yeats also, like Donne, evolved a kind of metaphysic of love that sought to make *one* both the individual lovers and the body and soul. In Donne's "The Extasie" two souls merge in a kind of Plotinian union and form a new soul. Yeats's lovers in "Summer and Spring" have a similar conception of their love:

> And when we talked of growing up
> Knew that we'd halved a soul
> And fell the one in t'other's arms
> That we might make it whole;

In Donne's "The Good-Morrow" two lovers join to form a perfect sphere. There is the same notion in Yeats's "Among School Children," but then Yeats, in a characteristic gesture, reinterprets Plato in a homely figure:

> . . . and it seemed that our two natures blent
> Into a sphere from youthful sympathy
> Or else, to alter Plato's parable,
> Into the yolk and white of the one shell.

Donne's "The Sunne Rising" dramatizes the idea that two lovers are all and everything else is nothing. The world is contracted to their room, and "Nothing else is." Similarly Yeats's "Solomon to Sheba" says, "There's not a thing but love can make/The world a narrow pound." Several of Yeats's poems, like Donne's "The Extasie," insist on a union of soul and body in love. Love must "take the whole/Body and soul," declares "Crazy Jane on the Day of Judgment." "The Three Bushes" presents a more complex relationship. A young man loves a lady spiritually and her maid physically, but body and soul become one as the bushes springing from them join to produce a rose. "Love cram love's two divisions/Yet keep his substance whole," the lady has sung.

Along with this integration of learning and life in the treatment of a philosophy of love and other subjects, Yeats used a number of metaphysical techniques after his study of Donne. These included the extended metaphor linking the inner and outer, the abstract and concrete, and the various realms of being Yeats knew through his familiarity with correspondences. "Chosen," which develops the familiar theme of a complete union in love, employs a single dynamic abstract metaphor throughout the poem in much the manner of Donne. The first stanza presents lovers caught on a "whirling Zodiac." The woman remembers that her lover scarcely sank "from the west" to find a "subterranean rest" on the "maternal midnight" of her breast before she "marked him on his northern way." But her "utmost pleasure with a man" occurred

> Where his heart my heart did seem
> And both adrift on the miraculous stream
> Where — wrote a learned astrologer —
> The Zodiac is changed into a sphere.

In an extended figure in "Easter, 1916" the "Hearts with one purpose alone," sacrificed too long for Irish nationalism, are compared to an unchanging stone in the midst of "the living stream," while horses and moor-hens live and change minute by minute around it. As often in modern metaphysical figures, ironic overtones ring out from the extended conceit about which "High Talk" is built. Yeats's poetry is thought of as a procession in which "high talk," like "high stilts," is necessary to catch the eye. He is "Malachi Stilt-Jack" — "All metaphor, Malachi, stilts and all." A similar tone pervades "The Circus Animals' Desertion," in which the poet recalls that his "circus animals were all on show" but that he must now be satisfied with the "foul rag-and-bone shop of the heart." Yeats modified the metaphysical conceit even further in "The Long-Legged Fly," in which the working of a genius like Caesar or Michelangelo, slow and seemingly trivial but ultimately of the greatest significance, is compared to the fly through the refrain:

> *Like a long-legged fly upon the stream*
> *His mind moves upon silence.*

Yeats's metaphysical tendencies are evident in a number of poems which depend entirely on extended metaphors that make an abstraction completely concrete. They bear some resemblance to seventeenth-century emblem poems, but are more strikingly similar to poems like George Herbert's "The Altar" and "The Windows," in which the external objects of the temple image inner qualities. In fact, Herbert is a possible source for Yeats's technique in these poems. "The Witch" and "The Peacock" are his first poems in this style. The latter treats one who "has made a great peacock/With the pride of his eye" and concludes:

> His ghost will be gay
> Adding feather to feather
> For the pride of his eye.

The most compact of these poems is "The Balloon of the Mind":

> Hands, do what you're bid:
> Bring the balloon of the mind
> That bellies and drags in the wind
> Into its narrow shed.

The mind's pride is embodied in "The Hawk" as the poet is ashamed that he gave to his friend a "pretense of wit." "I made my coat a song," says the poet in "The Coat," but since the fools caught it and wore it, there is now "more enterprise/In walking naked." "The Spur," "Spilt Milk," and "The Friends of His Youth" employ a similar technique.

Yeats was also like the metaphysicals in his use of wit. He particularly resembled Donne and Marvell in using various witty devices with serious expression and also in a kind of open-minded, all-encompassing approach to his material. This is not so much ambiguity as a free play of the mind, often a sophisticated intellectual play in the choice of words or imagery. This learned but tongue-in-cheek approach occurs in the flattery of Donne's "The Dreame" or in the mischievous teasing of "Aire and Angels." It is found in his late poems as he thinks of himself as a "flatt mappe" in his illness or puns on his own name as he asks God for forgiveness for his last sins. There is a similar quality in the Olympian detachment and satiric pointedness with which Marvell's soul and body argue their cases or in the intellectual implications of "vegetable love" and "quaint honour." [9]

Very much this same open minded, all-inclusive approach is evident in Yeats's use of conventional witty figures or in his phrasing and imagery. He used the paradox to develop the proposition that "Hatred of God may bring the soul to God" and to insinuate that despite the bishop's contentions Crazy Jane's seducer, Jack the Journeyman, was the real "solid man" and the bishop the "coxcomb." In thinking of his imagination as a centaur lured into perilous territory, he made a punning reference to its "horse-play." [10] This tone pervades some of Yeats's finest poems. In "Sailing to Byzantium," for instance, his mind continuously plays lightly over deep feeling as well as the ponderous philosophical problems of being and becoming and the relation of the body and soul. There is a mature vision, alert and urbane, in his treatment of the body-soul dilemma as he refers to himself in "Monuments of unageing intellect" and knows that for his soul there is no "singing school but studying/Monuments of its own magnificence." Intellectual subtlety and an impressive erudition dance lightly together as Yeats, considering Byzantium as a symbol of art's transcendence of change, asks to be gathered into the "artifice of eternity" and imagines that he himself is the Emperor's artificial bird of "golden handiwork" of which he has read. Although some of his poems like "All Souls Night" have an astringent irony that is more distinctively modern, the light free play of the intellect over serious problems and deeply felt experience links Yeats with the tradition of metaphysical wit.

Yeats's interest in Donne and his followers came as a result of the nineteenth-century metaphysical revival that culminated in the Grierson edition of Donne. He was a close friend of Symons, who wrote metaphysical poetry and wrote about metaphysical poetry, and knew Lionel Johnson, who wrote an essay on Donne. More important was his friendship with Grierson, who gave new impetus to Yeats's study of Donne when he presented him with his edition of the poems. His lifelong interest in correspondences and "unity of being" complemented his concern with Donne, and it was in fact Donne's union of the spiritual and sensate, of "his pedantry and his obscenity," that most fascinated Yeats, who felt harried by modern science's tendency toward multiplicity and abstraction. Although Yeats was subject to a number of influences besides Donne and the metaphysicals, he apparently sometimes imitated Donne and Herbert directly and wrote poems that were simultaneously intellectual, passionate, precise, direct, and complex under the metaphysical influence. He often used metaphor and wit as the metaphysicals had, but while Donne made a show of his learning and dialectic, Yeats was so studiedly casual that the metaphysical quality of his work may frequently go unnoted.

VIII

Eliot and the
Twentieth-Century Revival

As THE high priest of the modern metaphysical revival, T. S. Eliot has been consistently honored but often misunderstood. His followers have repeated his theories about the unified sensibility in metaphysical poetry without realizing how Eliot's ideas had been developed or how much they had changed. Similarly, they have both imitated and explicated the "metaphysical" techniques in his poetry without a clear conception of metaphysical poetry or of the important differences between Eliot and the seventeenth-century poets. In short, his followers have usually not understood the ways in which Eliot, as critic and poet, crystallized and vitalized—then partly abandoned—a *new* but very fruitful interpretation of metaphysical poetry.

Actually, tracing the history of Eliot's ideas about metaphysical poetry shows both how indebted he was to earlier critics in formulating his theories and how much less sympathetic he became to Donne and his followers during the later 1920's. A major change in Eliot's poetry paralleled this change in his attitude toward the metaphysicals. However, the new metaphysical poetry created by Eliot can best be understood if it is analyzed, first, in relation to his own conceptions of metaphysical poetry and, then, in the light of seventeenth-century conceptions. This approach reveals both the close connection between his earlier interpretation of the metaphysicals and his earlier poetry and also the appearance of seventeenth-century techniques throughout most of his work. It reveals, too, the important sharp distinction between Eliot's modern interpretation and the seventeenth-century conception of metaphysical poetry.

ELIOT'S CRITICISM OF METAPHYSICAL POETRY

Immediately after the First World War, during the period 1919–1923, Eliot wrote his "The Metaphysical Poets," "Andrew Marvell," and "John Donne," three essays presenting a highly sympathetic modern interpretation of seventeenth-century metaphysical poetry. For Eliot's numerous disciples these essays became a new critical gospel, often not clearly understood but seldom doubted.

Eliot had apparently begun to study metaphysical poetry a number of years before he wrote any of these essays. He has said that he was already attracted to Donne while he was a freshman at Harvard and has described his early criticism as a "prolongation of the thinking that went into the formation of my own verse." [1] During this formative period he was also becoming familiar with a number of writers with whom he felt an intellectual affinity. He apparently had some knowledge of critics such as Grosart, Symons, Stephen, and Brooke, who had developed similar conceptions of the merging of thought and feeling, psychological realism, and the modernity of the metaphysicals. As a friend and admirer of Ezra Pound, Eliot may also have been influenced by Pound's definition of an image as "an intellectual and emotional complex in an instant of time." Another relatively early influence was the thought and style of F. H. Bradley. Eliot held that Bradley found the ideality of the finite, which is the life of the mind, in the incessant union of intellect and emotion, and disclosed that "the secret of Bradley's style . . . is the intense addiction to an intellectual passion." [2]

Depending, then, on past work and his own fresh perceptiveness, Eliot gradually crystallized his conception of metaphysical poetry. His interpretation of the metaphysical style derives most directly from his concern with the interrelationships of the senses, feelings, and thought. In fact, this interest has been more fundamental and persistent than his interest in any particular poets. In discussing these psychological interrelationships in his essay "Hamlet" (1919), he introduced the concept of the "objective correlative," a "formula" for a particular emotion: the theory is that a set of external facts given in a work of art terminates in a sensory experience that immediately evokes the emotion. Eliot was probably adapting to his own critical needs Pound's conception of poetry as a "sort of inspired mathematics, which gives us equations, not for abstract figures, triangles, spheres, and the like, but equations for the human emotions." Anticipating his later remarks on the metaphysicals in an essay on Henry Adams (also 1919), Eliot noted that "many men will admit that their keenest ideas have come to them with the quality of a sense-perception, and that their keenest sensuous experience has been 'as if the body thought'" (an allusion to Donne's "The Second Anniversary"). The next year, in an essay on Philip Massinger, he referred to the period of Donne and Webster "when the intellect was immediately at the tips of the senses." Eliot explained that Massinger initiated a different attitude. He later was to define this as the "dissociation of sensibility." [3] Thus, before actually writing about the seventeenth-century metaphysical poets, Eliot had been pondering some of the conceptions that were to prove most important in his interpretation of metaphysical poetry.

In his three essays on the metaphysicals Eliot's most original contribution was to approach metaphysical poetry and the modern theories concerning it as a historian of styles and as a professional poet. The older conceptions which he redefined were the relatively familiar ones of psychological realism achieved through a fidelity to changing thoughts and feelings, the close interrelationship of intellectual, emotional, and sensuous experience, and the modernity of the metaphysicals, especially in relation to the French symbolist poets. From these he drew implications that were essentially his own discoveries and that gave added significance to these previously formulated conceptions. First, he made entirely his own the conception of a metaphysical sensibility, which is a kind of mechanism for processing vast varieties of experience into new wholes. Then, in holding that one of the chief aims of writing was to convert the frontiers of experience into poetry, he gave an ultimate aesthetic justification to this sensibility. Second, Eliot applied these new psychological theories to the charting of literary history. He thus regarded the earlier seventeenth century as predominantly a period of unified sensibility and the later seventeenth century and afterward as a period of dissociated sensibility, in which Dryden was merely witty, Milton was magniloquent, and Tennyson and Browning were ruminative. Finally, Eliot in substance called upon modern poets to study these earlier poets and to write a complex modern kind of metaphysical poetry.

In these essays also, Eliot reached the peak of his admiration for the metaphysical poets, and by the middle 1920's his enthusiasm for them had cooled considerably. Probably the chief reasons for this change were that Eliot, now in his later thirties, was probing more deeply into religious problems and was also searching for a new stimulus in solving new aesthetic problems. This altered attitude is evident in his "Lancelot Andrewes" (1926) and in "Deux Attitudes Mystiques" (1927), partly an adaptation from the unpublished Clark Lectures delivered at Cambridge in 1926. It is even more evident in his writings on the metaphysicals published during the 1930's and in his "Milton" (1948). One of the first indications of this change in taste was Eliot's comparison of Donne the preacher with Lancelot Andrewes — to Donne's discredit. He asserted that Donne lacked spiritual discipline, was less traditional than Andrewes, was possibly a dangerous influence on those fascinated by "personality," and appealed to readers with "a certain wantonness of the spirit." [4]

But the clearest evidence of Eliot's changed point of view was his tendency to disparage Donne and the metaphysicals in contrasting them with his new ideal, Dante. Eliot's early interest in Dante became much more marked in the middle 1920's and bore fruit in his "Dante" (1929) and "Ash Wednesday." Donne paled in the radiance of Dante chiefly because of the contrast in the two poets' use of belief and thought-feeling relationships in their poetry. "I cannot see," Eliot declared, "that poetry can ever be separated from something which I should call belief, and to which I cannot see any reason for refusing the name of belief, unless we are to reshuffle names completely." And he thought Dante's poetry was founded on real belief, but Donne's was not. Eliot noted that Dante, like Lucretius and other "philosophical" poets, had one orderly theory about life and the universe and made poetry of it, while Donne, somewhat like Poe and Mallarmé, enjoyed and made use of many systems, but expressed "no settled belief in anything." Eliot further reasoned that Dante, because he dealt with everything in a religious spirit, was a great and major poet, while George Herbert, Crashaw, and presumably Donne as a religious poet, were minor since they dealt with religion only as an isolated part of the total subject matter.[5]

Eliot also held that Dante not only had "the most *ordered* presentation of emotions that has ever been made," but that in the progress toward the beatific vision there was an exact and consistent correspondence between this system of emotions and discursive thought. But in Donne, there was "hardly any attempt at organization; rather a puzzled and humorous shuffling of the pieces." There was "a manifest fissure between thought and sensibility" and sometimes a conscious contradiction between thought and feeling. Consequently he held that, while Dante's style was lucid and always clarified, Donne's could be tortuous and affected. In Donne's "The Extasie" he found "un des plus fâcheux mélanges des comparaisons," and found fault with both fundamental conceptions and numerous figures in the poem. While Dante, Eliot explained, stressed the unity of the spirit and the body, Donne heretically separated them.[6]

Dante's more ordered relationship of thought and feeling, dependent upon his more consistently and sincerely held belief, led Eliot to find Dante's sensibility more highly developed and valuable than Donne's. Because Dante had explored new degrees of degradation and exaltation, Eliot placed him first among the poets who had enlarged the domain of the sensibility and proceeded to an expansion of reality. But Donne achieved no similar expansion. "A modern, Donne is a prisoner of the narrowness of his own feelings." Eliot felt that Dante, like Guinicelli and Cavalcanti, had achieved his own ideal of impersonal expression in suggesting the effect on a lover through the beauty and dignity of the beloved. But in Donne there was never any sign of adoration. He and Edward Herbert, it seemed to Eliot, tended merely "to describe the object of their love, or to note complacently their emotions and their sensations." They were, he suggested, in seeking the absolute in the corporeal and the ephemeral, approaching the kind of spiritual bankruptcy in "le bon mariage à la Tennyson." Crashaw also was incomplete in comparison with Dante. "While Dante," Eliot explained, "was aware of every shade of human and divine love, Crashaw's passion for heavenly objects is incomplete because it is partly a substitute for human passion." Eliot thus found not only that Dante's inner life was vaster and his sensibility more valuable than those of the seventeenth-century metaphysicals, but that Dante represented a "civilization often superior to ours, superior also to the civilization of the world of Donne."[7]

Although Eliot did not entirely forsake Donne and the metaphysicals, a comparison of his "The Metaphysical Poets" with "Donne in Our Time" reveals the extent to which his attitude toward them changed within ten years. In his series of BBC talks in the spring of 1930 he continued to consider the interaction of thought and feeling as a distinguishing characteristic of metaphysical poetry. However, he asserted that the "two great creative acts of Donne," through which he achieved his intellectual music, were his introduction of a new vocabulary and his introduction of fresh meters into Elizabethan and Jacobean poetry. Eliot's essay written in connection with the Donne tercentenary in 1931 reveals still more clearly his changed attitude toward Donne and the metaphysical revival. While in 1921 Eliot was recommending the metaphysical poets as a valuable new discovery, by 1931 he no longer regarded Donne's poetry as a concern of the future. "Our enjoyment of Donne," he wrote, "was a fashion" (his use of the past tense seems significant). Commenting on the fissure between Donne's thought and sensibility, Eliot characterized Donne's learning as "just information suffused with emotion or combined with emotion not essentially relevant to it." While in 1921 Eliot approved of the metaphysicals as models for a generation of poets groping with modern complexities, by the time he wrote his Donne tercentenary essay he had already declared that there was no poet in any tongue so fit for a model for all poets as Dante. Within about another decade Eliot could speak of "our undue adulation of Donne and depreciation of Milton," and within a few more years he reversed completely his original attitude toward Milton and cast doubt on his own theory of the dissociation of sensibility. Implying that Donne and the metaphysicals were to be numbered among the "smaller, imperfect poets with whom later poets discover an affinity," he included Milton with Dante and Racine among the "great poets from whom we can learn negative rules" and recommended the study of his poetry to modern poets.[8]

ELIOT'S METAPHYSICAL POETRY AND HIS CRITICISM

Eliot has never concealed the close relationship between his critical thinking, his study of other poets, and his own poetry. What the poet "writes about poetry," he said, "must be assessed in relation to the poetry he writes," for "he is not so much a judge as an advocate" (i.e., of the kind of poetry he wishes to write himself). He has also insisted that making use of others' work was not sterile imitation, but that "the most original parts of his work may be those in which the dead poets, his ancestors, assert their immortality most vigorously."[9]

Most of Eliot's earlier poetry and some of his later work seem organically related to his criticism of the early 1920's. In fact, while the metaphysicals have asserted their immortality in Eliot's poetry, in a rather surprising phenomenon Eliot's poetry has apparently been more directly and extensively influenced by the modern critical approach to metaphysical poetry that he himself crystallized than by seventeenth-century metaphysical poetry itself. Both in his criticism and in his own poetry he has been more deeply and consistently interested in thought-feeling-sense relationships and in the unification and dissociation of the sensibility than in any particular poetry, and has examined not only the metaphysical poets but Dante, the seventeenth-century dramatists, Baudelaire, and others in the light of these conceptions.

These ideas, central to his criticism and to most modern writing about the metaphysicals, quite naturally became central also to the poetry he was writing at about the time he was working out these theories. Almost all the problems of sensibility are anatomized. Eliot's only portrait of a contemporary figure with a unified sensibility like that he attributed to the seventeenth-century metaphysicals is "Mr. Apollinax." His vitality and sexuality are clearly manifest but controlled, and his intellectual conversation is infused with drive and passion. Through portraying him sensuously (as in "the beat of the centaur's hoofs over the hard turf") and wittily (as in "the head of Mr. Apollinax rolling under a chair"), Eliot has clearly tried to make the poem itself an embodiment of unified sensibility. But Eliot's earlier poetry most characteristically presents the most painful examples of dissociated sensibility. "The Love Song of J. Alfred Prufrock" is the impotent whine of a prototypal character whose thoughts and emotional desires are in agonizing conflict with each other. Then "Burbank with a Baedeker: Bleistein with a Cigar" and the Sweeney series portray not so much characters whose sensibility is divided but those whose sensibility is sadly truncated. "The Waste Land," with its appalling revelation of lust without love, thought without meaning, and activity without direction, unfolds a vast panorama of dissociated sensibility. In Eliot's later poetry the shadow of dissociation continues to fall, but the quest for a higher spirituality dwarfs and partly solves the problem of the dissociated sensibility.

Relationships between thought, feeling, and sense largely determine the tensions and internal structures of Eliot's poetry. Although his terminology is imprecise and his concepts are aesthetic counters rather than psychological realities, it was chiefly through Eliot's own interpretation of the metaphysicals in the light of conceptions such as these that he was influenced by them. While there is considerable overlapping, it is possible to distinguish seven types of thought-feeling-sense relationships applicable to the poetry of Eliot, Donne and the metaphysicals, or both.

1. *A system of thought, such as Dante's, can lead to the perception of another plane (usually the spiritual) of emotional or sensual experience.* Although Eliot has noted that Donne did not usually depend on a fully believed philosophical system, in "The Second Anniversary" Donne did pass from his scarcely disconsolate grief over the death of Elizabeth Drury to a profound state of spiritual dedication through a meditation on the Christian eschatology. A similar relationship appears on a smaller scale in some of his "Holy Sonnets" written under the influence of the Ignatian *Exercises*. On a smaller scale and with a less solid structure of thought, this occurs in the sexual-religious parallels in poems like Donne's "The Canonization." In Eliot's work, this type probably appears most clearly in poems like "Marina" and "Journey of the Magi," in which the concrete and sensuous imagery of the settings suggests a spiritual level in accordance with established patterns of Christian thought. More ambiguously, there is the suggestion of a higher plane in the erotic experience of "Dans Le Restaurant."

2. *Complex thought, even philosophical analysis, may be converted into a feeling or expressed in sensuous terms (the thought is followed by emotional images, rhythms, etc.).* Eliot, for example, has said that "the witty union of ideas" in Donne's "The Prohibition" "gives the emotional equivalent of a state of mind." [10] The flat abstractions and ponderous polysyllables of "Mr. Eliot's Sunday Morning Service" similarly communicate an emotional state, even if scarcely understood. Particularly in longer poems, reasoning may be fired by emotion that either belongs to the original experience or — perhaps more often — is generated through the creation of the poem. In the "Anniversaries" Donne's imagery, rhythm, and voice breathe life into his anatomizing of the world and his tracing of the soul's progress. In Eliot's "Gerontion," "Ash Wednesday," and *Four Quartets* the intellectual strivings and

turnings are emotionally or sensuously expressed or are suddenly transformed into deeply felt emotional experience, as in "Burnt Norton," I.

3. *An emotional equivalent of a thought may be expressed without an effort to express the thought itself (the emotional equivalent is generated by the thought).* This does not occur in Donne's poetry, but is found in Eliot's "Preludes," "Morning at the Window," and other early non-discursive statements about the monotony, mechanism, and dissociation of sensibility characteristic of modern life.

4. *Emotional experiences may lead to intellectual speculations which evoke new feelings (which may lead to more intellectual speculations, etc.).* This occurs in Donne's "The Relique," where his thinking of a "bracelet of bright haire about the bone" as a relic leads to the somewhat forced second stanza about relics, but then to the inexpressible mystery of "what a miracle she was." Similarly in "A Nocturnall upon S. Lucies Day" thoughts about his lady's illness and the shortest day lead to learned abstractions concerning degrees of nothingness, which evoke a refined and deeply felt sense of desolation and dedication. Though the type of emotion generally differs, there is a similar thought-feeling relationship in Eliot. In "Prufrock" desire continuously produces thought which leads only to the pangs of frustration. In particularly poignant passages Prufrock perceives his relation to John the Baptist or to Lazarus, only to see the irony in the comparison and be reminded again of his own frustration.

5. *An emotional experience may lead to an intellectual defining of it, especially through the metaphysical conceit.* This appears in the familiar compass figure of Donne's "A Valediction: Forbidding Mourning" and in many other poems by Donne. Eliot sometimes employs the strict logic of the extended conceit, as in the figure of "the wounded surgeon" in "East Coker," IV. But the analysis is sometimes less logical and consistent, as in the fog figure in "Prufrock" or in the coalescing of the Pentecostal dove and the bomber in "Little Gidding," II.

6. *Passionate feeling may change to reflective thought.* In this

process there is a tendency toward a dissociation of sensibility. Donne's poems sometimes do not end as well as they begin, but they never lapse entirely into flat ruminating or empty rhetoric. Despite some of the long abstract passages in *Four Quartets*, this change probably does not occur when Eliot speaks unmistakably with his own voice. It does occur, however, when Eliot speaks as the Prufrock of "a hundred visions and revisions" or as the disappointing gallant in "Portrait of a Lady," who ponders "things that other people have desired."

7. *Passionate feeling may change to a conscious conflict between the feeling and the intellectual interpretation of it.* This kind of thought-feeling relationship tends to create ambiguity and an ironic view. It occurs seldom if ever in Donne, but frequently appears in some way in Eliot. In one of his apparently more personal poems, "A Cooking Egg," a disillusioned intellectual mocks the "penny world" of his youthful desires, and in "The Hollow Men" the "shadow" of abstract negation falls across all spontaneous feeling.

Although Eliot found these ideas of the relationship between thought and feeling more vital to his aesthetic thinking than Donne or any particular poet, he nevertheless found in the work of the seventeenth-century metaphysicals, particularly Donne, stimulating and suggestive examples of these tensions between thought and feeling in action. From Donne, Eliot apparently received hints about the poetic use of this kind of elusive yet inescapable psychological relationship, hints that were more fruitful than those provided by any particular images or conceits. But Eliot has gone beyond Donne in the development of these subtle, shifting relationships, and his theories of thought-feeling relationship and the unified sensibility, while providing one perceptive approach to the poetry of Donne and others, are most valuable in illuminating his own poetic methods and aims. In the poetry of Eliot the range and consistency of these relationships are greater than in the verse of the seventeenth-century metaphysicals or in that of other modern metaphysicals. He clearly exploited these processes much more self-consciously and deliberately than the earlier poets did and nurtured much more tenderly those tensions and ironies that develop when thought and feeling either preserve a kind of armed truce or break into open conflict.

Eliot also infused into his own poetry the kind of psychological realism that he attributed to the seventeenth-century metaphysical poets. While Donne is always the more dramatic, the resolution of psychological conflict is much more difficult in Eliot. In most of Donne's religious sonnets, based on the general pattern of the Ignatian *Exercises*, a confession of hopeless depravity is neatly and quickly balanced by a sublime faith in salvation, and even in the last sonnet ("Oh, to vex me, contraryes meet in one") the conflict between what he would do and does do is resolved in the "best dayes, when I shake with feare." However, in Eliot's "Ash Wednesday" the struggle is more protracted and the sense of spiritual tension, effort, and exhaustion much greater, as there is a gradual hard-won progress from complete doubt and despair to self-abnegation, past the temptation of renewed hope, to a recognition of the need of grace and a renewal of the will toward God. Just as Donne cried "that when I would not/I change in vowes, and in devotion," Eliot notes that "though I do not wish to wish these things" the reawakened "lost heart" at the last minute seems unable to forsake the world.

Besides charting these turnings and twistings of a modern mind trying to break its bonds, Eliot has been faithful to the modern dissociated sensibility with its real ambiguity of attitude. Prufrock, trapped between fear and desire, simultaneously accepts and rejects love, as does the gentleman of "Portrait of a Lady," whose undernourished sensibility does not know what to feel nor feel what it knows. While Donne's attitude toward a woman may be ambiguous, there is never this simultaneous acceptance and rejection that leads only to procrastination and frustration. While Eliot has not attained Donne's passion or dramatic intensity, he has excelled in epitomizing the subtle spiritual and erotic conflicts in modern man.

In discussing the seventeenth-century metaphysicals' expression of the flux and ambiguity in their thinking and feeling, Eliot cited their use of structures "sometimes far from simple," a "development by rapid association of thought" and imagery, and the use of surprises and "sudden contrasts." Eliot certainly found these techniques in his study of Donne and the metaphysicals, but used them more frequently and more radically than had his metaphysical predecessors. In Donne the structural complexity is logical; in Eliot it is psychological. Although Donne, unlike Eliot, may jump from the logical development of one idea to that of another, the logical progression of the poem is seldom really lost, even if it may be obscured by ellipses and technical terminology. This is true of poems as varied as "The Good-Morrow," "The Extasie," and "A Valediction: Forbidding Mourning." In Eliot the structures are complex because the thought is concealed behind images and the psychological leaps are sometimes so demanding that the reader may go off in the wrong direction or lose the trail completely. In "Prufrock" — to mention only some of the necessary leaps between stanzas — one must jump from the women talking of Michelangelo to the cat-like yellow fog to the remembered eyes and arms to "lonely men in shirt-sleeves," "ragged claws" scuttling through "silent seas," and to the "mermaids singing, each to each." Equally strenuous are the sudden transitions between sections of "The Waste Land," "A Cooking Egg," and "Mr. Eliot's Sunday Morning Service."

As would be expected, the rapid manipulation of thought and imagery is more audacious and more difficult in Eliot than in Donne. Eliot cited "A Valediction: Of Weeping" as an example of rapid association in Donne. Here there is not much regard for connotation in the images, but there is a thread of logic connecting the comparison of his mistress's tears (bearing her stamp) to both coins and spherical maps. In Eliot a state of mind may be expressed through highly connotative shifting images with no logical connection with each other. For instance, the impression of Mr. Apollinax on the poet is imaged through references in quick succession to "Priapus in the shrubbery," "an irresponsible foetus," "the old man of the sea," "the head of Mr. Apollinax rolling under a chair," and "the beat of centaur's hoofs over the hard turf." Like Donne, Eliot is indeed full of surprises, particularly in the early poetry. Instead of Donne's a "sun dyall in a grave," Prufrock feels his "nerves in patterns on a screen," his life "measured out . . . with coffee spoons," and his body "pinned and wriggling on the wall." The surprises, like the rapid juxtaposition of ideas and images, tend to be more connotative and ironic than in Donne.

Eliot, then, took suggestions from techniques he analyzed in the work of the seventeenth-century metaphysical poets, but modified these techniques in his own way, often introducing a note of modern discord through his experiments. Exploring problems of sensibility, thought-feeling-sense relationships, and psychological realism, Eliot became a metaphysical poet according to his own definition.

ELIOT'S POETRY AND THE SEVENTEENTH-CENTURY VIEW

If Eliot was a metaphysical by his own definition, was he also a metaphysical poet in accordance with what may be called the seventeenth-century interpretation of metaphysical poetry? While there is some overlapping between the modern and the earlier interpretation, the chief characteristics of metaphysical poetry that were understood in the seventeenth century are a dependence on correspondences, an extensive use of logic, metaphors (often elaborately extended) linking disparate realms of being, witty devices (often in a serious context), and the witty grotesque.

Most of these characteristics belong as much to Eliot's later poetry as to his earlier work. Correspondences, for instance, played a relatively minor role in Eliot's poetry until he needed them in an intensified search for integration. In *Four Quartets*, however, he showed a fascination with systems of correspondence, analogical reasoning, and incarnational symbolism that was remarkably in the spirit of the seventeenth century. The *Quartets* are based upon the three-way analogy between the earth, man, and the *Quartets* themselves and upon the more fundamental analogy between the changing external world and the unseen spiritual world that are joined through man. Each of the earth's four elements symbolizes an element in man and becomes the key symbol of one of the quartets. "Burnt Norton" represents man's powers of abstraction as air; "East Coker," his body as earth; "Dry Salvages," his river of blood as water; and "Little Gidding," his spirit as fire. Man is a reflection of God and a part of the intricately repeated pattern of the universe. He is the "visible reminder of Invisible Light." Furthermore,

> The dance along the artery
> And circulation of the lymph
> Are figured in the drift of stars
> Ascend to summer in the tree . . .[11]

Other correspondences are explored in "East Coker" as the paradoxical "In my beginning is my end" links Eliot's family origin and his return to England, human history, the nonhuman history of the earth and sea, and spiritual history. There is a pattern in the midst of change, and unity in the midst of diversity.

Linking all of these various spheres to each other and to God is the principle of incarnation. In his sense of deity manifested at different levels of correspondence and in different ways, Eliot resembles Crashaw and also the nineteenth-century Catholic metaphysicals. This immanence is suggested in the moments of rapt intensity in the *Quartets* when the Annunciation, Incarnation, or Pentecost are felt to join the changing world of time and the unchanging world of eternity. Incarnation may be symbolized in "the winter lightning/Or the waterfall" — only hints.

> The hint half guessed, the gift half understood,
>   is Incarnation.
> Here the impossible union
> Of spheres of existence is actual . . .

One symbol of incarnation is the saint, pondering the "intersection of the timeless/With time." Another kind of transcendent fulfillment comes through art, like the Chinese jar of "Burnt Norton" that moves perpetually in its stillness.[12] *Four Quartets* may be thought of as offering this kind of revelation, with their complex patterns of correspondence mirroring an ultimate pattern. Better than any other contemporary poet, Eliot has been able to recapture the sacramental relationships between nature and history, time and eternity.

Eliot's resemblance to the seventeenth-century metaphysicals in the use of metaphor preceded his development of correspondences. Like Donne and other earlier poets, he used "unpoetic" figures from medicine, business, mathematics, and other fields seemingly widely separated from the subject of the poem, but he mixed and juxtaposed connotations much more self-consciously. Several modern scientific conceptions enter Prufrock's feeling that his morbid self-consciousness is "as if a magic lantern threw the nerves in patterns on a screen." Merging in the closing lines of "Gerontion" are figures suggesting business, medicine, and physics: the senses "Protract the profit of their chilled delirium." One of the principal figures in "Mr. Eliot's Sunday Morning Service" is based upon the fertilization of flowers by bees. Geometrical imagery runs all through *Four Quartets*, where there is a constant concern with "the point of intersection of the timeless/With time" and with the "union/Of spheres of existence," as referred to in "Dry Salvages," V.

The most distinguishing characteristic of seventeenth-century metaphysical poetry, the extended conceit, is employed by Eliot, but less often and in a different way. Eliot has shown less interest in defining an inner experience through a conceit or in exploring an analogy for its own sake, but considerably more interest in employing the objective correlative to evoke a complex, often ironic, cluster of thoughts and feelings. This is evident in Eliot's first extended conceit, the fog-cat figure in "Prufrock":

> The yellow fog that rubs its back upon
>   the windowpanes,
> The yellow smoke that rubs its muzzle on the
>   windowpanes
> Licked its tongue into the corners of
>   the evening,
> Lingered upon the pools that stand
>   in drains,
> Let fall upon its back the soot that falls
>   from chimneys,

Slipped by the terrace, made a sudden leap,
And seeing that it was a soft October night,
Curled once about the house, and fell asleep.

There is a minimum of logic in this comparison of the yellow fog and cat with the atmosphere of indecision and inhibition in which Prufrock exists. But the suggestions and emotional overtones seem incalculable. Everything is perceived with repugnance. The fog, like the forces suffocating Prufrock, is all-obscuring and everywhere, yet formless and intangible. The cat that merges with it shows only a desire that ends in inertia. The whole mood is one of confusion, frustration, and inaction. Eliot's method is very different from that of Donne in, for instance, the compass figure of "A Valediction: Forbidding Mourning," where the analogy is logical and definitive and the figure's sexual connotations are probably to be ignored. However, the attempts in both figures to describe an inner experience in terms of a widely separated outer reality are basically similar.

Much closer to the seventeenth-century metaphysical manner is the Good Friday section of "East Coker," but a comparison of this with Donne still reveals marked differences. It apparently owes a part of its seventeenth-century quality to some dependence on Marvell's "A Dialogue between the Soul and Body." Both poems have similar metrics, rhythm, and tone, and both treat a spiritual purification as a physical fever which paradoxically leads to spiritual health through death. The scope of the analogy is made clear in the third stanza of Eliot's lyric:

> The whole earth is our hospital
> Endowed by the ruined millionaire,
> Wherein, if we do well, we shall
> Die of the absolute paternal care
> That will not leave us, but prevents
> us everywhere.

The "ruined millionaire" is Adam. Within the hospital we are cared for by the "dying nurse" and the "wounded surgeon" with "bleeding hands" whose "sharp compassion" resolves the "enigma of the fever chart." The nurse is apparently the church and the surgeon, Christ, but all of these figures tend to merge as examples of sufferers who alleviate suffering. It is in the description of the desired purification itself that the poem deviates most conspicuously from seventeenth-century techniques:

> If to be warmed, then I must freeze
> And quake in frigid purgatorial fires
> Of which the flame is roses, and the
> smoke is briars.

The rich concentration of connotation here may suggest Crashaw, but is essentially Eliot's own. It is a kind of incantation, and reveals a new experience fusing both extreme pain and extreme ecstasy. The rose suggests love, Christ's wounds (symbolized in Hopkins and others by the five-petaled rose), martyrdom, and probably for Eliot the whole of Dante. The briars suggest among other things the crown of thorns. This incorporation of a multifoliate symbolism into a metaphysical structure again is different from Marvell's technique in the dialogue or from Donne's closest parallel, "Good Friday: Riding Westward." Here a witty but serious casuistry is maintained to the end when the poet explains he has turned his back "but to receive/Corrections till thy mercies bid thee leave" and, when Christ's image is restored in him, he will turn his face.

Frequently one of the chief functions of Eliot's conceits, unlike those of Donne and Marvell, is to give an added dimension of ironic connotation. Eliot first made use of naïve imagery for a satiric effect in "The Hippopotamus," where there is an extended contrast of the hippo, representing quite materialistic ways, and the True Church, but it is the hippo who among the saints "shall be seen/Performing on a harp of gold" and who "shall be washed as white as snow,/By all the martyr'd virgins kist." In "A Cooking Egg" the speaker, mourning like Villon his lost youth, represents himself as a somewhat stale egg that appropriately is found among the "weeping multitudes" that droop in a hundred Aerated Bread Company tearooms. The irony slashes deeper in "Little Gidding," written during the Second World War, as the Pentecostal dove and the enemy divebomber merge in a single figure:

The dove descending breaks the air
With flame of incandescent terror
Of which the tongues declare
The one discharge from sin and error.

We can make a choice of "pyre or pyre" and "be redeemed from fire by fire."[13] Sin can be discharged through hatred and revenge or through the purifying fires of God. The analogy, set off by the contrast, extends beyond the superficial comparison of the dove and bomber, tongues and gunfire; for purification, like war, involves pain, and the divebomber, like the Pentecostal tongues, is a call to repentance and salvation. Donne too, of course, wrote dramatically of the paradoxical kinship of suffering and salvation, but never with the same ironic clash.

A type of conceit appearing more often in Eliot, particularly the earlier poetry, than in Donne is the compressed figure with its surprising union of widely separated realms. "Prufrock" abounds in these. The familiar etherized patient figure is of course an example. Sometimes an inner state is revealed through an exaggerated externalization of a gesture. There are hands that "lift and drop a question on your plate" and "eyes that fix you in a formulated phrase." Prufrock wonders if he should "have bitten off the matter with a smile." But side by side with these is a kind of fantastic, perhaps surrealistic figure. Prufrock imagines himself "pinned and wriggling on the wall" and his "head [grown slightly bald] brought in upon a platter." In "Choruses from the 'Rock'" the Rock proclaims, "The desert is squeezed in the tube-train next to you" (I) and the chorus later speaks of "Dividing the stars into common and preferred" (III).

Both in his prose and poetry Donne was fond of the paradox, and Eliot has resorted a number of times to the same device. Donne's "Good Friday: Riding Westward" and most of his *La Corona* sonnets are built around a paradox, but perhaps his most paradoxical poem is "Upon the Annunciation and Passion Falling Upon One Day," in which the poet sees Christ "nothing twice at once, who's all." Donne is referred to directly in one of Eliot's most carefully developed paradoxes, "Whispers of Immortality," which was in fact probably suggested by Donne's "bracelet of bright haire about the bone" ("The Relique"), which paints so vividly the contrast between the skeleton and the living flesh. There is an antithesis between Donne and Webster and the modern world. A similar antithesis between thought and carnality is suddenly resolved in a paradox: they are really of the same nature because they can be experienced in the same way. Thought can be felt — in fact was felt by Donne and Webster — just as the material world can be felt. "The Hippopotamus" follows a similar pattern as the contrasted hippo and True Church finally exchange destinies as the hippo takes wing while the True Church remains below in the "old miasmal mist."

Antithesis and paradox are the underlying patterns that give form to the poetic music of *Four Quartets*. There is a continuous play upon the contrast between movement and stillness, past and present, sickness and health, and particularly beginning and end. The paradoxical "In my beginning is my end" is the core about which meaning gathers in "East Coker" and to a lesser extent in the other quartets. If we trace back our history, our journey's end is the garden in which we began. In a kind of pun "end" can also come to mean purpose or final cause. The metaphysical lyric in "East Coker" depends as much on paradox as on the extended conceit. In the Marvell dialogue that apparently suggested it, the soul complains that "ready oft the port to gain," it is "shipwrecked into health again," while Eliot observed that "if we do well, we shall/Die of the absolute paternal care."

Eliot, like Donne, also sometimes used puns in a serious context or employed other ways of wringing the utmost meaning out of words. There is a double pun in "the unstilled world still whirled" in "Ash Wednesday," V, and in "East Coker," III, a play on "the hollow rumble of wings" which comes like the "darkness of God" in a theater. But word-play, like other metaphysical techniques, is often used in Eliot with an ironic twist foreign to the seventeenth century. In "A Cooking Egg" the "penny world" described both the naïve world of success the speaker sought and also the monotonous room of the A.B.C. tearooms he has obtained. In the

"Please, will you/Give us a light?" of "Triumphal March" the trivial request and the anguished prayer coalesce. A similar witty irony is gained through allusion. While Marvell proposes to his "coy mistress," "Let us roll all our strength and all/Our sweetness up into one ball," Prufrock asks himself if he should "have squeezed the universe into a ball?/To roll it toward some overwhelming question." The many allusions in "The Waste Land" often function similarly. The double allusion to *The Inferno* and Sherlock Holmes's adventures with the hound of the Baskervilles provides an ironic commentary on the treatment of deception at the conclusion of "East Coker," II.

Dry bones sometimes rattle in Eliot's poetry, very much as in Donne's, to infuse a grotesque element that can add both to the wit and seriousness of a poem. In its witty but realistic treatment of death, Eliot's "Whispers of Immortality" approaches nearer than any of his other poems to the spirit of Donne's "The Relique" and "The Funerall" and Marvell's "To His Coy Mistress." Donne's "bracelet of bright haire about the bone" is matched by Eliot's "skull beneath the skin." While Marvell reminded his coy mistress that "worms shall try/That long preserved virginity," Eliot juxtaposed Grishkin's "promise of pneumatic bliss" with "breastless creatures under ground/Leaned backward with a lipless grin." In a rather grim grotesquerie Donne's "The Autumnall" mentioned "winter faces . . . Whose mouths are holes, rather worn out than made" while Eliot more seriously imaged despair in describing a stair in "Ash Wednesday," III, as "Damp, jagged, like an old man's mouth dribbling, beyond repair." In "Ash Wednesday" and elsewhere various other forms of the grotesque add an insistent note of reality to the recurring variations on the life-death antithesis.

With considerable justice Eliot may be regarded as the high priest of the twentieth-century revival of metaphysical poetry. Although he evidently derived his theories of metaphysical poetry partly from earlier critics, he expanded and refined these more significantly than anyone else. While he reacted against Donne and the seventeenth-century metaphysicals more sharply than has generally been realized, he continued to value highly the fusion of thought and feeling that he had found in the metaphysicals. In fact, Eliot's own theories often provided a prism through which Donne and his followers worked on his imagination. It is almost impossible to understand his techniques apart from either the older or the modern interpretations of metaphysical poetry. Eliot is most clearly a metaphysical poet in accordance with his own definition, although he went beyond Donne in his experimentation with thought-feeling relationships and in his attempts to capture the flux and flow of experience, especially in his earlier poetry. Eliot, however, is also a metaphysical poet in accordance with what may be called the seventeenth-century interpretation of metaphysical poetry; but, measured by these standards, he seems in many ways very different from Donne. Eliot's poetry certainly shows deep thinking and a lively wit. Still it lacks two of the prime characteristics of Donne's poetry: the natural, almost spontaneous development of logical thought for its own sake and the frequent, easy use of the extended conceit as the structure of a poem. Correspondences and metaphors are utilized to contribute to the total pattern of a poem, but there seems to be no particular pleasure in the perception of the relationship itself. Instead, it is usually the ironic overtones of the figures that are important, so that in place of the "tough reasonableness beneath a slight lyric grace" that Eliot attributed to Marvell there is often an abrasive irony beneath a lyric grace that is deliberately deceptive. Eliot probably absorbed the spirit and techniques of Donne and the metaphysicals more thoroughly than any other recent poet; but, also, his transmutation of these has been more original than that of other modern poets. Eliot's work is a quite new, revitalized metaphysical poetry.

IX

Metaphysicals and Critics
since 1912

AFTER the Grierson edition in 1912 the chorus of praise for Donne and the metaphysicals swelled to a great crescendo during the Donne tercentenary in 1931 and has in fact continued. The movement was given impetus by Eliot's writings on the metaphysical poets, other publications, and various special events, but was relatively unaffected by Eliot's change of taste during the 1920's. These later critics proceeded from the interpretations of the earlier period of the revival, but their key conception became that of Donne the modern. They greatly extended the base of the movement and seemingly proclaimed almost everywhere that Donne with his tensions and conflicts was a modern and that his poetry could best be understood through the most modern methods of analysis.

SCHOLARS, TERCENTENARIES, AND "FOR WHOM THE BELL TOLLS"

Besides new editions of various works by Donne, there were during this period new editions of the poetry of George Herbert, Edward Herbert, King, Marvell, Crashaw, and Vaughan. Two anthologies of "metaphysical" verse testified to a growing tendency to regard as "metaphysical" as much good poetry as possible. Grierson's *Metaphysical Lyrics and Poems of the Seventeenth Century* included poems by Milton and Butler and held that metaphysical poetry in its fullest development, as in *The*

Divine Comedy, was inspired by a philosophical conception of the universe.[1] Genevieve Taggard's *Circumference*, treating "varieties of metaphysical verse 1456–1928," included poems by Milton, Bunyan, Pope, Gray, Burns, Wordsworth, Shelley, Swinburne, and Whitman.

Since the 1930's scholars have produced a number of major works on the metaphysical poets, their reputations, and influence. George Williamson's *The Donne Tradition* (1930), representing metaphysical poetry as characterized by wit, surprise, and conceit, traced religious and secular lines of development in the seventeenth-century metaphysical movement. Two English works, Joan Bennett's *Four Metaphysical Poets* and John Blair Leishman's *Metaphysical Poets*, appeared in 1934. Miss Bennett contrasted metaphysical analysis with nineteenth-century sensuousness, and Leishman contributed to the growing appreciation of the metaphysicals by including many carefully selected quotations. Book-length studies of individual authors have also appeared. Arthur H. Nethercot's *Abraham Cowley, The Muse's Hannibal*, appeared in 1931; Austin Warren's *Richard Crashaw*, in 1939, and Joseph H. Summers' *George Herbert*, in 1954. Leishman, in *The Monarch of Wit* (1951), painted the familiar picture of Donne as a tortured Hamlet-like individual, but related him to his seventeenth-century background rather than to modern poetic theories. The revolt against metaphysical poetry was examined in Robert L. Sharp's *From Donne to Dryden*, while the reputations of the metaphysicals during the late seventeenth century and the eighteenth century were traced by Nethercot in a series of articles (1922–1930). Then in *Sense and Sensibility in Modern Poetry* (1948), William Van O'Connor reviewed the influence of the seventeenth-century metaphysicals on modern poets expressing the tensions of our time.

The most important stock-taking of the revival was provided by Theodore Spencer's and Mark Van Doren's *Studies in Metaphysical Poetry* in 1939. The work listed 540 titles of books and articles about the metaphysical poets for the years 1912–1938, and showed a sharp increase in metaphysical studies during the early 1920's. Although the list was not complete, Spencer was correct in his surmise that it was "at least twice as long as a similar list would be for the whole nineteenth century." [2] Since 1939 annual bibliographies of studies of the poets, particularly Donne, have continued long, while poems by seventeenth-century metaphysical poets have often been reprinted in some of the more popular magazines.

A series of tercentenaries created new waves of interest. The 300th anniversary of Marvell's birth was celebrated in March 1921, at Kingston-upon-Hull, in observances that included a meeting of about 2000 students to hear recitations of Marvell poems and a public celebration at the guildhall highlighted by an address by Augustine Birrell. Those attending could see a special Marvell exhibit, receive a Marvell medal, and ride in "two new tramcars suitably decorated with historic designs" that added "a novel and arresting feature to the celebration." [3] The tercentenary of Donne's death in 1931 was celebrated chiefly in print, but received a great deal of attention. The most important tribute was *A Garland for John Donne*, composed of a number of critical and scholarly essays. *The Bookman* offered a prize for the best sonnet on Donne, and the winner, a Mary Hacker, exulted that Donne's voice "will not fall mute again." [4] John Peale Bishop's poem "John Donne's Statue," appearing later, also marked the Donne tercentenary. The tercentenary of George Herbert's death was celebrated quietly at Bemerton in June 1933, and the tercentenary of Crashaw's death was observed at Peterhouse, Cambridge, in July 1949, when a memorial lecture was delivered by Basil Willey.

Donne's reputation received a new and quite unexpected boost in 1941 with the publication of Hemingway's best-selling *For Whom the Bell Tolls*, whose title and motto were from Donne's prose devotions. As *Time* reported, after the 1000-odd copies of Donne's poems on hand were sold, "Best-Seller Donne was O.P." (out of print). Fifteen hundred sheets ordered by Random House from England were bombed out of existence while the Oxford

Press here anxiously hoped their editions of Donne would elude Nazi planes and submarines.[5]

MODERN CONCEPTIONS OF DONNE AND THE METAPHYSICALS

The earlier ideas about Donne and the metaphysicals continued after 1912. Virginia Woolf, for instance, in a tercentenary essay, represented Donne as rebelling against both his elders and the temper of his times, found his "riddle too difficult to read," felt Donne's figure seemed "too entirely itself to turn to common clay," and stressed his fidelity to thought and feeling.[6] But the ideas about Donne as a rebellious, mysterious, and unique individual were gradually funneled into the conception of Donne the modern. Courthope had detected a modern note in Donne's rebellion, and perhaps Victorian readers had identified themselves somewhat timidly and subconsciously with Donne's revolt against his times. However, more recent readers, openly in revolt against "Victorian" conventions, were boldly and self-consciously ready to identify themselves with the Donne that seemed a modern rebel. In an inevitable reaction against corporate life in everything, explained John Bailey, Donne attracted the young as "the most self-willed individualist of all our older poets."[7] Donne's mystery was largely solved too in the discovery that he was the first of the moderns. As F. O. Matthiessen noted, "the sudden juxtapositions of experience . . . the jagged brokenness of Donne's thought has struck a responsive note in our age." The paradox of Jack Donne and Dean Donne seemed the less puzzling since modern taste could find an affinity simultaneously with Donne's plain-spoken "passion without sentiment" as well as with his "note of fear" and his struggle toward faith through doubt. Twentieth-century critics also prized his distinctive originality as a modern virtue. During the tercentenary Alan Porter attributed Donne's fame to his originality — even his oddness and perversity — and S. Addleshaw asserted that the "modern flair for originality" led us to admire Donne, like D. H. Lawrence, as "himself triumphantly."[8]

The idea that Donne and the other seventeenth-century meta-physicals were modern had of course existed before 1912. This modernity was usually found in the comparison of the earlier poets with "modern" poets such as Thompson and Brooke. With a broader conception of Donne's modernity, Stephen had explained that Donne's deep feeling, "neurotic constitution," and philosophy appealed to modern taste. Since 1912 the tendency to compare seventeenth-century and twentieth-century metaphysical poets has become so habitual that about seventy poets have been regarded as in some way metaphysical. But the more characteristic tendency in this later criticism has been to enlarge on conceptions like that of Stephen and present Donne not simply as like certain modern poets, but as the prototype of modern man.

This idea of Donne the modern was proclaimed in high school weeklies as well as in English studies and in both scientific journals and religious quarterlies. It absorbed all the older conceptions of Donne the man and of the psychological realism in his work. The discovery of the modernity of Donne became a nucleus for detailed comparisons of the earlier seventeenth and twentieth centuries as similar periods marked by world disorders, social breakdowns, scientific advances, and religious skepticism.[9] It also brought into focus not only all the conflicts and tensions that moderns thought they shared with Donne but qualities that they felt Donne possessed but they lacked. By a kind of totemism, twentieth-century readers in studying Donne sought not only themselves, but Donne's unified sensibility, his essential heroism in dealing with mistresses, God and himself (despite Eliot's remark that metaphysical poetry tends to be anti-heroic), and sometimes his hard-won faith. The twentieth century discovered that Donne was a modern and then that moderns needed to be more like Donne.

The disillusionment and crumbling of values that followed the First World War provided a congenial climate for the conception of Donne's modernity, but the seminal ideas about Donne and the metaphysicals certainly existed before the war. In any case, during the postwar period an increasing number of critics saw their own moods mirrored in Donne. Lost between old and new values, they envisioned Donne as similarly torn between two worlds. By 1919 H. J. Massingham could write that the seventeenth-century poets, like moderns, "lived under the shadow of corruption and disintegration, and their poetry as well as ours feels, fears, and runs from the darkness." Allen Tate later noted Donne's awareness of frustration and bewilderment, and Ashley Sampson recognized in Donne the "world-weary melancholy of today." Michael F. Moloney saw Crashaw and other metaphysicals as responding to a universe rent by temporal and spiritual conflicts.[10] For most, seventeenth-century "melancholy" and twentieth-century "anxiety" seemed the same malady.

Critics tended to believe that these tensions and conflicts that made Donne a modern had three main closely related aspects: Donne's interest in science and the "new philosophy," his skepticism, and his probing self-analysis. Donne's interest in science was first noticed by Gosse, who represented Donne as "completely captivated by the recent epoch-making discoveries in the science of astronomy" and discussed Donne's knowledge of Copernicus, Brahe, Galileo's *Sidereus Nuncius* and Kepler's *Dissertatio cum Nuncio Sidereo*. However, it was not until the 1920's and 1930's that Donne students gave much specific attention to his scientific interests and regarded these as modern. Although Bush has concluded that Donne was "no scientific modernist," scientific interests fitted very neatly into the portrait of a modern Donne and provided a modern explanation for Donne's "skepticism." Earlier critics such as Hugh I'Anson Fausset and Laurence Binyon wrote of the disturbing effects that Donne's "restless scientific curiosity" had on him, while the more scholarly studies of Marjorie Hope Nicolson and Charles Monroe Coffin testified further to the twentieth century's concern with the seventeenth century's reaction to the "new philosophy."[11]

"The new Philosophy calls all in doubt," cried Donne and endeared himself to a future generation. Some earlier critics had considered Donne as more or less of a skeptic. Even Jessopp in his idealized life of Donne as a religious leader had characterized him as "always seeing objections, always surprising others with unexpected doubts and difficulties." Gosse portrayed the youthful Donne as cynical, skeptical, contemptuous, heartless, and arrogant without relating him to the philosophical conflicts of his period, while Grierson later pointed out his emancipated attitude toward religious problems. This conception of Donne as a skeptic mushroomed rapidly at about the same time that readers were discovering Donne's scientific interests and concluding that in the seventeenth century, as in the twentieth, science bred skepticism and relativism. After all, besides the passage about the "new Philosophy," Donne had said "doubt wisely" and more explicitly had written:

> Ther's nothing simply good, nor ill alone,
> Of every quality comparison
> The onely measure is, and judge opinion.[12]

One of the most significant aspects of this conception of Donne as a modern skeptic was its widespread popularity. All of Donne's biographers echoed it. Fausset explained that Donne escaped from Catholicism to agnosticism. He expressed a representative view in declaring that as one who "went into the wilderness to seek religion from life, he is essentially modern," and found the example of Donne's life "pre-eminently bracing" today. F. W. Payne wrote that in his youth Donne had no religious belief, and Richard Ince in his popular life of Donne asserted that "young Jack emphatically had no codes" and was a modern. In some more sophisticated criticism, Marius Bewley recently sought to uncover as yet unsuspected depths of religious cynicism in Donne's poetry, while in a related field, Hiram Haydn's intellectual and cultural history of the "Counter-Renaissance" represented Donne as familiar with all the relativistic thought of his day. Although this contagious habit of regarding Donne as a modern skeptic continues, a corrective has been sounded by writers who recalled that he advised doubting wisely as a way of reaching truth that *does* stand "on a huge hill,/Cragged, and steep" and that he did not wonder whether to believe, but what to believe. Modern critics who "kidnap" Donne and make him a modern skeptic received a very

171

erudite scolding from Merritt Y. Hughes, who emphasized the vast differences between Donne's revolt against the Stoic conception of natural law and modern cosmic relativism.[13]

To their portrait of a modern Donne critics usually added his studied self-analysis, often feeling that bewilderment about the new science and the resulting skepticism had made him turn within. In the age of psychoanalysis Donne came to be regarded as psychoanalytic. Of the various characteristics attributed to Donne, this was the most firmly rooted in earlier criticism. Carpenter had referred to Donne's "self-consuming subjectivity" and "passionate introspection" and in the criticism of Stephen, Brooke, and others a conscious self-analysis was usually implied in the conception of psychological realism. Then in 1919 Massingham mentioned the "introspective cast" Donne gave to sexual love, and Logan Pearsall Smith spoke of "a subtlety of self-analysis, an awareness of the workings of his own mind" in the sermons. The idea was developed in the 1920's by Payne, Fausset, and many others. By the tercentenary Addleshaw could write: "Donne is the most introspective of all writers." Expressing the relationship of Donne's introspection to other aspects of his modernity, Coffin asserted that the drama of his response to the new science was enacted in his own soul, and Matthiessen noted "a reflection of our own problem in the manner in which his passionate mind, unable to find final truth in which it could rest, became fascinated with the process of thought itself." [14] To the exaggerated conception of Donne's probings of himself, Miss Rosemond Tuve and others have objected. Although there was some basis for the modern view in the Renaissance conception of the poet as a physician to himself, this was quite different from the modern notion of the poet as his own psychiatrist.

Despite the widespread idea of Donne as skeptical and tortured, there was also at the same time a persistent but less evident tendency, particularly in religious publications, to emphasize the contemporary spiritual and theological significance of Donne and some of the other metaphysical poets. The studies of the mysticism and religious experience of the metaphysical poets by Itrat

Husain and Miss Helen C. White reflect this tendency. Donne was regarded as an important figure in ecclesiastical history who had something to say to the twentieth century through his life, theology, and devotional poetry. Donne, wrote W. H. Hutton, "belongs to the company of S. Paul and S. Bernard and S. Francis, and Hooker and Wesley and Pusey and Newman." He was praised as "a devoted pastor and penitent, a priest whose faith in God was as near as that of any man living on earth to sight." John Sparrow emphasized that Donne was not a skeptic and that his religious dedication in later life simply showed the "unfolding of certain traits which had always been an important part of his nature." Eleanor Johnson agreed that the same mind spoke all through the poetry and prose and pointed out that Donne's treatment of "the strange alchemy of right and wrong" was pertinent today. F. E. Hutchinson acclaimed Donne for taking issue with the Calvinists, Thomas Foster praised the Catholic elements in Donne's poetry, and Henry Newbolt asserted that "when there shall come another religious poet as great as Donne, he will speak like him." [15]

Meanwhile, Crashaw and Herbert were similarly interpreted. Just after the First World War, Constance Spender spoke of the value of Crashaw's undimmed ecstasy and his "immortal freshness" to "weary, war-torn mortals." M. Whitcomb Hess contrasted Crashaw's spiritual influence with the dehumanizing and dechristianizing influence of his contemporary, Descartes. During the Crashaw tercentenary Moloney stressed the importance of the poet to the "Catholic man of letters of our time" because of his singleness of purpose in an age of turmoil. A similar note was sounded during the Herbert tercentenary by Gilbert Thomas, who said Herbert's piety "overflowed the limits of his time and is still vital for ourselves." [16]

CRITICAL TRENDS

While critics were regarding Donne and other metaphysical poets as modern or particularly valuable to the twentieth century, they were also relating these conceptions to an analysis of metaphysical poetry according to the most recent techniques. They retained many of the earlier ideas about metaphysical poetry, but they also modified and reinterpreted some of the conclusions of Eliot and his predecessors to form some essentially new conceptions of metaphysical writing. This reinterpretation reached its peak in a revaluation that sought to rewrite English literary history in accordance with the new discoveries of the nature and significance of metaphysical poetry.

Conceits and wit were praised and the familiar conceptions of a thought-feeling relationship and psychological realism were developed with variations by a number of writers. In the 1920's Herbert Read depended on Eliot's ideas in his attempt to define the thought-feeling relationships in metaphysical poetry more precisely and thoroughly than Eliot had done. He explained clearly that in metaphysical poetry thought produced emotion while in "a vaguer, easier process" emotion produced thought. Growing from these ideas and from his conception of the merging of percept and concept and of experience and thought in metaphysical poetry was his more original conclusion that "the whole meaning of metaphysical poetry" was in an anagogic interpretation. He found this relation of lyricism to philosophical quest well exemplified in Donne's "The First Anniversary." [17]

John Crowe Ransom, too, made use of some of Eliot's ideas in working out his own conception of metaphysical poetry. He was concerned with relationships between thought and feeling, but felt that the unified sensibility, once shattered, could not be put together again. He preferred to approach metaphysical poetry ontologically. Trying to define types of poetry by examining what they really dealt with, he contrasted metaphysical poetry with "physical poetry," which dealt with things as in imagism, and "platonic poetry," which dealt with ideas alone and was allegorical, Victorian, and scientifically abstract. Metaphysical poetry, he felt, did not claim "scientific" truth, but comprehended and transcended both things and ideas in a "miraculism" that occurred when a poet worked from a partial analogy to a complete identification. Ransom thus became the leading champion of the notion that the one defining characteristic of metaphysical poetry was the extended conceit that became identical with the poem itself. He related this belief to the problems of thought and feeling in explaining that metaphysical poetry worked directly through the hard thought of the bold extended conceit to an extinction of the original feelings, but presumably to feelings of resolution.[18]

Meanwhile many of these ideas popularized by postwar critics were leading to a related but new and distinct definition of metaphysical poetry as a way of treating and resolving conflicting impulses. This new conception was formulated by selecting a part of the earlier ideas about conceits and psychological realism, reinterpreting and expanding these, and regarding them as the defining characteristics of metaphysical poetry. Contributing in some way to the development of this emphatically psychological interpretation were Brooke, Eliot, Richards, Empson, Ransom, Tate, and — most important — Brooks.

Brooke and Eliot had noted that in metaphysical poetry experience was presented in the round. Brooke spoke of Donne's ability to view experience both intellectually and emotionally, to see it from the other side, and Eliot discussed the levity that increased seriousness and the disparate if not necessarily opposed experiences that the unified sensibility could form into a new whole. However, Richards and his disciple Empson gave a greater impetus to the development of this new conception of metaphysical poetry. Richards formulated many of his ideas by working out dynamically and psychologically Coleridge's essentially logical conception of the reconciliation of opposites. Maintaining that the most valuable effects of poetry must be described in terms of "the resolution, interanimation, and balancing of impulses," Richards distinguished two ways of organizing impulses in a poem: by exclusion and by inclusion. Although he did not generalize about metaphysical poetry, he cited Donne's "Nocturnall" and Marvell's "The Definition of Love" as examples of the poetry of inclusion or synthesis.[19]

Empson, too, found metaphysical poetry exceptionally rich in praiseworthy ambiguities that reflected opposing psychological impulses. He included Donne's "A Valediction: Of Weeping," for instance, as an example of the fourth type of ambiguity, occurring when "statements do not agree among themselves, but combine to make clear a more complicated state of mind in the author." He explained that the poem was enriched by "the variety of irrelevant, incompatible ways of feeling about the affair." Empson discussed Crashaw's praise of St. Teresa's chastity in copulative metaphors as an instance of the seventh type of ambiguity that shows "a fundamental division in the writer's mind." He took a mischievous delight in uncovering unsuspected elements in the poetry of "holy" George Herbert. "The Pilgrimage," he explained, reflects two distinctly different moods, "Affliction" (I) reveals a mixture of submission and revolt, and "The Sacrifice" pictures Christ as "loved because hated" and "torturing his torturers because all merciful." Marvell's "The Garden," he said, contrasts and reconciles conscious and unconscious states, intuitive and intellectual modes of apprehension, and he concluded that only a metaphysical poet, "with so complete a control over the tricks of the style, at the end of its development, could actually dramatise these hints as he gave them." [20] While Empson's methods of analysis seemed to enhance metaphysical poetry particularly, metaphysical poetry provided many of the best illustrations of the virtues of Empson's methods.

Several other critics, particularly Brooks, went a step further to regard the inclusion of conflicting attitudes as a definitive characteristic of metaphysical poetry. Ransom's "metaphysical poetry" and Tate's "poetry of the imagination" bore some resemblance to the poetry of inclusion. But Tate, referring to Empson, approached the new conception of metaphysical poetry more directly in noting that in metaphysical poetry the "varieties of ambiguity and contradiction beneath the logical surface are endless" and in pointing out how Donne guarded himself against our irony. Working along related lines, Spencer saw in metaphysical poetry a resolution of conflict through wit. It remained for Brooks, identifying metaphysical poetry and Richards' poetry of inclusion, boldly to proclaim that metaphysical poetry was "a poetry in which the opposition of the impulses is extreme, or, to base oneself directly on Coleridge: it is a poetry in which the poet attempts the reconciliation of qualities which are opposite or discordant in the extreme." The metaphysical poet achieved sincerity, he said, by attempting to fuse conflicting elements into a harmonious whole. The use of wit, particularly the "unpoetic" conceit, gave the poem an "ironic contemplation" that protected it from the criticism of an opposing point of view. He went further than Eliot in declaring that symbolist poetry, with its irony, wit, and realistic diction, coalesced with metaphysical poetry.[21] Admittedly eclectic, Brooks crystallized some incompletely formulated ideas into a new conception of metaphysical poetry in somewhat the same way that Eliot had crystallized ideas of earlier critics in the 1920's.

Brooks's description of metaphysical poetry in terms of attitudes, Leonard Unger concluded, was the only recent definition substantiated by an analysis of Donne's *Songs and Sonets*. Brooks's broad definition, however, opened the way for even more generalized descriptions. Moloney suggested that what "distinguished the 'metaphysicals' more than their craftsmanship was their vital reaction to the problems with which their troubled world presented them." Miss Sona Raiziss considered "the predicaments of a troubled epoch, as well as subtle crises in the personality of an individual artist" as incentives to metaphysical expression.[22]

This new conception of metaphysical poetry, emphasizing psychological conflicts, is evidently another aspect of the idea of a modern Donne. The new approaches to metaphysical poetry provided by Brooks and others gave new fuel to the revival after the Donne tercentenary enthusiasm was dying down and were beneficial in encouraging a careful reading of metaphysical poems that demand a careful reading. But they also enticed the reader to lose sight of the logical, even abstract unity that the seventeenth-century metaphysicals presumably intended and to search with varying degrees of success for a new psychological unity derived from ambiguities, ironies, and impulses of which the poet was probably unaware. Opposition developed not only from seventeenth-century specialists but from what might seem an unexpected source: T. S. Eliot. Objecting specifically to some of the methods of Richards and Empson, Eliot exposed the dangers of the "lemon-squeezer school" of criticism that sought to "extract, squeeze, tease, press every drop of meaning" from a poem.[23]

In any event, almost all of these critics from Eliot to Brooks found their new evaluations and interpretations of metaphysical poetry so significant that they called for a radical revision of critical histories of English poetry. This movement was inaugurated by Eliot's discussion of the unified sensibility that vitalized the work of the metaphysicals but became dissociated in the poetry of Milton, Dryden, and Tennyson. Read restated virtually the same theory. This reinterpretation of critical history was reflected in the widespread exaltation of Donne at the expense of Milton and even of Shakespeare. Ransom, for instance, in his discussion of Donne and Shakespeare at sonnets, concluded that "structurally, there is no firmer architect of lyric anywhere in English than Donne," while Shakespeare "would not quite risk the consequences of his own imagination" and "developed poetically along lines of least resistance." [24]

Leavis and Brooks, however, contributed most to this "new look" given English literary history. Elaborating on the ideas of Eliot, Leavis described an aesthetically valuable "line of wit" running from Donne and Jonson through Carew and Marvell to Pope and then through Hopkins, Eliot, Yeats, and Empson. He found this line of development more important than the conventional Spenser-Milton-Tennyson line or Waller-Denham-Dryden-Pope line, and suggested that English poetry in the future must develop along this line of wit rather than in the tradition running from the romantics through Tennyson, Swinburne, and Housman. In his "Notes for a Revised History of English Poetry" Brooks again gave the boldest challenge to intrenched opinion. Such a sketch, he said, should begin with sixteenth-century metaphysical poetry, as in Wyatt, and trace the tradition of wit through Donne, Jonson, the Cavalier poets, some of Pope's work, and *The Beggar's Opera*. He explained that Blake, Coleridge, Keats, and Hardy possessed many of the characteristics of metaphysical poets and that the best of the modern poets were metaphysical. Orthodox histories of English poetry, he insisted, "will have to be rewritten." [25] This general change of taste and perspective, reflected by scholars, critics, and undergraduates, indicates the real significance of Bush's statement that the metaphysical revival was "the main single factor in effecting the modern revolution in taste."

THE REACTION AGAINST THE REVIVAL

There has gradually developed a reaction against metaphysical poetry and its most conspicuous champions, the "new critics." "As the nineteen-thirties drew on," M. C. Bradbrook has recollected, "the fashion for Donne gradually went out." Though the vogue for Donne, somewhat abated, continues today, there was indeed evidence of a waning interest. Striking an off-key note in the Donne tercentenary *Garland*, Eliot described Donne's poetry as "a concern of the present and recent past, rather than of the future." Then Spencer, four years after editing this volume honoring Donne, ventured to suggest that "modern poetry has learnt all it can from the metaphysicals; we need a fresher source of inspiration." A few years later he wondered "if, for our generation at least, the study of Donne has not now reached a kind of saturation point." [26]

Continuing during the 1940's and 1950's, this opposition to metaphysical poetry and the "new criticism" has been threefold: scholarly, aesthetic, and socio-political. The assaults on the "new critics" on any of these grounds are only indirectly and often unintentionally directed at the metaphysicals, but they are in a sense flanking attacks on metaphysical poetry since they tend to undermine the reputations of its champions and the interpretations of the poetry that have proved most meaningful to the twentieth century. After Hughes's attack on Donne's "kidnappers," historical scholarship's most potent blast at recent critics was Miss Tuve's *Elizabethan and Metaphysical Imagery*, which went far toward demolishing some of the most cherished modern conceptions of Donne and metaphysical poetry. For Miss Tuve,

Donne was clearly not rebellious, mysterious, or unique. Neither was he a skeptic driven to the analysis of his own thought processes. Renaissance poets, she said, considered truth as "disturbingly unrelativistic" and had no conception of the portrayal of the process of interpreting or feeling. These poets, she explained, could not think in terms of relationships between thought and feeling or regard images as conditioned by experience or a sensibility, rather than by logic. In fact, she feared that metaphysical poets were "sciencing, devouring idealists," writing the kind of Platonic poetry that Ransom had opposed to metaphysical poetry. Similarly, she objected to Brooks's thinking of it in terms of opposed impulses. Most important of all, she maintained that the seventeenth-century metaphysicals did not exist, distinct and original, as they were pictured by moderns, but worked within an accepted Renaissance tradition. More recently another writer asserted that there was no metaphysical style as there were Elizabethan and Augustan styles, while Geoffrey Walton's *Metaphysical to Augustan* stressed the continuity in the poetic tradition.[27]

During the same period some critics and poets were disparaging metaphysical poetry or displaying marked interest in a movement toward a more classical verse. Yvor Winters ridiculed the "young and decadent romantics of our own period . . . convinced that they are in the tradition of Donne," while Van Wyck Brooks revived the old accusation that the metaphysicals "were closest to chess and to crossword puzzles." Meanwhile a number of poet-critics have been writing in a more classic style and some have approved a return to classicism. Louise Bogan and Richard Wilbur have defended classicism, and Peter Viereck attacked the "new critics" and their methods and then predicted that "the American poetry of the future, like the classicism of the ancient past, will again see art as a groping search for the good, the true, the beautiful."[28]

Aesthetic considerations were strongly colored by socio-political interests in the work of another school of criticism. The awarding of the Bollingen prize to Pound, accused of treason in the Second World War, crystallized opposition to the "new critics" and to poetry showing complexity and technical skill rather than a clear presentation of approved opinions. Many of the disparaging allusions dropped by these critics apply unmistakably to metaphysical poetry. In two *Saturday Review of Literature* articles, Robert Hillyer assailed the Pound-Eliot "stranglehold on American poetry through the so-called 'new criticism.'" He scorned particularly these critics' insistence on irony, regarded by Brooks and others as a precious ingredient of metaphysical poetry, and linked the "new criticism" with the "new fascism" and the "new estheticism" as well as with old-fashioned anti-Semitism. Charging a conspiracy to "damn all literature that is even slightly humanistic," Russell Hope Robbins sharply criticized not only Eliot himself but Ransom and Tate and in fact all pro-Eliot critics. Eliot, usually regarded as the poet-critic leader of the metaphysical revival, was described as "a poet of minor achievement, emotionally sterile and with a mind coarsened by snobbery and constricted by bigotry." [29]

Just as the revival, then, gloried in the modernity of Donne and in modern interpretations of metaphysical poetry, the reaction against it has grown largely from opposition to these ideas. This opposition is in many ways indirect and exploratory. Also, the predictions of a twentieth-century neoclassicism may easily be the result of critics' overemphasizing the parallels between the seventeenth and twentieth centuries. Nevertheless this reaction seems symptomatic of a gradual change in taste. Even more symptomatic of such a change is the fact that, while many specialized studies of the metaphysicals continue to appear, during the last fifteen years there has been almost no major criticism of the metaphysical poets and much less popular writing about them. They have been virtually abandoned by such early champions as Eliot, Read, Leavis, Ransom, Tate, and Brooks. Apparently the metaphysical intrenchments will yield to the exhaustion of a form, boredom with the established, and a natural love of novelty — aided by growing opposition to the "new criticism" — rather than to any direct assault. Though the revival's early death was predicted some twenty-five years ago, it still seems far from moribund.

X

The Metaphysical Florescence

A
s CRITICS evaluated poetry more and more in relation to
its metaphysical qualities, a host of modern poets turned
more and more to metaphysical techniques. Influenced
partly by fad and partly by a desire to be true to themselves and
the contemporary spirit, these poets went back to Donne, hailed
Eliot as their master, or evolved their own metaphysical style.
Although a diligent search would probably turn up something
metaphysical in a majority of modern poets, particularly significant interpretations of the metaphysical style occur in the work
of Wallace Stevens, the Fugitives, Elinor Wylie, Read, Edith Sitwell, and Empson.

WALLACE STEVENS

Wallace Stevens has long been recognized as a "metaphysical"
poet in the philosophical sense of the word. He was also, though
less obviously, a "metaphysical" poet in the literary sense. These
two aspects of his work are of course related. Both Donne and
Stevens, for instance, described and defined many kinds of individual experience in philosophical or scientific terms. But the
characteristic emphasis was different. Donne did not develop in
his poetry a consistent philosophy nor explore persistently a single philosophical problem, but utilized knowledge and techniques
from many fields in the development of his poems. However,
Stevens did treat consistently and persistently the relation of the
imagination and reality. Usually the accent is on the abstract
problem, and aspects of individual experience become examples

182

of a principle. Nevertheless, in a number of poems the emphasis shifts, and Stevens' work suggests Donne's or, more exactly, Marvell's "The Garden," which discusses problems very similar to those that haunted Stevens. Other bonds between Stevens and the metaphysicals were their use of correspondences, conceits, paradox, and wit.

Some of Stevens' poems treating philosophical ideas are metaphysical in their use of conceits and packed logic. In a somewhat grotesque treatment of perception in "Tattoo," light is compared to a spider whose webs are spread under one's eyelids and extend to "the surface of the water" and to "the edges of the snow." "The Glass of Water," which would melt in heat or freeze in cold, is seen to be like a state "in the centre of our lives," between two poles. In "So-and-So Reclining on Her Couch" the sensuous imagery of the curving hip and "dripping blue" eyes is subordinated to the tautly reasoned abstract discussion of "the thing as idea and/The idea as thing."

In some other poems Stevens treated a more personal kind of experience through metaphysical techniques. The relation between lovers is defined in a manner reminiscent of Donne in "Re-Statement of Romance":

> Only we two may interchange
> Each in the other what each has to give.
> Only we two are one, not you and night,
>
> Nor night and I, but you and I, alone . . .

In a concluding astronomical figure the lovers are regarded as casting a pale light upon each other against a night that is "only the background of our selves." "Last Looks at the Lilacs" juxtaposes a romantic theme and coldly scientific imagery very much as in Donne's compass figure, but the connotations of the imagery are much more important in Stevens:

> To what good, in the alleys of the lilacs,
> O caliper, do you scratch your buttocks
> And tell the divine ingénue, your companion,
> That this bloom is the bloom of soap
> And this fragrance the fragrance of vegetal?

The unimaginative gentleman is not even a complete scientific instrument, since calipers must be used in pairs to measure objects successfully. Metaphysical, too, in their attempts at a laboratory-like precision in the dissection of a fleeting mood are the descriptions of gaiety in "Of Bright & Blue Birds & the Gala Sun" and of "sudden time in a world without time" in "Martial Cadenza."

Although Stevens approached Baudelaire and the French symbolists in his interest in the imagination's discovery of relationships and in the translation of one sense impression into another, he sometimes regarded man as a little world with secret affinities with the universe. In "Asides on the Oboe" Stevens' important "central man" becomes the "human globe." Again the life of man and the earth are compared in "Anatomy of Monotony." "But in yourself is like," cried the poet, observing the "Stars at Tallapoosa"; and in "Nomad Exquisite," as "the immense dew of Florida" brings forth rich tropical life,

> So, in me, come flinging
> Forms, flames, and the flakes of flames.

Twice Stevens, like Marvell, employed the geometric figure of two parallel lines, but Stevens' lines converge. At the end of "Notes toward a Supreme Fiction" the soldier's war and the "war between the mind/And sky" are compared:

> Two parallels that meet if only in
>
> The meeting of their shadows or that meet
> In a book in a barrack, a letter from Malay.

And in "To an Old Philosopher in Rome":

> The threshold, Rome, and that more merciful Rome
> Beyond, the two alike in the make of the mind.
> It is as if in a human dignity
> Two parallels become one, a perspective, of which
> Men are part both in the inch and in the mile.

There is the hint of another geometric metaphor in the description of the concentric circles of his fellows that ring the wounded soldier in "Esthétique du Mal," VII.

Stevens also twice used extended figures from the theater. In

"Of Modern Poetry" the "poem of the mind in the act of find-ing/What will suffice" is compared to an actor whose emotions become one with those of the audience, while in "Credences of Summer" the "personae of summer play the characters/Of an inhuman author." In a similar style, "Academic Discourse at Havana" compares passing life to "an old casino in the park" and that "serener myth" to a passing circus. Other extended conceits occur in "Two Tales of Liadoff" and "The Pediment of Appear-ance." A more condensed metaphysical conceit relies on astron-omy:

> High poetry and low:
> Experience in perihelion
> Or in the penumbra of summer night —

A heaping of condensed metaphors in the manner of Herbert oc-curs in several poems. Stressing the need for refreshing change, Stevens referred to

> A single text, granite monotony,
>
> One sole face, like a photograph of fate,
> Glass-blower's destiny, bloodless episcopus,
> Eye without lid, mind without any dream —[1]

There is a similar style in "The Curtains in the House of the Metaphysician" and "What We See Is What We Think."

Because of the very nature of Stevens' highly self-conscious search into teasing epistemological mysteries, antithesis, paradox, and a qualifying comic or ironic tone became an important part of his poetry. His poems frequently grow from conscious antith-eses, such as the opposition between man and nature, mind and passion, and order and chaos. As in some of Donne's and Eliot's poems, a paradox is the cornerstone of some by Stevens. "Con-noisseur of Chaos," for instance, develops this proposition:

> A. A violent order is disorder; and
> B. A great disorder is an order.

Donne's ponderings on aspects of nothingness in his "Nocturnall" are suggested in "The Snow Man" as the listener, "nothing him-self, beholds/Nothing that is not there and the nothing that is."

The Revival of Metaphysical Poetry

A paradox is central to Stevens' conception of the "supreme fiction," independent of reality and imagination and yet a product of both, and to his interpretation of the *felix culpa* in "Esthétique du Mal" — pain "never sees/How that which rejects it saves it in the end." In addition, the way in which the tough seriousness of Stevens' work is offset by wit and grace suggests the metaphysicals, but the precise tone of this wit is closer to that of the French symbolists, while urbane coinages such as "coiffeur of haloes" and "beau caboose" are, after all, Stevens' own.

THE FUGITIVES

Some poets associated with the Fugitives, a Southern literary group that sprang up in the early 1920's, were linked with the seventeenth-century metaphysicals early in their careers. The most important of these have been Ransom, Tate, and Robert Penn Warren. They were clearly familiar with Donne and Marvell, and their elaborate conceits and verbal play are very much in the seventeenth-century style. Yet these poets are much more interesting for their subtle metamorphosis of the formal elements of metaphysical poetry than for their polished imitations of the earlier style.

Some of the poems of this group show a clear influence of Donne and other metaphysicals in phrasing or theme. Tate in "Epilogue to Oenia" referred to "the sapphire corpse undressed by Donne" and was apparently influenced by some well-known lines about Elizabeth Drury in Donne's "Second Anniversary" in writing of "a body vanished into a thought." Surely when in "Winter Remembered" Ransom described his fingers as "frozen parsnips hanging in the weather" he recalled Donne's lines:

> And like a bunch of ragged carrets stand
> The short swolne fingers of thy gouty hand.

But even here the difference is striking and symptomatic. In his "The Comparison" Donne was using images logically to deprecate his rival's mistress. Ranson was employing similar imagery to gain the right nuance of tone in a self-satiric plaint. Donne's "The Extasie" was also clearly imitated — and reinterpreted — by Warren and Tate. Warren's "Picnic Remembered" is very similar to the Donne poem in subject, mood, and figures as well as in its close punctuation, repetition of key words, and general rhythm. While Donne described bodiless souls negotiating, Warren similarly wrote of released souls,

> . . . sped where each with each patrols,
> In still society, hand in hand . . .

But here too there is a modern note in the sudden exclamation: "The bright deception of that day!" Tate's "Shadow and Shade" and "Pastoral" also belong in the tradition of "The Extasie."

The relations between the soul and the body and between love, death, and religion — central in the work of Donne and Marvell — reappear in the poetry of the Fugitives, but almost always with a pale cast of disillusion and frustration. In "The Extasie" and "To His Coy Mistress" the lovers are positive and confident, but in a representative poem like Ransom's "The Equilibrists," "Their flames were not more radiant than their ice," and they are entombed still "untouching in each other's sight." Like "two painful stars . . . orbited nice," they were held in a "torture of equilibrium." Body and spirit did not animate each other, but rather frustrated one another. In Warren's "Love's Parable," as so often happens in Donne, love and religion are virtually equated. Love is a "miracle" of a "garden state" and the poet hopes to master love's grace through prayer. But the love has been lost in a world that reflects the lovers' ruin.

In both subject matter and development the conceits of this group strikingly resemble those of the seventeenth-century metaphysicals. In "Love's Parable," for instance, the lovers are described in scientific figures:

> That time, each was the other's sun,
> Ecliptic's charter, system's core;
> Locked in its span, the wandering one,
> Though colder grown, might yet endure
> Ages unnumbered, for it fed
> On light and heat flung from the source
> Of light that lit dark as it fled:
> Wonder of dull astronomers.

> For joy sought joy then when we loved,
> As iron to the magnet yearns.

But the use of conceits with new or added functions clearly reveals the differences between the seventeenth-century style and the Fugitives' modern metaphysical style. Frequently, for instance, a metaphor indicating differences as well as similarities may be selected to make an ironic or satiric comment. Two could-be lovers in Ransom's "Good Ships" are described as "Fleet ships encountering on the high seas," but the note of irony creeps in with the reference to "the loud surge/Of one of Mrs. Grundy's Tuesday teas" and the realization that the couple will only exchange the "nautical technicalities." After all, "A macaroon absorbed all her emotion." In the extended figure of Tate's "The Paradigm" there is not only sustained precision but an amused though sympathetic satire as two quarreling lovers seal themselves in their icy land (a few square feet) until their fleeting enmity is crashed like a hard mirror. There is irony, too, in the concluding reference to their "ignorant paradigm." A metaphysical conceit may similarly suggest a mood or the poet's way of apprehending an experience. The appropriate mood is created by Ransom's description of his "Spectral Lovers," "immaculate angels" that "haunted a thicket of April mist," though there is also a very gentle satire on the hesitant idealism of the lovers paradoxically "frozen asunder." In his "Triumph" all the connotations of Greece and Rome color the lovers' union and the soul-body relation.

Both in their subject matter and their use of metaphor the Fugitives often imitated the seventeenth-century metaphysicals more directly—though less originally—than Eliot. But they have strongly resembled Eliot in their almost obsessive concern with Prufrockian characters with divided sensibilities, their use of irony, and their presentation of the poet as observer (sometimes of himself) rather than as active protagonist.

ELINOR WYLIE

Along with learning much from Shelley and other romantics, Elinor Wylie showed a familiarity with the seventeenth-century metaphysicals and depended on them in her use of sacramental correspondences, logic, wit, and metaphor. But her metaphysical techniques, like those of the Fugitives, are most interesting for their creation of new effects through old devices. She could, indeed, "enjoy with Donne a metaphysical frolic." Donne's "bracelet of bright haire about the bone" probably inspired descriptions of a face "fretted into paper-lace/About a brittle skull" and a hand "frayed into a ravelled band/Around a silver ring." [2] The conversation between the body, mind, heart, and soul in "This Corruptible" strongly suggests Marvell's "Dialogue between the Soul and Body."

Incarnational and sacramental correspondences and a play on theological or philosophical conceptions appear in Mrs. Wylie's work very much as in Donne's. She said of the china figure in "The Broken Man":

> Ah, poor anatomy, the type and token
> Of mortal love, how often were you broken!

Associated with her lover, the broken figure is also a "type" of Christ. Compounded of clay and pierced with iron, he is "miraculously lost" only to be "lifted from drifted dust." She continued, like Donne and Emily Dickinson, often to attribute divinity to a lover. In "One Person," XII, the lover is conceived of as Christ and then as Adam, and in "The Loving Cup" he transforms wine to blood. A Platonic conception apparently provides the basis for the assertion in "The Lie" that his countenance is "the elemental stuff/Of Beauty perfected, and the mask put off," while there is a characteristically metaphysical play on philosophical conceptions in the desire to cherish her lover twice,

> Once in a mist made matter; once again
> In my true substance made ethereal: [3]

In her most metaphysical work, logic, wit, metaphor, and psychological penetration coalesce to create a poetry whose seriousness and complexity is shot through with a genuine lightness and grace in the seventeenth-century manner. In "The Loving Cup" (there is a pun on the "loving") she treated an amorous triangle while preserving a kind of tart affection for the lover. The ladies are his vessels and he drinks from both. He and her rival "drink division" from the cup's "sole brim." The rival drinks despair and disease, he drinks health and joy; for he has blessed his own drop, which "converts it all," and "The cup is loving, having kissed you once." "The Lie" shows a similar ability to relieve seriousness by a conceit:

> A fortnight past you looked at me and lied:
> Then my heart fainted, and I thought it died.
> But O, that engine's not so simply stilled
> Burns you for fuel, so I was not killed!

Wit punctuates a more somber mood in "To A Cough in the Street at Midnight":

> God cure your cold,
> Whether it be but a cold in the head
> Or the more bitter cold which binds the dead.

Like the Fugitives, Mrs. Wylie frequently employed metaphysical metaphors, but with aims and results different from those of the seventeenth century. Throughout the four sonnets composing "A Red Carpet for Shelley" the weaving, coloring, and laying down of the carpet are compared to the creation of poetry in homage to Shelley. In "Nameless Song" the poet's heart is a shell, "cold and weather-worn," but alive with a mysterious voice, while in "Bells in the Rain" falling rain, tinkling bells, sleep, and death merge in a sleepy, semiconscious association. A similar state is expressed in "Viennese Waltz" as,

> . . . falling, falling, feather after feather,
> The music spreads a softness on the ground.

HERBERT READ

In elaborating on Eliot's theories of metaphysical poetry, Herbert Read was stimulated by his own enthusiasm about Donne and his interest in writing his own metaphysical poetry. After discovering Blake and Yeats, Read has explained, he experienced the impact of Donne and Browning. Donne, whose conceits appealed to him, he described as "an influence apart . . . an education in emotional rectitude," and Browning he admired because of his "expression of intellectual concepts in the language of feeling." Read's Browningesque dramatic monologue "John Donne Declines a Benefice" was apparently a product of this double admiration and shows his sensitive attempt to probe Donne's character. Read also praised Crashaw, "the true type of the divine poet," and Herbert, who "more than any other member of the group shows how the poetry of metaphysical wit can be transmuted into the poetry of religious experience." [4]

Although asserting that in metaphysical poetry thought produced emotion, rather than *vice versa*, Read also significantly credited Donne with showing that "the material of philosophy was also the material of poetry" and explained that Donne recognized "that there was often more poetic value in the thought about an emotion than in the emotion itself." [5] This bias is reflected in Read's own poetry, which usually lacks the high-tension voltage of Donne's and often consists chiefly of thoughts about emotions or even thoughts about thoughts.

He not infrequently used conceits of rather low imaginative power to state essentially abstract propositions:

> Mind wins deciduously,
> hibernating through many years.

> Reason like a lily
> fed by sense and feeling
> blooming eternally [6]

Twice through virtually the same conceit he expressed the characteristically metaphysical attitude of viewing experience intellectually, but failed to work through the thought to a release of emotion. In "The Retreat" mind is a "mirror, passively receiving/ The body's ritual," and again in "A World Within a War":

> Mind looks into a mirror pois'd
> Above body: sees in perspective
> Guts, bones and glands: the make of a man.

This tendency toward the intellectualization of experience often led Read to work with correspondences, conceits, and other metaphysical techniques. In "Summer Rain" the earth is the macrocosm whose "warm breath/issues from the nostrils beneath/the mask of death." Again, "mind simulates/The crystal in the cooling rock/The theorem in the beetle's eye," and a haze quivering on the horizon suggests the "ultimate harmony of the world" and "all that's known/In the deep percipient heart of man." [7] In "My Company" his men, sweating, blaspheming, and bloody, are "modern Christs."

Mathematical figures in the style of Donne and Marvell occur also in Read. His "Equation" is probably unique. The stanzaic order corresponds to the equation $a + b + c = x$. Statements of the essential unity of (a) the world and God, (b) man and woman, and (c) the mind and the body add up to (x) the impossibility of the mind's developing a system of ethics outside the totality of the universe. Read's several circle figures are less striking than Donne's, but he thought of a conscience as circling the mind until walled in, of the self as "exfoliated from an infinite center," and of the way of life before Dunkirk as "a centre to the circle/of all our wanderings" from which the mind was free "to range in thought and fantasy." [8] Read appropriately imagined Donne, pondering on God, to speak through a scientific conceit:

> He is one and has none higher to enhance
> Enormously the wavering needle of a will.
> But he to man is a magnetic North, a call
> For conscience to settle toward,
> And through the tossings of stormy run
> Rest as quiescent as it can
> Till it attain its set attraction in death. [9]

In a homelier conceit in the style of Herbert everything — "wind-woven branches," "fray'd nerves," and "interrupted speech" — is "ragged ends" and "Death is the only even skein." In a similar spirit, the soul is regarded as

> . . . a distilled essence, held
> in a shaking cup, spilt
> by a spit of lead . . . [10]

Read, then, like his masters Donne, Blake, and Yeats, has viewed the universe in terms of analogies between related spheres of being. With not too adventurous an imagination, he has never-theless written a number of completely consistent and unified metaphysical poems like "Equation" and "The Even Skein," while usually lacking the dramatic sweep or emotional intensity of Donne.

EDITH SITWELL

It was partly Dame Edith Sitwell's long affinity with the meta-physicals and the seventeenth century that gave a rare blend of toughness and poignancy to her finest poems, particularly those inspired by the Second World War. In her earlier criticism she confessed that her "peculiar personal passion" was for Marvell. In both Marvell and Eliot she found the same "controlled and terrible passion." More recently she has shown an increasing in-terest in Donne, and in a number of her poems depended on passages from Donne's sermons. Perhaps, too, she was stimulated by her brother Sacheverell Sitwell, who worked for more than ten years on his unfinished narrative poem, *Doctor Donne and Gargantua*. Though one critic has regarded Crashaw as her only visible predecessor, she herself has shown no real interest in his poetry.[11]

Edith Sitwell's poetry is usually infused with the desire to bring together in meaningful patterns all the varied life of the universe. In this she approached very closely the seventeenth-century point of view. She was familiar with Browne, Burton, and Burnet as well as with the metaphysical poets, and thought in terms of cor-respondences and sacred symbols linking God, the universe, and man. Comparing the patterns of ferns and frost, snowflakes and rock crystals, she attempted to see what "material phenomena . . . revealed to us of the spiritual world."[12] She noted the "um-bilical cords that bind us to strange suns/And causes," the veins' equator and the heart's solar system, and held that "the beat of the earth/And beat of the heart are one."[13] Similarly related, in "Medusa's Love Song," are

> . . . the curvature
> Of Space and the hump of the cripple; the blood's
> fever-microbe
> And the criminal, microbe of the world's fevers.

Frequently, as in the poetry of Hopkins and Thompson, an incarnational or sacramental symbolism electrifies an all too earthly reality with new meaning. In the early "Gold Coast Customs" the "murdered God" is seen in the eyes of the drunkard and the outstretched arms of the hungry. Crashaw is suggested in "The Two Loves" as "Christ's wounds weep in the Rose on the wall." In "Still Falls the Rain," perhaps the finest of her war poems, an air raid becomes another crucifixion:

> Still falls the Rain
> Still falls the Blood from the Starved Man's
>   wounded Side:
> He bears in His Heart all wounds, — those of the
>   light that died,
> The last faint spark
> In the self-murdered heart, the wounds of the sad
>   uncomprehending dark,
> The wounds of the baited bear, —

The rain, the falling bombs, human bloodshed and Christ's shed blood merge symbolically in this modern epiphany of man's depraved violation of innocence, his punishment, and redemption through suffering. Similarly, in "Holiday,"

> Old people at evening sitting in the doorways
> See in a broken window of the slum
> The Burning Bush reflected, and the crumb
> For the starving bird is part of the Broken Body
> Of Christ Who forgives us —

Edith Sitwell has adapted the metaphysical style to the poetic scrutiny of modern warfare more distinctively and successfully than any other poet. This is perhaps her greatest triumph. A number of the poems prompted by the Second World War and the atomic bomb combine at explosive tensions the searching analogies, wit, and complexity of metaphysical poetry. Much of the poignancy of "Still Falls the Rain" is caught also in "Serenade: Any Man to Any Woman." The theme of "To His Coy Mistress" is inverted and the poem is built around a fundamental paradox as the lovers look to death rather than to life. The irony is increased by the crisp metrics of the love-song, conceits, and wit.

194

The lover, the "cannon's mate," can compliment his lady only in terms of the shining cannon and "armoured wind." Her serenade must be the starving's howls and her canopy, lies. There is a mordant wit in the ironic twist on Marlowe in "Then die with me and be my love." A similar tension between the form and the theme in "Lullaby" verges on the grotesque. The modern air raid and loathsome prehistoric struggle are equated as the bomber is compared to a primitive bird that lays steel eggs in mother-earth and then fouls its nest. The mother is replaced by Jonson's Babioun, which can sing only "Do, do" in a flat, meaningless, and hopeless world. Edith Sitwell, like Donne, made poetic use of the latest scientific discoveries, and so in "The Shadow of Cain" Christ, man, and the atomic bomb are brought together in a conceit. Nuclear fission is compared to the fission in man, faced now more than ever before with his potentiality for good or for evil. But the poem envisions the fission as the basis for a new wholeness, from which Christ arises as from a split sepulcher.

Some other poems not directly connected with war depend heavily on metaphysical techniques. In "The Song of the Cold," much as in Donne's "Nocturnall," death is treated in a mathematical figure:

> Their huge arithmetic is but the endless
> Repetition of zero — the unlimited
> Eternal.

"Eurydice" is based on the paradox of the rejuvenating power of death, for "the great rays of the heart/Are ripened to wisdom by death." Various other forms of wit, including antithesis and word-play, help mold Edith Sitwell's characteristic poetic line. Her mastery of another metaphysical effect, the witty grotesque, is seen in such grisly reminders as "And my love, that white lady, is but a thin white bone," and "The worm's a pallid thing to kiss." [14]

Seeing both her own troubled times and an expanding universe in a metaphysical perspective was particularly rewarding for Edith Sitwell. She was able to write about the desolation of modern life and the devastation of modern war with a penetrating sensitivity and a mature complexity, but yet with a broadening vision of a universe in which divine love holds all things together in a natural kinship.

WILLIAM EMPSON

William Empson, just turned twenty in the middle 1920's, made a sudden impact on Cambridge society much like that Donne made on Elizabethan England. Like Donne, he began writing primarily for a small intellectual group and allowed his poems to be passed around, copied, quoted, and discussed long before they were published. Working out and debating their obscurities became a favorite game at Cambridge teas. Empson was admired for his wit, condemned for his daring, and finally accepted as a brilliant smart-alec.

Empson's poetry resembles Donne's also in its intellectualism, particularly its concern with philosophy and science, and its union of obscurity with a strong "masculine" line. Both the new physics of Planck and Einstein and the crossword puzzle became very popular in educated circles during the 1920's, and Empson captured the appeal of both in his poetry. The traditional emphasis on science and mathematics at Cambridge and Richards' and Leavis's sharp reaction against the irresponsible subjective interpretation and the stock response led Empson to a very self-conscious awareness of the need for a complex intellectual structure to shape and direct the poem's emotional force. Both Donne and Empson apparently sought to challenge their readers to the intellectual concentration necessary to break through the puzzle barrier in their poetry. Though Empson is more consistently cerebral than Donne, the pleasure in reading Empson is very much like that in reading Donne. There is a triumph in mastering the intellectual structure and then a sudden liberation of emotion and an appreciation of the hard packed lines.

If Donne perplexed the fair sex, Empson would certainly do so too. Yet, like Donne, through his careful reasoning he could reveal conscientiously defined feelings and his own distinctive tenderness. "Letter V," addressed to a lady, is about his way of knowing her and her effect on him despite the fact that he feels he does not really know her essential inner self. The poem defines and explores his attitude toward the lady through some rather complex mathematical and philosophical reasoning. His way of knowing her is compared to defining a surface by tangents rather than by lines, by "Paths of light not atoms of good form." However, paradoxically,

> Such tangent praise, less crashing,
>   not less warm.
> May gain more intimacy for less hope.

The same idea is qualified through other figures:

> Wide-gasping glass in which to gaze alone
> Your curve bars even fancy at the gates;
> You are the map only of the divine states
> You, made, nor known, nor knowing in,
>   make known.

She is like a wide-reflecting mirror that, while revealing nothing of itself, reflects his image in an incredible non-Euclidean scene. There seems to be a clear pun on the "states" (geographical and psychological) which she as map discloses, although paradoxically she is not really known in them and knows nothing about them. She is described in philosophical terms and then the poem is resolved through the original geometrical figure:

> Yet if I love you but as Cause unknown
> Cause has at least the Form that has been shown,
> Of love what you imply but to exclude
> That vacuum has your edge, your attitude.

> Duality too has its Principal.
> These lines you grant me may invert to points;
> Or paired, poor grazing misses, at your joints,
> Cross you on painless arrows to the wall.

Never really known as herself, she is a vacuum that is nevertheless clearly defined. The last stanza is loaded with very condensed and somewhat casuistical implications. The principle of duality in mathematics states that every proposition of a certain kind about points has a corresponding one about lines, and this implies that the lady could after all be known in other, apparently more satisfactory ways. Perhaps the poem itself helps in this since the "lines" are also its lines. But the poem is more concerned with another "principle" (principle, cause, and chief) of duality, that in sexual relations. This principle, like the mathematical one, may be made to work. There is a playful tenderness as the original figure takes a paradoxical turn at the conclusion. Just as tangents can define a surface and arrows confine one while missing their mark, the poet can still know and hold his lady while remaining quite separate from her.[15]

Though more condensed and more dependent on ambiguity than most of Donne's work, "Letter V" is nevertheless like Donne's poems in its use of geometrical imagery and learned reasoning as well as a light playfulness to express fundamentally serious feelings. As the separated lovers are yet united in Donne's familiar compass conceit, Empson's lady — so unknowable and perplexingly separate — is at last known and caught through the logic of his geometry. The poem also fits into the later metaphysical tradition in suggesting the two touching spheres in Browning's "Beatrice Signorini" and the compass figure treating the epistemology of love in Hopkins' *Floris in Italy*.

Empson wrote directly about philosophical problems more often than Donne. Like Donne, however, he treated these through metaphysical techniques. His poems frequently center upon the universe of the new physics and the new ethics, the isolation of the individual, and man's paradoxical position in the universe. Though these are of course modern themes, they are reminiscent of Donne's anxiety in "The First Anniversary" about the new science, the loss of coherence and a unifying balm, and the degeneration of man. "Plenum and Vacuum" indicates that objects are now so empty and meaningless that a system of things nothing in themselves is all that is left. This is stated metaphysically — and characteristically for Empson — through comparisons of Darwin's scorpions under a glass, the outdated "void-centred" eye muscles, the space outside our space-time, and "the glass firmament's airholes" (the universe as a bubble in glass). "Earth Has Shrunk in

the Wash" foresees the dangers of scientific discovery. The man
with all the answers may

> Dowser be of his candle as of springs,
> And pump the valley with the tunnel dry.

Partly because of these dangers and partly because of the isolation
of modern civilization ("They pass too fast. Ships . . ."), the
earth has "shrunk" to an asteroid, without gravity or atmosphere,
where men starve on plants with the mirror images of ours. "Letter I," in a similar vein, compares persons with nothing in common
to stars with no "dark spaces" that "carry glances" between them.
This is "Too non-Euclidean predicament." There are some similar
ideas in "Letter II" and "To An Old Lady," while "Your Teeth
Are Ivory Towers" treats the peculiar isolation of poets.

Searching paradoxes disclose man's place — or lack of place — in
the universe and modern civilization. "Arachne" presents the
human predicament. Man, who for Donne was "a little world
made cunningly/of Elements, and an Angelike spright," is seen
by Empson to partake of all and yet to have to stand between all
and avoid all:

> Twixt devil and deep sea, man hacks his caves;
> Birth, death; one, many; what is true, and seems;
> Earth's vast hot iron, cold space's empty waves:

He is "King spider," walking on a "gleaming bubble between void
and void," who "Must bird and fish, must god and beast avoid."
In "Legal Fiction," "Law makes long spokes of the short stakes
of men" as the "well fenced out real estate of mind" extends to
"land in Heaven and Hell," to the earth's center and "all stars as
well." The approach is wittier, but the problems just as serious
in "High Dive." Modern man contemplating the universe, like a
high diver observing the pool, must either jump into action or
surrender to fear and neurosis. As "Doctrinal Point" asserts in a
different context,

> The duality of choice becomes the singularity
> of existence;
> The effort of virtue the unconsciousness of
> foreknowledge.

Pondering on these problems was bound to lead Empson sooner or later to face the problem of religion in this modern "asteroid" world. He did this somewhat tentatively in "To An Old Lady," but very squarely in "This Last Pain." In this world of paradox, he finds that religion presents us with a double paradox. Man has conceptions of divine states that he cannot attain; these conceptions are supported by fictions, yet these very conceptions support the values that seem truest and most meaningful. This is stated in a metaphysical conceit that probably owes something to Eliot's magic-lantern figure in "Prufrock":

> All those large dreams by which men long
> > live well
> Are magic-lanterned on the smoke of hell;
> > This then is real, I have implied,
> > A painted, small, transparent slide.
>
> These the inventive can hand-paint at leisure,
> Or most emporia would stock or measure;
> > And feasting in their dappled shade
> > We should forget how they were made.

To read Empson's poetry is to conclude that he has one of the most analogizing minds of the century. With apparent ease, he seems always to perceive a world welded together by scores of resemblances that would never occur to the ordinary man. Some of these are deeply revealing, some obviously forced, and others trivial though evidently spontaneous. In general, Empson's figures depend less than Donne's upon systems of thought and more upon odd bits of information. Figures such as those in "Letter V," "Earth Has Shrunk in the Wash," and "This Last Pain," though highly ingenious, also yield fresh feelings and new insights. In some similar conceits the inbreeding, self-conscious mind in "Dissatisfaction with Metaphysics" is compared to incest, opposing mirrors with an infinite number of reflections, and a dotted line ("and so on") as contrasted with "safe straight lines." Then in "Arachne" human society is considered in terms of the molecular action in a bubble. Empson's analogical virtuosity is best exemplified in his three-page "Bacchus," in which the myth of Bacchus, the distillation of liquor, and human history are compared simultaneously. In "Description of a View," where there is a comparison only of the physical with the physical, resemblances may be enjoyed just for their own sake. An unfinished white building with a rusting crane suspended over it suggests a biological specimen, Milton's bridge to hell, the beam of justice, a zeppelin over a river, light brown hair on white flesh, and dry grass on chalk downs.

Empson's poetry abounds with puns, paradoxes, antitheses, and other witty or humorous metaphysical devices used in a highly serious context. The poetry illustrates his persistent interest in ambiguities as well as his prose writings. In the first two stanzas of "Bacchus," for instance, there are puns on "cymbal," "retort," "whirled," "coping," "groyned," "miner," "equitation," "bar," "helled," "boxed the compassing," "ether," "wheal," and probably some other words. While this kind of punning is in the spirit of poems like Donne's "The Crosse," it far exceeds any similar paranomastic exhibitions in seventeenth-century poetry. Measured by his own standards, most of Empson's puns fall within his first four types of ambiguity and do not show contradiction or a division in the author's mind. Allusions also sometimes give poems a humorous twist and an added dimension. In "This Last Pain," after careless self-deceit is boldly compared to the mock-regal crown of thorns, the thorns are thought of as "woven into knots" for a fire and the old adage about a watched pot's not boiling is introduced. In "Earth Has Shrunk" Douglas Fairbanks, jumping from motor to express, is intended to suggest the lack of cohesion in a fast-moving machine age, while in "Reflection from Anita Loos" a line from *Gentlemen Prefer Blondes* becomes a refrain. In general, Empson has depended less than most of his metaphysical contemporaries upon the modern stock response to irony and has gained the multi-dimensional effects in his poetry more through genuine wit and a kind of humor.

With apparent ease and delight, Empson has resembled Donne in utilizing a vast erudition, cogent logic, and a lively intellectual play in treating significant personal experience and the most vital philosophical problems of his age. However, his poetry seems more self-consciously intellectual, less patently emotional, than Donne's. Empson gives the impression of being torn between being himself and being a showoff — but perhaps he is most himself when he is something of a showoff. So sometimes was Donne.

Retrospective

THROUGHOUT the history of the metaphysical revival — the history of a style — the metaphysical style has continued both to maintain its identity and integrity and to stimulate fresh critical interpretation and vital poetic experimentation. As the stylistic embodiment of an idea or attitude, the metaphysical style has sought a hard-won integration from the disturbing complexity and diversity in the universe and in the individual. This quest for integration has given function and meaning to the correspondences, conceits, ambiguity, and thought-feeling relationships that have helped express it. The metaphysical revival, beginning as part of an antiquarian dusting off of older writers, has thrived on new interpretations growing often from a new view of persistent problems.

These new interpretations have tended to focus on problems of the nature and role of analogy and personal expression in metaphysical poetry. The average seventeenth-century reader would have taken it for granted that the poet treated a world knit together by correspondences and analogies. Although the average nineteenth-century reader found many of the metaphysicals' commonplace assumptions quaint and fantastic, the philosophical and religious idealism of the earlier nineteenth century was nevertheless congenial and conducive to a revival of metaphysical work. The nineteenth and twentieth centuries, like the seventeenth, apparently seized upon the analogies of metaphysical poetry as an instrument for patching and reinforcing an ordered system that was called in doubt. Browning and the Catholic group illustrate this tendency. Hopkins and Eliot went the furthest in repossessing a sacramental outlook uniting God, man, nature, and history. Edith Sitwell exhibited very much a seventeenth-century approach to correspondences, Yeats plundered esoteric thought in constructing his own unifying myth, while Empson — perhaps despairing of contriving any real unity — ranged the most widely and came up with the most analogies, if not always the most meaningful ones.

Poets and critics also tended to seek in metaphysical poetry a psychological, as well as a cosmological, integration and inclusiveness. Earlier nineteenth-century critics usually exaggerated the personal frankness and spontaneous feeling in metaphysical poetry while feeling that conceits and other intellectual devices ruined these. Metaphysical techniques were gradually understood only as there was a loss of faith in the imaginative and a growing reliance on the intellectual. Browning was one of the first to appreciate Donne's intellectual subtlety in the treatment of experience. Emily Dickinson achieved some of her most personal poetry by bare analysis. In the twentieth century, sincere and valuable personal expression became associated with the complexity and probing self-analysis that produced a "unification of sensibility" or a "poetry of inclusion." Metaphysical poetry was defined and evaluated chiefly in terms of its expression of thought-feeling relationships, psychological impulses, and ambiguities. Eliot and the Fugitives, like Donne, were admired for their anatomy of sensibility and for a fidelity to the complexity of experience. Stevens combined convincing personal insight with epistemological analysis, and Empson nurtured his own ambiguities in the apparent conviction that they helped express the whole truth of an experience. But if moderns have too much appreciated Donne "the human corkscrew" (as one recent critic put it), they have frequently felt that an understanding of his intellectual gyrations could liberate a wine of sincere lyricism.

The metaphysical revival has apparently sprung from a broad philosophical outlook and need rather than from specific events and influences, though certainly the Catholic revival, the First and Second World Wars, and the "waste land" era have helped to shape and color it. Both seventeenth-century and modern readers have had to deal with a world breaking loose from its old religious and philosophical moorings. Nineteenth and twentieth century readers found guidance in the seventeenth-century metaphysical poets' use of analogies to link the fragments of the universe together into a meaningful whole, and they found solace in what they regarded as the soul-baring expression of complex experience similar to their own. The metaphysical poets sometimes appeared as the champions of older religious values, particularly during the Catholic revival and after the Second World War. But Donne also seemed the champion of social rebels. Gosse, Stephen, and Symons evidently identified themselves with a Donne of their own creation in part of a complex revolt against strict Victorianism. Later of course Donne towered as a tortured, skeptical modern born three centuries too soon. Metaphysical poetry has thrived on a search for cosmological and psychological integration. Though there has been some reaction against it, as the embodiment of this quest it will live until the search is ended or the goal is appreciably changed.

NOTES AND INDEX

Notes

INTRODUCTION

[1] Merritt Y. Hughes, "Kidnapping Donne," *University of California Publications in English*, IV (1934), 61; Douglas Bush, *English Literature in the Earlier Seventeenth Century* (London, 1945), p. 135; Mario Praz, "The Critical Importance of the Revived Interest in Seventeenth-Century Metaphysical Poetry," *English Studies Today*, ed. C. L. Wrenn and G. Bullough (London, 1951), pp. 165–66.

I. EARLY CONCEPTIONS OF METAPHYSICAL POETRY

[1] *The Autobiography of Edward, Lord Herbert of Cherbury*, ed. Sidney Lee (London, 1906), p. 35.

[2] David Masson, *Drummond of Hawthornden* (London, 1873), p. 357.

[3] *Ben Jonson*, ed. C. H. Herford and Percy Simpson (8 vols., Oxford, 1925–47), I, 138, 144.

[4] *The Poems of John Donne*, ed. Sir Herbert Grierson (2 vols., London, 1912), I, 378–80.

[5] *The Poems of Edward, Lord Herbert of Cherbury*, ed. G. C. Moore Smith (Oxford, 1923), pp. 57–59.

[6] John Sampson, "A Contemporary Light Upon John Donne," *Essays and Studies by Members of the English Association*, VII (1921), 82–91.

[7] *Wilson's Arte of Rhetorique*, ed. G. H. Mair (Oxford, 1909), p. 113.

[8] *The Rhetoric of Aristotle*, trans. J. E. C. Welldon (London, 1886), iii. 11. 264.

[9] Ronsard, *Oeuvres Complètes*, ed. Prosper Blanchemain (8 vols., Paris, 1857–67), III, 26–27; Du Bellay, *Oeuvres Françaises*, ed. C. Marty-Laveaux (2 vols., Paris, 1866–67), I, 54–55.

[10] Fraunce, *The Arcadian Rhetorike* (London, 1588), Bk. I, ch. i.; Cowley, *Poems*, ed. A. R. Waller (Cambridge, 1905), p. 214.

[11] Hoskins, *Directions for Speech and Style*, ed. Hoyt H. Hudson (Princeton, 1935), p. 39.

[12] *The Scholars Guide from the Accidence to the University* (London, 1665), pp. 110–11; *A Briefe of the Art of Rhetorique*, quoted from W. L. Ustick and H. H. Hudson, "Wit, 'Mixed Wit' and the Bee in Amber," *The Huntington Library Bulletin*, VIII (Oct. 1935), 110; Fuller, *The History of the Worthies of England*, ed. P. A. Nuttall (3 vols., London, 1840), II, 240.

[13] Peacham, *The Garden of Eloquence* (London, 1577), pp. Bii–Ci.

[14] *The Poems of Richard Crashaw*, ed. L. C. Martin (Oxford, 1927), p. 242. See Joseph Anthony Mazzeo, "A Critique of Some Modern Theories

The Revival of Metaphysical Poetry

of Metaphysical Poetry," *Modern Philology*, L (Nov. 1952), 88–96, and "Metaphysical Poetry and the Poetic of Correspondence," *Journal of the History of Ideas*, XII (April 1953), 221–33. For a discussion of the distinction between a poetry of correspondence and an ornamental baroque style, see F. J. Warnke, "Marino and the English Metaphysicals," *Studies in the Renaissance*, II (1955), 160–75.

[15] See Malcolm Mackenzie Ross, *Poetry and Dogma* (New Brunswick, 1954).

[16] Aristotle, *Rhetoric* iii. 9–11. 255–66.

[17] Cicero, *On Oratory and Orators*, trans. and ed. J. S. Watson (London, 1896), ii. 54–63. 283–96; Quintilian, *Institutes of Oratory*, trans. and ed. J. S. Watson (London, 1892), vi. 3. 6–7. 431–33; Charles Sears Baldwin, *Ancient Rhetoric and Poetic* (New York, 1924), pp. 87–100, and *Medieval Rhetoric and Poetic* (New York, 1928), pp. 75–98.

[18] Castiglione, *The Book of the Courtier*, trans. Thomas Hoby ("Everyman's Library," London, 1948), pp. 148–68.

[19] *The Works of Gabriel Harvey*, ed. A. B. Grosart (3 vols., London, 1884), III, 33.

[20] Cornwallis, *Essayes*, ed. D. C. Allen (Baltimore, 1946), pp. 70, 155, and "Introduction."

[21] T. W. (Thomas Walkington), *The Optick Glasse of Humors* (London, 1663; 1st. ed. 1607), pp. 81–82, 94–95.

[22] Hoskins, pp. 15–16.

[23] Quoted from Ustick and Hudson, p. 116.

[24] Puttenham, *The Arte of English Poesie*, ed. Joseph Haslewood (London, 1811), p. 39; Felltham, *Resolves* (London, 1670), p. 107; *Elizabethan Critical Essays*, ed. G. Gregory Smith (3 vols., Oxford, 1904), II, 366.

[25] Izaak Walton, *Lives* (London, 1927), p. 314; *Critical Essays of the Seventeenth Century*, ed. J. E. Spingarn (3 vols., Oxford, 1908), II, 81, 85.

[26] Puttenham, pp. 123–24; *Ben Jonson*, VIII, 625; *Elizabethan Critical Essays*, I, 335; Arnauld, *Logique*, III, 9, quoted from Morris W. Croll in *Schelling Anniversary Papers* (New York, 1923), p. 95.

[27] Eliot, *Selected Essays* (New York, 1950), p. 246.

[28] Donne, *Letters to Severall Persons of Honour*, ed. Charles Merrill, Jr. (New York, 1910), pp. 141, 95, 61; see Burton, *The Anatomy of Melancholy* (3 vols., "Everyman's Library," London, 1948), pp. 374–76.

[29] Burton, I, 160–62; George Sidney Brett, *A History of Psychology* (2 vols., New York, 1921) II, 74; *Elizabethan Critical Essays*, I, 249; Puttenham, p. 36.

[30] Donne, *Letters*, pp. 47–48, 233; Donne, *Poems*, I, 393, 381; *Minor Poets of the Caroline Period*, ed. George Saintsbury (3 vols., London, 1905–21), I, 328, *The Complete Works in Verse and Prose of George Herbert*, ed. Grosart (London, 1874), II, cix–x.

[31] Quintilian *Institutes* vi. 3. 1. 430; Cicero, *On Oratory* ii. 58–67. 289–302; *The Apologye of Syr Thomas More, Knyght*, ed. Arthur Irving Taft (London, 1930), p. 194; Blount, *De Re Poetica* (London, 1694), p. 155.

[32] More, pp. xxv–lvi; Willard Farnham, "The Medieval Comic Spirit in the English Renaissance," *John Quincy Adams Memorial Studies*, ed. J. G. McManaway *et al.* (Washington, D.C., 1948), pp. 430–31; Erasmus, *The Praise of Folly*, trans. John Wilson and ed. Mrs. P. S. Allen (Oxford, 1925), p. 177.

[33] Castiglione, pp. 45–49.

[34] W. Fraser Mitchell, *English Pulpit Oratory from Andrewes to Tillotson* (New York, 1932), pp. 150–53.

[35] Henri Brémond, *Histoire littéraire du sentiment religieux en France* (11 vols., Paris, 1916), I, 308–16; Tesauro, *Il Cannochiale Aristotelico* (Rome, 1664), pp. 586–87, 315.

[36] Cicero, *On Oratory* ii. 56. 287; Quintilian, *Institutes* vi. 3. 46–54. 440–42; More, p. 194; *The English Works of Sir Thomas More*, ed. W. E. Campbell *et al.* (2 vols., New York, 1927–31), II, 2–3.

[37] Mitchell, p. 352; T. W., "To the Reader."

[38] Donne, *Letters*, pp. 95–96; *Poems*, I, 325, 345.

[39] *Poems*, I, 145. See also *Letters*, pp. 89, 156, 170, 197, 206.

[40] *The Works of George Herbert*, ed. F. E. Hutchinson (Oxford, 1941), pp. 102, 54, 233–35.

II. SEEDS OF THE REVIVAL

[1] See G. C. Moore Smith, "Wordsworth and George Herbert," *Notes and Queries*, Twelfth Series, XII (Jan. 13, 1923), 30; Hallam Tennyson, *Alfred Lord Tennyson, A Memoir by His Son* (New York, 1897), II, 335, 500–1; William Davies, "The Laureate and George Herbert," *The Athenaeum*, Aug. 26, 1893, p. 288.

[2] Hunt, *The Town* (London, 1858), p. 14; Macdonald, *England's Antiphon* (London, 1868), p. 192.

[3] Coleridge, *Notes, Theological, Political, and Miscellaneous*, ed. Derwent Coleridge (London, 1853), pp. 251–53; *The Complete Works of Samuel Taylor Coleridge*, ed. W. G. T. Shedd (7 vols., New York, 1844), IV, 286–87; *Notes*, pp. 253–55.

[4] *Notes*, pp. 258, 261, 289.

[5] John Livingston Lowes, *The Road to Xanadu* (Boston, 1930), p. 25; *Works*, IV, 286.

[6] *Notes*, p. 388; *Works*, IV, 392; *Biographia Literaria*, ed. J. Shawcross (2 vols., Oxford, 1907), II, 73; *The Table Talk and Omniana of Samuel Taylor Coleridge*, ed. T. Ashe (London, 1909), pp. 321–22.

[7] Richards, *Coleridge on Imagination* (New York, 1935), p. 232.

[8] *Biographia Literaria*, II, 12.

[9] Richards, *Principles of Literary Criticism* (New York, 1928), pp. 249–50.

[10] Brooks, *Modern Poetry and the Tradition* (Chapel Hill, 1939), p. 42.

[11] *The Complete Works of William Hazlitt*, ed. P. P. Howe (21 vols., London, 1930–34), XII, 36; XVII, 122–25; Charles Lamb, *Mrs. Leicester's School and Other Writings in Prose and Verse*, ed. Alfred Unger (New York, 1886), p. 358; *The Works of Charles and Mary Lamb*, ed. E. V. Lucas (7 vols., New York, 1903–5), VI, 82–83.

[12] *The Works of Charles and Mary Lamb*, V, 50, 23.

[13] *The Collected Writings of Thomas De Quincey*, ed. David Masson (14 vols., Edinburgh, 1889–90), X, 99–100.

[14] Hazlitt, *Works*, VI, 49–57.

[15] *The Complete Works of Walter Savage Landor*, ed. T. Earle Welby (16 vols., London, 1927–36), IV, 158–71.

[16] *The Works of the English Poets*, ed. Chalmers (21 vols., London, 1810), V, 123; Campbell, pp. 83–84; Hallam, *Introduction to the Literature of Europe* (14 vols., London, 1839), III, 493.

[17] "John Donne," *The Retrospective Review*, VIII (1823), 35; Jameson, *Memoirs of the Loves of the Poets* (Boston, 1885), p. 328; Gilfillan, *Speci-*

mens with Memoirs of the Less Known British Poets (3 vols., Edinburgh, 1860), I, 202–3.

[18] *The English Nation*, ed. Cunningham (5 vols., Edinburgh, 1863–68), II, 458; Hunt, *Men, Women, and Books* (London, 1876), p. 227; Craik, *Sketches of the History of Literature and Learning in England*, Second Series (6 vols. in 2, London, 1845), III, 168–69.

[19] *The Retrospective Review*, VIII (1823), 32.

[20] Hartley Coleridge, *Lives of the Northern Worthies*, ed. Derwent Coleridge (3 vols., London, 1852), I, 97.

[21] Hazlitt, *Works*, VI, 23–24; "Herbert's Poems," *The Retrospective Review*, III (1821), 221; Coleridge, *Works*, IV, 151–56; Hunt, *Wit and Humour* (London, 1846), pp. 9, 52; *The Retrospective Review*, VIII (1823), 39; Craik, IV, 119; Macdonald, pp. 119, 176; Brown, *Lectures on the Atomic Theory and Essays Scientific and Literary* (2 vols., Edinburgh, 1858), II, 122.

[22] *The Retrospective Review*, VIII (1823), 32.

[23] *The Florence Miscellany* (Florence, 1785), pp. 46, 132–33, 143.

[24] Herbert, *Works*, p. 206, and *Keble's Lectures on Poetry, 1832–41*, trans. Edward Kershaw (2 vols., Oxford, 1912), II, 99.

[25] "George Herbert," *The Penny Cyclopaedia of the Society for the Diffusion of Useful Knowledge* (27 vols., London, 1833–43), XII, 147; *Keble's Lectures on Poetry*, II, 99; "George Herbert and His Times," *The Christian Remembrancer*, n.s. XLIV (July 1862), 131.

[26] Keble, "Sixth Sunday After Trinity," *The Christian Year* (London, 1927), p. 136; Herbert, "The Flower," *Works*, p. 167.

[27] *The Works of Thomas Lovell Beddoes*, ed. H. W. Donner (London, 1935), p. 642; Donner, *Thomas Lovell Beddoes: The Making of a Poet* (Oxford, 1935), pp. 192, 229.

[28] *Works*, pp. 533–34.

[29] *The Complete Poetical Works of Thomas Hood*, ed. Walter Jerrold (London, 1906), p. 63.

[30] *Works*, pp. 434, 176, 372, 187.

III. JOHN DONNE AND ROBERT BROWNING

[1] *The Complete Poems of John Donne D.D.*, ed. Grosart (2 vols., London, 1872), II, xlv; Gosse, *The Life and Letters of John Donne* (2 vols., New York, 1899), II, 353; Gwynn, *The Masters of English Literature* (New York, 1904), p. 400.

[2] Schelling, *Two Essays on Robert Browning* (Philadelphia, 1890), pp. 17–18; Brooke, *The Poetry of Robert Browning* (New York, 1902), p. 47; Herford, *Robert Browning* (New York, 1905), p. 8; Griffin and Minchin, *The Life of Robert Browning* (3rd ed., London, 1938), p. 47.

[3] Orr, *Life and Letters of Robert Browning* (Boston, 1908), p. 8; *Robert Browning and Julia Wedgwood, A Broken Friendship as Revealed by Their Letters*, ed. Richard Curle (New York, 1937), p. 86.

[4] *The Letters of Robert Browning and Elizabeth Barrett Barrett, 1845–1846* (2 vols., New York, 1899), I, 27, 195, 417, 437, 145; II, 115.

[5] *Letters of Robert Browning, Collected by Thomas J. Wise*, ed. Thurman L. Hood (New Haven, 1933), p. 205; *Rossetti Papers, 1862–1870*, compiled by William Michael Rossetti (New York, 1905), p. 378; Colvin, *Memoirs and Notes of Persons and Places, 1852–1912* (London, 1905), p. 82.

[6] *The Works of Robert Browning*, ed. F. G. Kenyon (10 vols., Boston, 1912), IX, 147; Donne, *Poems*, I, 308; *The Complete Poetical Works of Robert*

Browning, ed. Augustine Birrell (rev. ed., New York, 1924), p. 1339. All subsequent references to Browning's poetry will be to the Kenyon edition.

[7] "To Sir Henry Goodyere," *Poems*, I, 183.

[8] "Browning's Essay on Shelley," *The Browning Society's Papers* (London, 1881–84), vol. I, pt. I, p. 18; *Works*, I, 80, 153, 340; VII, 98.

[9] See C. N. Wenger, *The Aesthetics of Robert Browning* (Ann Arbor, 1924), esp. pp. 36–37, 42–54, 90–94, 125, 166–67, 251.

[10] Donne, *Poems*, I, 111, 204–5; Browning, *Works*, IX, 22, 97, 111–12.

[11] Browning, "Childe Roland to the Dark Tower Came," st. 45, *Works*, III, 406, and Donne, "A Valediction: Forbidding Mourning," *Poems*, I, 49.

[12] Browning, *Works*, V, 145; IV, 203; Donne, *Poems*, I, 51.

[13] "Fifine at the Fair," st. 86, *Works*, VIII, 236.

[14] "La Saisaiz," ll. 525–26, *Works*, IX, 147.

[15] "The Family," "Charles Avison," *Works*, X, 84, 239.

[16] "Beatrice Signorini," *Works*, X, 328.

[17] *Works*, X, 183; IV, 162–63.

[18] *Works*, I, 163. Donne's "To Sir Edward Herbert, at Iulyers" says, "Man is a lumpe where all beasts kneaded bee," and his verse letter to the Countess of Bedford ("T'have written then") explains that "first seeds of every creature are in us."

[19] Donne, *Poems*, I, 273; Browning, "Fifine at the Fair," st. 129, *Works*, VII, 272; *Works*, IX, 139; VIII, 222. See Donne, "To the Countesse of Huntington" ("That unripe side of earth"), a poem sometimes attributed to Donne, in which the countess is praised as a straight line (*Poems*, I, 420).

[20] *Works*, VII, 97, 104, 113.

[21] Donne, *Letters*, p. 54.

[22] *Works*, VII, 368; IV, 305; VI, 198; VII, 333–34; V, 3–4; VIII, 220.

[23] *Works*, VII, 197, 202.

[24] *Works*, III, 378; Donne, *Poems*, I, 252.

[25] "Elegie VI," l. 11; *Poems*, I, 88; "The Flight of the Duchess," and "Fifine at the Fair," *Works*, III, 358; VII, 164. In "The Statue and the Bust" the duke is described as riding past "empty and fine like a swordless sheath" (III, 393, l. 15) and "Sordello" explained that "the singer's proper life was 'neath/The life his song exhibits, this a sheath/To that" (I, 250). See also *Works*, V, 103–4; VII, 249; IX, 50; IX, 124.

[26] "The Ring and the Book," Bk. IX, *Works*, VI, 223; *Works*, IX, xii.

[27] *Works*, VI, 230; VII, 287, 297.

IV. THE BEGINNINGS OF THE REVIVAL IN AMERICA

[1] *The Complete Works of Edgar Allan Poe*, ed. James A. Harrison (17 vols., New York, 1902), XII, 140; IX, 100–1; *Life of Henry Wadsworth Longfellow*, ed. Samuel Longfellow (3 vols., Boston, 1891), II, 40, 87; Eleanor M. Tilton, *Amiable Aristocrat* (New York, 1947), pp. 211, 367; Holmes, *The Poet at the Breakfast Table* (Boston, 1900), p. 110.

[2] *The Writings of James Russell Lowell* (10 vols., Cambridge, 1890–92), III, 35, 171; V, 108; II, 79, 160; III, 35; *Letters of James Russell Lowell*, ed. Charles Eliot Norton (2 vols., New York, 1894), II, 319, 385–86.

[3] *The Works of John Greenleaf Whittier* (7 vols., Boston, 1892), VI, 94; *Prose Writings of William Cullen Bryant*, ed. Parke Godwin (2 vols., New York, 1901), I, 153; Fuller, *Papers on Literature and Art* (2 vols., London, 1846), I, 21.

[4] Quoted from William Irving Bartlett, *Jones Very, Emerson's "Brave*

Saint" (Durham, 1942), pp. 132–33; *The Journals of Bronson Alcott*, ed. Odell Shepard (Boston, 1938), p. 214; Lowell, *Writings*, I, 381; *The Writings of Henry David Thoreau* (Boston, 1906), VII, 467.

[5] "Nature doth Have her Dawn Each Day," *Collected Poems of Henry David Thoreau*, ed. Carl Bode (Chicago, 1943), p. 70; pp. 109, 71.

[6] "I am a parcel of vain strivings tied," *Poems*, p. 81; p. 125.

[7] *Writings*, VII, 153; *Poems*, p. 182.

[8] George Willis Cooke, *Ralph Waldo Emerson: His Life, Writings, and Philosophy* (Boston, 1881), p. 236; Holmes, *Ralph Waldo Emerson* (Boston, 1885), pp. 169–70, 21.

[9] *Journals of Ralph Waldo Emerson*, ed. Edward Waldo Emerson and Waldo Emerson Forbes (9 vols., Boston, 1909), II, 253–54; III, 428; V, 254; *The Letters of Ralph Waldo Emerson*, ed. Ralph L. Rusk (6 vols., New York, 1939), VI, 52–53; I, xxxv, 264; *Parnassus*, ed. Emerson (Boston, 1875), pp. iv, vi.

[10] *The Complete Works of Ralph Waldo Emerson*, with introduction and notes by Edward Waldo Emerson (12 vols., Boston, 1903–4), X, II; IX, 43, 139; VI, 32–33; VIII, 15, 91.

[11] *Parnassus*, p. vii; *Journals*, IV, 254; *Works*, VIII, 98; II, 184; X, 462.

[12] *Works*, IX, 359, 510.

[13] *Works*, IX, 70, 350, 121, 192.

[14] "Manners," *Works*, IX, 227; "The Mower's Song," *Poems and Letters of Andrew Marvell*, ed. H. W. Margoliouth (2 vols., London, 1927), I, 45. These and other similarities between Emerson and Marvell are discussed in Norman A. Brittin's "Emerson and the Metaphysical Poets," *American Literature*, VIII (March 1936), 1–12.

[15] "The Poet," I, "Fragments on the Poet and the Poetic Gift," V, and "Life," *Works*, IX, 309–10, 327, 352.

[16] "Inscription for a Well," *Works*, IX, 376; IX, 137.

[17] George Frisbie Whicher, *This Was A Poet* (New York, 1939), p. 210. Mr. Jay Leyda kindly provided me with the probable source of Emily Dickinson's copy of "Mattens" and his dating of her letter to Colonel Higginson.

[18] Martha Dickinson Bianchi, *The Life and Letters of Emily Dickinson* (Boston, 1924), p. 244.

[19] *The Poems of Emily Dickinson*, ed. Thomas H. Johnson (3 vols., Cambridge, Mass., 1955), pp. 148, 792.

[20] *Poems*, pp. 428–29; Bianchi, pp. 24–25; Whicher, p. 48.

[21] *Poems*, pp. 790, 444.

[22] *Poems*, p. 668.

[23] "At half-past three a single bird," *Poems*, p. 1084.

[24] *Poems*, pp. 656, 89, 184, 71, 222–23, 614–15.

[25] *Poems*, pp. 501–2, 579, 353, 712, 495.

[26] *Poems*, pp. 1157, 1169, 699.

[27] Bianchi, p. 25.

[28] *Poems*, pp. 1134, 236–37, 191, 366.

[29] "To know just how he suffered would be dear," *Poems*, p. 479; *Poems*, p. 1169.

[30] "Unfulfilled to observation" and "Delight's despair at setting," *Poems*, pp. 703, 905.

[31] *Poems*, pp. 666, 654, 321, 470, 911, 1158, 710.

[32] "Further in summer than the birds" and "These are the days when birds come back," *Poems*, pp. 752, 92–93.

[33] *Poems*, pp. 273, 20, 1082, 901, 575.

[34] *Poems*, pp. 423, 1168, 144.

[35] "Extol thee – could I – then I will," *Poems*, p. 1125; pp. 183, 581.

[36] *Poems*, pp. 511, 504; "I'm ceded – I've stopped being theirs –," *Poems*, p. 390.

[37] *Poems*, pp. 771, 456, 838.

[38] *Poems*, pp. 682, 198, 655.

[39] *Poems*, pp. 238, 721, 908, 440, 858, 986, 519, 449, 208, 452, 168, 365, 406.

[40] *Poems*, pp. 1010, 170, 473, 74, 201, 238, 568, 429, 300.

[41] Whicher, pp. 175–80; Genevieve Taggart, *The Life and Mind of Emily Dickinson* (New York, 1930), p. 376; *Emily Dickinson's Letters to Dr. and Mrs. Josiah Gilbert Holland*, ed. Theodora Van Wagenen Ward (Cambridge, Mass., 1951), pp. 165, 175.

[42] "Consulting summer's clock," *Poems*, p. 1157.

[43] *Poems*, pp. 918, 174, 793, 758, 136, 307; Whicher, pp. 99–112.

[44] *Poems*, pp. 380, 317, 395–96, 409.

V. THE CATHOLIC REVIVAL AND THE METAPHYSICALS

[1] Hoxie N. Fairchild rejects the common view that the Catholic revival was the legacy of the romantic revival. See his *Religious Trends in English Poetry*, IV (New York, 1957), 3–17, 240–301; Newman, *Apologia pro Vita Sua*, ed. Charles Frederick Harrold (New York, 1947), p. 88; *Literary Criticisms by Francis Thompson*, ed. Terrence L. Connolly (New York, 1948), p. 546.

[2] Newman, p. 89, and *Further Letters of Gerard Manley Hopkins*, ed. Claude Colleer Abbott (London, 1938), p. 20.

[3] Newman, pp. 9, 16; unpublished manuscript, quoted in John Pick, *Gerard Manley Hopkins, Poet and Priest* (London, 1942), p. 49; *The Collected Works of Francis Thompson*, ed. Wilfrid Meynell (3 vols. in 1, Westminster, Md., 1947), III, 83, 25; II, 9; Everard Meynell, *The Life of Francis Thompson* (New York, 1913), p. 191.

[4] Thompson, *Works*, III, 3; *Post Liminium: Essays and Critical Papers by Lionel Johnson*, ed. Thomas Whittemore (New York, 1912), pp. 112–20.

[5] Alice Meynell, "Some Memories of Francis Thompson," *The Dublin Review*, CXLII (Jan. 1908), p. 172; Thompson, *Literary Criticisms*, p. 79; *The Poetical Works of Henry Alford* (London, 1845), p. 107.

[6] Eleanor Ruggles, *Gerard Manley Hopkins, A Life* (New York, 1944), p. 73, and *The Correspondence of Gerard Manley Hopkins and Richard Watson Dixon*, ed. Claude Colleer Abbott (London, 1935), pp. 23–24.

[7] *The Notebooks and Papers of Gerard Manley Hopkins*, ed. Humphry House (London, 1937), pp. 161, 79–80, 126; *The Letters of Gerard Manley Hopkins to Robert Bridges*, ed. Claude Colleer Abbott (London, 1938), pp. 82, 97, 169, 133, 225; *Further Letters of Gerard Manley Hopkins* (London, 1938), pp. 222, 239, and *The Correspondence of Gerard Manley Hopkins with Richard Watson Dixon*, p. 20.

[8] *Poems of Gerard Manley Hopkins*, ed. W. H. Gardner (3rd ed., London, 1948), pp. 65, 76.

[9] See Donne, I, 421, 243, and Hopkins, *Poems*, p. 99.

[10] *Poems*, p. 142.

[11] *Poems*, p. 56.

[12] *Poems*, pp. 107, 105, 37, 86, 109, 112; Herbert, pp. 130, 90, 41, 57.

[13] Donne, I, 238, and *Poems*, pp. 70, 72, 75, 110, 107.

[14] *Poems*, pp. 28, 38, 58; Herbert, "Affliction" (1), *Works*, p. 48.

[15] Crashaw, "A Hymne of the Nativity, sung by the Shepheards," p. 107; Donne, "Holy Sonnets" (XIV), 1, 328; Herbert, "Paradise," p. 133.

[16] *Poems*, pp. 52, 62–63.

[17] "St. Winefred's Well," Act II, and ("Margaret Clitheroe") *Poems*, pp. 155, 160–61.

[18] *The Correspondence of Gerard Manley Hopkins and Richard Watson Dixon*, pp. 26, 153.

[19] Thompson, *Literary Criticisms*, pp. 31, 182; "The Preacher Poet," *The Academy and Literature*, LXIV (Feb. 28, 1903), 198, and Tynan, "Francis Thompson," *The Fortnightly Review*, n.s. LXXXVII (Feb. 1, 1910), p. 354.

[20] Thompson, *Works*, III, 23, 175–77; *Literary Criticisms*, pp. 63, 68, 251, 149, 282; "Abraham Cowley," *The Academy*, LXIX (Oct. 7, 1905), 1027; "Andrew Marvell," *The Academy*, LXIX (Sept. 23, 1905), 976–77.

[21] Thompson, *Works*, I, 125–26; II, 21, 26.

[22] *Works*, I, 206; II, 4.

[23] *Works*, II, 57, 58.

[24] "All Flesh," *Works*, II, 225.

[25] *Works*, II, 215, 13.

[26] "Sister Songs," Part the Second, *Works*, II, 58.

[27] *Works*, I, 19; II, 226, 14.

[28] "The Hound of Heaven" and "A Judgment in Heaven," *Works*, I, III, 190.

[29] "Any Saint," *Works*, II, 47–48; Herbert, "Affliction" (IV), *Works*, p. 90.

[30] Thompson, "The Hound of Heaven," *Works*, I, 111.

[31] *Works*, I, 111, 206; II, 105.

[32] *Works*, I, 4; II, 61.

[33] Everard Meynell, p. 13.

[34] *Ibid.*, pp. 212, 163.

[35] *Literary Criticisms*, p. 65; "A Dead Astronomer," *Works*, I, 215; Everard Meynell, p. 126.

[36] Alice Meynell, *The Dublin Review*, CXLII, 167, 163; Thompson, "To the Dead Cardinal of Westminster," *Works*, I, 133.

[37] *Works*, II, 117.

[38] *Works*, I, 169; II, 132–34.

[39] Viola Meynell, *Alice Meynell, A Memoir* (New York, 1929), pp. 207–8; *A Seventeenth Century Anthology*, with an introduction by Alice Meynell (Boston, 1904), p. iv.

[40] "'Fair and Flagrant Things,'" *The Pall Mall Gazette*, April 14, 1897, p. 6; *A Seventeenth Century Anthology*, p. vi, and Anne Kimball Tuell, *Mrs. Meynell and Her Literary Generation* (New York, 1925), pp. 206, 208, 22.

[41] "Henry Vaughan," *The Pall Mall Gazette*, Sept. 8, 1897, p. 3; *The Pall Mall Gazette*, April 14, 1897, p. 6, and Tuell, p. 243.

[42] *The Flower of the Mind* (London, 1897), p. 334; "Abraham Cowley," *The Pall Mall Gazette*, April 28, 1897, p. 3, and "Andrew Marvell," *The Pall Mall Gazette*, July 14, 1897, p. 3.

[43] *The Poems of Alice Meynell* (London, 1941), p. 152.

[44] Viola Meynell, p. 320.

VI. THE METAPHYSICAL REVIVAL, 1872–1912

[1] *The Complete Poems of John Donne D.D.*, I, x; "Intimate Glimpses from Browning's Letter File," ed. A. J. Armstrong, *The Baylor Bulletin*, XXXVII (Sept. 1934), 58, 61.

[2] See Wightman Fletcher Melton, *The Rhetoric of John Donne's Verse* (Baltimore, 1906), p. 206.

[3] See Thompson, *Literary Criticisms*, p. 149; John White Chadwick, "John Donne, Poet and Preacher," *The New World*, IX (March, 1900), 48; and Truman J. Backus, *Shaw's New History of English Literature* (rev. ed., New York, 1884), pp. 143–44.

[4] In a letter to the writer on January 31, 1951, Grierson wrote that it had occurred to him during the 1890's that Donne's poems needed textual study similar to that he had recently given Aristotle's Nicomachean Ethics while studying at Oxford. He recalled that criticisms of Donne by Edward Dowden and William Minto had stimulated his interest in the poet and that he had first read Donne with interest in E. K. Chambers' edition of 1896. He explained that he had been asked to write the article on Donne in *The Cambridge History of English Literature* because of his treatment of the poet in his *The First Half of the Seventeenth Century*, published in 1906. While occupied on these two studies, he said, he realized that both the canon and text of Donne's poems needed careful re-examination. He wrote that in his early work on Donne he had relied in some measure on Grosart, that he had later become interested in Craik's criticism, and that Gosse had given him some help when he undertook to edit Donne's poems. He added that he had known George Herbert's poetry well before reading a line of Donne's.

[5] Courthope, *A History of English Poetry* (6 vols., London, 1911), III, 167–68.

[6] Chambers, "The Poems of John Donne," *Modern Language Review*, IX (April 1914), 269; "The Poetry of John Donne," *The Spectator*, CX (Jan. 18, 1913), 102; Brooke, "John Donne the Elizabethan," *The Nation* (London), XII (Feb. 15, 1913), 826; "The Poems of John Donne," *Times Literary Supplement*, Jan. 30, 1913, p. 13.

[7] Minto, "John Donne," *The Nineteenth Century*, VII (May 1880), 848.

[8] Carpenter, *English Lyric Poetry*, 1500–1700 (London, 1897), pp. lvii–lviii.

[9] Gosse, *John Donne*, II, 330–34; Symons, "John Donne," *The Fortnightly Review*, n.s. LXVI (Nov. 1, 1899) 735–40; H. M. Sanders, "Dr. Donne," *Temple Bar*, CXXI (1900), 624; Grierson, "John Donne," *The Cambridge History of English Literature*, ed. A. W. Ward and A. R. Waller (15 vols., New York, 1910), IV, 226, 254; Donne, *Poems*, II, xi–xvii.

[10] More, "George Herbert," *Shelburne Essays*, Fourth Series, pp. 74–75; Melton, pp. 166, 206; Chadwick, p. 35; Moody and Lovett, *A History of English Literature* (rev. ed., New York, 1926), p. 165.

[11] Palgrave, *The Treasury of Sacred Song* (Oxford, 1889), p. 333; "John Donne and His Contemporaries," *The Quarterly Review*, CXCII (July 1900), 231; Gosse, *The Jacobean Poets*, pp. 47–48; Symons, p. 735.

[12] Stephen, "John Donne," *The National Review*, XLV (Dec. 1899), 595–96; Chadwick, p. 33; "Briefs on New Books," *The Dial*, XX (May 1, 1896), 280.

[13] Minto, p. 848; Sanders, *Temple Bar*, CXXI (1900), 615; Brooke, *The Nation*, XII, 825.

[14] *The Complete Poems of John Donne D.D.*, p. xlvii; Child, "A Group of Old Authors," *Modern Language Notes*, XV (Jan. 1900), 62; Stephen, pp. 595–96.

[15] *A Book of Elizabethan Lyrics*, ed. Schelling (Boston, 1895), pp. xxii, lxviii; Martin G. Brumbaugh, "A Study of the Poetry of John Donne," unpubl. diss. (University of Pennsylvania, 1893), p. 98.

[16] *The Complete Verse and Prose of Andrew Marvell*, ed. Grosart (4 vols.,

London, 1872–75) I, lxvi; *The English Works of George Herbert*, ed. George Herbert Palmer (3 vols., Boston, 1905), I, 163; "The Cloister Library," *The Independent*, LV[2] (May 21, 1903), 1211.

[17] *The Complete Works of Richard Crashaw*, ed. Grosart (2 vols., London, 1872–73), II, lxx; *The Complete Poems of John Donne D.D.*, II, xxxix; *The Complete Works in Verse and Prose of Abraham Cowley*, ed. Grosart (2 vols., Edinburgh, 1881), I, xcv–xcvii. During the nineteenth century the passage from Donne's "The Second Anniversary" about Elizabeth Drury's speaking soul and almost thinking body was quoted much more than any other lines from Donne, and it apparently came to be regarded as Donne's expression of a psychological and aesthetic theory. In the nineteenth century the concept of the union of thought and feeling throve in an intellectual climate particularly sympathetic to the seventeenth century. Thoreau, referring to Donne's words, "one might almost say, her body thought," affirmed: "I quite say it." Quoted from F. O. Matthiessen, *American Renaissance* (London, 1941), p. 98.

[18] Symons, p. 741. In an even closer anticipation of Eliot's theories Symons wrote that Baudelaire's poetry was "made out of his whole intellect and all his nerves." *The Symbolist Movement in Literature* (New York, 1919), p. 115; Eliot, *Essays*, pp. 249–50; Stephen, p. 601; Grierson, *The Cambridge History*, IV, 245.

[19] Lowell, *Writings*, III, 171; *A Book of Elizabethan Lyrics*, p. xxii; Edward Bliss Reed, *English Lyrical Poetry* (New Haven, 1912), p. 241; Everard Meynell, p. 298; Thompson, *Literary Criticisms*, pp. 555, 188.

[20] Brooke, *The Nation*, XII, 825.

[21] Brooke, "John Donne," *Poetry and Drama*, I (June 1913), 186.

[22] *Essays*, p. 247.

[23] Brooke, *Poetry and Drama*, I, 186–87, and Eliot, *Essays*, pp. 247, 262, 255, 248.

[24] Brooke, *Poetry and Drama*, 186; See Eliot, *Essays*, pp. 246–49.

[25] *The Complete Works in Verse and Prose of George Herbert*, II, lxvii, lxix, and *The Complete Works of Richard Crashaw*, II, lxiv, lxxvii; Minto, p. 856.

[26] Gosse, *John Donne*, II, 339–40; Carpenter, p. lx.

[27] *The Poems of John Donne*, ed. Chambers, with an introduction by Saintsbury (2 vols., London, 1896), I, xxxii; Symons, p. 742–44; Donne, *Poems*, II, xxxiv–xxxv; Brooke, *The Nation*, XII, 826, and *Poetry and Drama*, I, 187; Chadwick, p. 46.

[28] *The English Works of George Herbert*, I, 155; Wendell, *The Temper of the Seventeenth Century in English Literature* (New York, 1904), pp. 120–25.

[29] See Eliot, *Essays*, p. 250, and *The Quarterly Review*, CXCII (July 1900), 239–40.

[30] Mégroz, *Francis Thompson*, p. 113; Bliss, "Francis Thompson and Richard Crashaw," *The Month*, CXI (1908), 1–12; Alice Meynell, *The Dublin Review*, CXLII (1908), 172; Symons, *Dramatis Personae* (Indianapolis, 1923), p. 162.

[31] Stephen, p. 613.

[32] Brooke, *Poetry and Drama*, I, 188.

[33] Walter De La Mare, "An Elizabethan Poet and Modern Poetry," *The Edinburgh Review*, CCXVII (April 1913), 385, and *Rupert Brooke and the Intellectual Imagination* (London, 1919), p. 27.

³⁴ Gosse, *John Donne*, II, 339; *The Quarterly Review*, CXCII, 240; Chadwick, p. 36.

³⁵ Gosse, *John Donne*, II, 339; Grierson, *The Cambridge History*, IV, 249; Eliot, *Essays*, pp. 248-49, p. 255. For Eliot's comparison of the sensibility of Donne and Mallarmé see "Note sur Mallarmé et Poe," *La Nouvelle Revue Française*, XXVII (Nov. 1926), 524-26.

³⁶ Both metaphysical and symbolist poets believed in a system of underlying analogies and in the relationship between man as microcosm and the universe as macrocosm. Both Baudelaire and Thompson, for instance, were influenced by Swedenborg. However, metaphysical poetry is more closely related to symbolist theory than to symbolist practice, and even when the symbolists practiced what they preached, their techniques differed in several ways from those of the metaphysicals. The metaphysicals' approach to analogy was primarily intellectual and logical; that of the symbolists was primarily anti-intellectual and intuitive. The symbolists were chiefly interested in the secret affinities of all things with an individual soul, rather than in the relations of things to each other and to God. Nevertheless, some of the symbolists, particularly Corbière and Laforgue, employed metaphors, puns, neologisms, and other devices similar to those in metaphysical poetry.

³⁷ *The Collected Poems of Edmund Gosse* (London, 1911), p. 279.

³⁸ *Poems by Arthur Symons* (2 vols., New York, 1902), I, 148; II, 219-20, 55.

³⁹ *Poems*, II, 71-92, 103, 157, 158.

⁴⁰ *The Collected Poems of Rupert Brooke*, with an introduction by George Edward Woodberry (New York, 1941), pp. 61-62.

⁴¹ *Poems*, p. 52.

⁴² *Poems*, pp. 73-74, 69, 82, 127-28, 142, 143.

VII. YEATS, DONNE, AND THE METAPHYSICALS

¹ *Essays by W. B. Yeats, 1931 to 1936* (Dublin, 1937), pp. 11, 33; H. J. C. Grierson, "Preface," V. K. Narayana Menon, *The Development of William Butler Yeats* (Edinburgh, 1942), pp. x–xiii; *The Letters of W. B. Yeats*, ed. Allan Wade (New York, 1955), pp. 570-71, 710, 902; W. B. Yeats, *Autobiographies* (New York, 1927), pp. 402-3.

² "To a Young Beauty," *The Collected Poems of W. B. Yeats* (New York, 1954), p. 138.

³ W. B. Yeats, *A Vision* (London, 1937), p. 172; *Essays* (London, 1924), p. 432; *Letters*, pp. 759, 836-37; Vivienne Koch, *W. B. Yeats, The Tragic Phase* (Baltimore, 1951), pp. 95-96.

⁴ *Letters on Poetry, from W. B. Yeats to Dorothy Wellesley* (London, 1940), p. 192; Norman Jeffares, *W. B. Yeats, Man and Poet* (New Haven, 1949), p. 237; *Autobiographies*, pp. 101, 142; Richard Ellmann, *The Identity of Yeats* (New York, 1954), pp. 216-17.

⁵ See Virginia Moore, *The Unicorn* (New York, 1954), pp. 24, 27, 81, 88, 103-4, 224; Jeffares, p. 106; Ellmann, p. 33.

⁶ *Autobiographies*, pp. 127, 188; Ellmann, pp. 129, 56; *Letters on Poetry*, pp. 94, 8, 64; *Essays*, p. 198; *A Vision*, p. 275.

⁷ Ellmann, pp. 24-38.

⁸ Donne, "You have refin'd mee," "Reason is our Soule's left hand," "The Dreame" and "The Canonization;" *Poems*, I, 193, 189, 37, 15.

⁹ Donne, "Hymne to God My God, in My Sicknesse" and "A Hymne to

God the Father," *Poems*, I, 368–69; Marvell, "A Dialogue between the Soule and Body" and "To His Coy Mistress," *Poems*, I, 20, 26.

[10] "Ribh Considers Christian Love Insufficient," "Crazy Jane and the Bishop," and "On a Picture of a Black Centaur, by Edmund Dulac," *Poems*, pp. 284, 251, 212.

VIII. ELIOT AND THE TWENTIETH-CENTURY REVIVAL

[1] *On Poetry and Poets* (New York, 1957), p. 117.

[2] Pound, *Pavannes and Divisions* (New York, 1918), p. 96; R. W. Church, in "Homage to T. S. Eliot," *The Harvard Advocate*, cxxv (Dec. 1938), 26; Eliot, *Selected Essays*, p. 395.

[3] Pound, *The Spirit of Romance* (London, 1910), p. 5; Eliot, "A Sceptical Patrician," *The Athenaeum*, May 23, 1919, p. 362; *Selected Essays*, p. 185.

[4] *Selected Essays*, pp. 302, 309.

[5] Eliot, "A Note on Poetry and Belief," *The Enemy*, I (Jan. 1927), 15–17; "Note sur Mallarmé et Poe," *La Nouvelle Revue Française*, xxvii (Nov. 1926), 525; "Rhyme and Reason: The Poetry of John Donne," *The Listener*, III (March 19, 1930), 502; *Selected Essays*, p. 145.

[6] *The Sacred Wood* (London, 1920), p. 152; *Selected Essays*, p. 226; "Deux Attitudes Mystiques: Dante et Donne," *Chroniques*, No. 3, *Le Roseau d'Or, Oeuvres et Chroniques*, xiv (1927), 153, 154.

[7] "Deux Attitudes Mystiques," pp. 160, 165, 149–151, 158, 168, 159; "Donne in Our Time," *A Garland for John Donne*, ed. Theodore Spencer (Cambridge, Mass., 1931), p. 8; *For Lancelot Andrewes* (London, 1928), p. 125.

[8] "Thinking in Verse," *The Listener*, III (March 12, 1930), 441–43; "Rhyme and Reason," pp. 502–3; "The Devotional Poets of the Seventeenth Century," *The Listener*, III (March 26, 1930), 552–53; *A Garland for John Donne*, pp. 5–6, 8; *Selected Essays*, pp. 248–49, 229; "The Music of Poetry," *Partisan Review*, IX (Nov.-Dec. 1942), 462; "Milton," *Proceedings of the British Academy*, xxxiii (1948), 10, 18.

[9] "The Music of Poetry," p. 452; *Selected Essays*, p. 4.

[10] "Rhyme and Reason," p. 503.

[11] "Choruses from the 'Rock,'" IX, and "Burnt Norton," II, *The Complete Poems and Plays 1909–1950* (New York, 1950), pp. 112, 118–19.

[12] "Dry Salvages," V, and "Burnt Norton," V, *Complete Poems and Plays*, pp. 136, 121.

[13] "Little Gidding," IV, *The Complete Poems and Plays*, p. 144. See also "Little Gidding," II.

IX. METAPHYSICALS AND CRITICS SINCE 1912

[1] Grierson, ed., *Metaphysical Lyrics and Poems of the Seventeenth Century* (Oxford, 1921), p. xiii.

[2] Spencer and Van Doren, eds., *Studies in Metaphysical Poetry* (New York, 1939), p. 3.

[3] William H. Bagguley, ed., *Andrew Marvell, 1621–1678: Tercentenary Tributes* (London, 1922), pp. 3, 13–14, 31.

[4] Hacker, "To John Donne," *The Bookman* (London), lxxx (May, 1931), 140.

[5] "John Donne, O. P.," *Time*, xxvii (Jan. 13, 1941), p. 76.

[6] Woolf, *The Second Common Reader* (New York, 1932), pp. 22–23, 37, 25–26.

⁷ Bailey, "The Sermons of a Poet," *The Quarterly Review*, ccxxxiii (April 1920), 317.

⁸ Matthiessen, *The Achievement of T. S. Eliot* (New York, 1947), p. 11; Porter, "Dean Donne," *The Spectator*, xlvi (April 4, 1931), 539-40; S. Addleshaw, "A Famous Dean: Dr. John Donne of St. Paul's," *The Church Quarterly Review*, cxii (Oct. 1931), 38-39.

⁹ For the most complete discussion of seventeenth- and twentieth-century parallels, see Sona Raiziss, *The Metaphysical Passion* (Philadelphia, 1952), esp. pp. 59ff, 107-10.

¹⁰ Massingham, ed., *A Treasury of Seventeenth Century English Verse* (London, 1919), p. xxii; Tate, *Reactionary Essays on Poetry and Ideas* (New York, 1936), p. 72; Sampson, "The Resurrection of Donne," *The London Mercury*, xxxiii (Jan. 1936), 308, 310; Moloney, "Richard Crashaw," *The Catholic World*, clxii (Oct. 1945), 44.

¹¹ Gosse, i, 257; Bush, *Science and English Poetry* (New York, 1950), p. 35; Fausset, "In Memory of John Donne," *The Bookman* (London), lxxxix (March 1931), 342; Laurence Binyon, "A Study of Donne," *The Bookman*, lxvii (Jan. 1925), 201.

¹² Donne, "The First Anniversary," l. 205, "Satire iii," ll. 77-80, and "The Progresse of the Soule," ll. 518-20, *Poems*, i, 237, 157, 316; Jessop, p. 61.

¹³ Fausset, *John Donne, A Study in Discord* (London, 1924), pp. 23-24; Payne, *John Donne and His Poetry* (London, 1926), p. 85; Ince, *Angel from a Cloud* (London, 1939), pp. 8-9; Bewley, "Religious Cynicism in Donne's Poetry," *The Kenyon Review*, xiv (Autumn 1952), 619-46; Haydn, *The Counter-Renaissance* (New York, 1950), p. 163; Hughes, "Kidnapping Donne," *University of California Publications in English*, iv (1934), 61-89.

¹⁴ Massingham, p. xviii; Smith, ed. *Donne's Sermons, Selected Passages* (Oxford, 1919), p. xxxi; Addleshaw, *The Church Quarterly Review*, cxii (Oct. 1931), 38; Coffin, *John Donne and the New Philosophy* (New York, 1937), p. 287, and Matthiessen, *T. S. Eliot*, p. 11.

¹⁵ Hutton, "John Donne, Poet and Preacher," *Theology*, ix (Sept. 1924), 165; Sparrow, "Donne's Religious Development," *Theology*, xxii (March 1931), 146-50; Johnson, "John Donne, 1572-1631," *The Congregational Quarterly*, x (Jan. 1932), 41, 45; Hutchinson, "Donne the Preacher," *Theology*, xxii (March 1931), 162-63; Thomas Foster, "The Tragedy of John Donne," *The Month*, clvii (May 1931), 404-9; Henry Newbolt, *Studies Green and Gray* (London, 1926), p. 288.

¹⁶ Spender, "Richard Crashaw, 1613-1648," *The Contemporary Review*, cxvi (Aug. 1919), 210; Hess, "Descartes and Richard Crashaw," *Commonweal*, xlii (Aug. 24, 1945), 455-57; Moloney, "Richard Crashaw, 1649-1949," *The Catholic World*, clxix (July 1949), 336-39; Thomas, "George Herbert," *The Contemporary Review*, cxliii (June 1933), 707.

¹⁷ Read, *Reason and Romanticism* (London, 1926), esp. pp. 45, 57.

¹⁸ Ransom, "Eliot and the Metaphysicals," *Accent*, i (Spring, 1941), 151-52; *The World's Body* (New York, 1948), pp. 111-42, 286-91.

¹⁹ Richards, *Principles*, pp. 113, 249-50.

²⁰ Empson, *Seven Types of Ambiguity* (London, 1949), pp. 133, 139, 217-18, 129, 183, 233; *Some Versions of Pastoral* (London, 1950), pp. 119, 145.

²¹ Tate, *Reason in Madness* (New York, 1935), pp. 68, 74; Spencer, *A Garland*, pp. 158, 160; Brooks, pp. 42-43, 37, 30, 50, 61, and *passim*.

²² Leonard Unger, *Donne's Poetry and Modern Criticism* (Chicago, 1950),

esp. pp. 63–67; Moloney, *The Catholic World*, CLXII (Oct. 1945), 44; Raiziss, p. 59.

[23] *On Poetry and Poets*, p. 125.

[24] Ransom, *The World's Body*, pp. 286–87.

[25] Leavis, *New Bearings in English Poetry* (London, 1950), 25, 171, and *passim*; *Revaluation* (London, 1936), pp. 29–33 and *passim*; Brooks, pp. 214–43.

[26] Rajan, ed., *T. S. Eliot, A Study of His Work by Several Hands* (London, 1949), p. 121; Eliot, in *A Garland*, p. 5; Spencer, "Poets in Their Fame," *The Saturday Review of Literature*, XII (May 4, 1935), 22, and *Studies*, 14.

[27] Tuve, *Elizabethan and Metaphysical Imagery* (Chicago, 1947), pp. 43–44, 164–65, 396, 420, and *passim*; "The School of Donne," *The Times Literary Supplement*, March 25, 1955, p. 182.

[28] Unger, ed., *T. S. Eliot, Selected Critiques* (New York, 1948), p. 88; Brooks, *Opinions of Oliver Allston* (New York, 1941), p. 245; Bogan, "The Pleasures of Formal Verse," *The Quarterly Review of Literature*, VII (1953), 176–85; Wilbur, "The Bottles Become New, Too," *The Quarterly Review of Literature*, VII (1953), 188–92; Viereck, *Dream and Responsibility* (Washington, D.C., 1953), p. 22.

[29] Hillyer, "Treason's Strange Fruit" and "Poetry's New Priesthood," *The Saturday Review of Literature*, XXXII (June 11, 1949), 11, and XXXII (June 18, 1949), 8; Robbins, *The T. S. Eliot Myth* (New York, 1951), pp. 190, 185, 200, 69.

X. THE METAPHYSICAL FLORESCENCE

[1] "Things of August," III, and "It Must Change," VI, from "Notes Toward A Supreme Fiction," *Collected Poems* (New York, 1955), pp. 490, 394.

[2] "Portrait in Black Paint" and "Madwoman's Miracle," *Collected Poems* (New York, 1938), pp. 276, 259.

[3] "One Person," VII, *Poems*, p. 178.

[4] *Annals of Innocence and Experience* (London, 1940), pp. 94–95; *Phases of English Poetry* (New York, 1929), pp. 67–68.

[5] *Phases*, pp. 67, 79.

[6] "Mutations of the Phoenix" and "The Nuncio," *Collected Poems* (Norfolk, Conn., 1946), pp. 177, 193.

[7] Read, "A World Within a War" and "The Retreat," *Poems*, pp. 97, 175.

[8] "John Donne Declines a Benefice" and "Ode Written During the Battle of Dunkirk," *Poems*, pp. 159, 92, 89–90.

[9] "John Donne Declines a Benefice," *Poems*, p. 159.

[10] "The Even Skein" and "Meditation of the Waking English Officer," *Poems*, pp. 126, 72.

[11] Edith Sitwell, ed., *The Pleasures of Poetry*, First Series (London, 1930), pp. 40, 43–44; *Aspects of Modern Poetry* (London, 1934), pp. 14, 51; Horace Gregory, "The 'Vita Nuova' of Baroque Art in the Recent Poetry of Edith Sitwell," *Poetry*, LXVI (June 1945), 154.

[12] *The Canticle of the Rose, Poems: 1917–1949* (New York, 1949), pp. xv–xvi; "One Day in Spring," p. 222.

[13] *Ibid.*, pp. 232, 230, 237, 158.

[14] "O Bitter Love, O Death" and "The Hambone and the Heart," *The Canticle*, pp. 213, 100.

[15] See *Collected Poems* (New York, 1949), for Empson's notes on this and other poems discussed.

Index